People to People Romania

Romania
People to People

Jim Haynes

Canongate Publishing
Edinburgh
in association with
Handshake Editions
Paris

First published in Great Britain in 1991
by Canongate Press PLC
14 Frederick Street, Edinburgh, Scotland
in association with Handshake Editions, Paris

Copyright © 1991 Jim Haynes
Cover art Copyright © 1991 Joseph Francis

British Library Cataloguing in Publication
Data:

Haynes, Jim
  Romania. — (People to People).
  I. Title II. Series
  914.9803

ISBN 0 86241 335 4 (Romania)

Typeset in Paris by Handshake Editions
Printed and bound in Poland by
Z.W. Okopowa, Warsaw.

Acknowledgements

So many people helped to make this book possible. They all know who they are; their help and energy are appreciated

In Romania, I must mention with gratitude:
Roxane and Dima

In Paris, I would like to thank:
Corine Berrevoets; Alain Champagnac; Joe Francis; Dorota Janiszewska Chrisp; Jack Henry Moore

Introduction

This series of travel guides will contain none of the usual tourist information that can be found in most guide books. No museums or galleries, no lists of hotels or restaurants, no suggestions on what to see or to do, and no potted histories. Instead we introduce you to over 1000 individuals who live, work, play in the villages, towns, and cities of the country. The people are of all ages and all professions. They want to meet you and to show you how they live, introduce you to their favorite restaurants, to share their friends and their interests with you. They speak English, French, German, Italian, Spanish, Esperanto, Russian, and many other languages. They play chess, bridge, and other games. They like to climb mountains, play tennis, swim, sail, and enjoy many other sports. They know more about their village, town, city, country than all the guide books combined. And their information is up to the minute. We suggest you write to them before you depart on your journey, to arrange with them your accommodation needs and requirements and finally meet them. They will help you to make your trip everything you could hope for. When you meet them and their friends, you will begin to participate in their life and they in yours.

We have entitled this new and innovative series of travel books: People to People. The title clearly states our aims. We wish to establish a warm relationship between travellers and the local population that will be based upon mutual passions and common interests — be it bridge, tennis, ballet, or gardening.

Unfairly, perhaps, I divide the traveling population into "tourists" and "travellers". A tourist usually arrives in a group with other tourists, stays in a tourist hotel, tours the city in a large bus, purchases trinkets from a tourist shop, spends a lot of time looking at monuments, being photographed and writing postcards. The tourist usually leaves the country without ever encountering the local population except when being served in a bar, restaurant or shop.

A traveller, on the other hand, usually stays with someone — an old friend or a new one. The traveller participates in the daily life of the host or hostess and contributes in many ways to an enriching exchange. The traveller is often met at the airport or train station. The traveller arrives with a gift or something the host needs or would appreciate. Often the host will have arranged appointments or theatre, ballet or opera tickets for the traveller. Both contribute to make the visit meaningful and enjoyable; both are sad when the visit ends. Rarely does anyone mark the departure of a tourist.

OK, these are two extreme portraits. Probably most of us are a little of both. The aim of this series is to help transform tourists into travellers.

In recent years we have heard a great deal of talk about living in a Global Village. People to People is a step toward its realization. Go forth and meet your neighbors. They're waiting for you. And they're nice...

ROMANIA

If one travels primarily to meet people, to participate in their life - this was almost impossible and even dangerous before December 1989 in Romania; it would only create problems for yourself and for Romanians. It would be the last thing anyone would wish. Therefore no trip to Romania for me during all my travels East in the 60's, 70's and 80's. Then December 1989 and the dramatic unfolding of events forced all of us to do some re-thinking.

This series of travel guides was already in preparation. In January I read Robert Culler's long and sensitive article in *"The New Yorker"*. He ends his report by asking Professor Virgiliu Constantinescu of the Bucharest Polytechnic Institute what the West could do for Romania. The professor replied : "but first we need contacts, personal contacts...". This was all I needed to confirm what I suspected. I decided to visit the country as soon as possible and to include it among the first group of books to be published in this series.

One trip of one week to Bucharest in July 1990 is not a lot of time and experience to qualify someone to edit a book on Romania, but this is not a normal travel book. Two friends from Bucharest have spent three months in Paris assisting in the preparation.

Now here is the book. We hope it will enable you to meet Romanians in all parts of the country. We also hope that at the same time it will enable Romanians to reach out to the world and travel abroad. The country has been closed for too many years. They need friends and contacts. We feel this book will help. I have asked Dima to write something that he feels should be said to travellers coming to Romania.

> Romania. The only country in Eastern Europe where people speak a language of Latin origin. A strange island of Latinity, striving through centuries to preserve its identity, in a sea of Slav cultures. And this is not the only curious thing.
>
> Romania is really more than the country of Dracula. Try to meet some people from up there, and they'll tell you much more amazing stories about their past and present history. You will be surprized to hear that they've been here, in the same world, all the time, in spite of the "iron curtain", that they speak foreign languages, they know the Western world, and most of all, they love to make friends and open their hearts.
>
> And this is what this book will try to achieve. Fourty five years of communism forced them to keep quiet and reserved, and now, as the political barriers are desintegrating, all this desire to speak and communicate with you is exploding. Everybody wants to show you how beautiful this country is (and it really is!) it has everything — mountain, sea, ruins, palaces, stadiums, you name it, and how entertaining they can be. After all this time, their potential and energy is tremendous. Just ready to overwhelm anybody who cares to touch them.
>
> So, a wonderful people in a wonderful country. However, what's wrong with this place? Things cannot be just so ideally beautiful. Well, communism was shaken out, but the marks of it remain. Once rich and prosperous, now Romania's economy is a mere shadow of what it used to be before World War II, it will take years to recover, and that makes a poor people too. But most of the people will accept their material misery with humour and hope, and though the shops don't offer much, everyone manages to fulfill their needs. Having a car, a colour TV and a VCR has became the ideal standard of living for the avarege middle class family, as it is now often realized. So, the Romanians are not "that poor" after all, when you come to think of it...or are they? Well, you will find out for yourself, if you would come to meet these interesting people, cherish their passions and hospitality, make more friends and a new experience.

Tips, Suggestions & Warnings

Write ahead to the individuals you wish to meet. Tell them about yourself, your needs, hopes, travel plans. You might ask them what you can do to contribute to their needs. Some people are in a position to have you stay, others are not. Do not assume that everyone will be able to look after you. All the people listed in this book wish to meet travellers. They would also like to be travellers and visit you. They can probably assist you with your accommodations, and in other ways. Ask them if they know a friend who would welcome a little money for having you to stay, or the name of a hotel or pension.

If you are a tourist or want to be a tourist, this book is not for you. There are dozens of books that deal with tourist information. This book is primarily for "travellers" — those individuals who wish to experience life as the locals live it, who wish to participate in the social, intellectual, and cultural life of the community. If you are primarily concerned with your comfort, if you need to take two showers daily, if you need to make international telephone calls, then you should not plan to stay privately in Romania. You need a hotel.

Nor is this book for people who wish to travel in groups. This book is for those individuals who wish to travel alone. Groups form their own social unit that is difficult for anyone to enter. Individuals are open for contact and are easier to integrate into the plans and activities of local hosts. A single traveller is always welcomed. From years of receiving guests in my home, it is always the individual traveller who adjusts to the rhythms and lifestyle far more easily than couples or groups. An individual is more involved, fits in easier, and participates easily. Recently a couple stayed for a week. When they got up in the morning, they fixed their own breakfast from things they purchased for themselves. Then they disappeared until late in the evening — at which time they retired straight away. After their one week here, there was very little one could say about them. Nor did they learn very much about us. There are exceptions of course.

Often one half of a couple wishes to travel quickly; the other half, slowly. They compromise. They neither travel quickly nor slowly, and both are unsatisfied.

Several years ago I travelled with a group to Russia. The first morning we were urged to board a large bus for the city tour. I forced myself — with great reluctance — to get inside. At the first opportunity, I defected. Escaped. Wandering off in search of friendly natives. Within a short time they were found. I never returned to the group. They were busy on endless tours to this and to that monument. With my new friends I participated, and hopefully, contributed to their lives. Who had the richer experience? Those who stayed with the group or myself? My way is more meaningful for me. I certainly suspect it is what a lot of other people desire as well.

If you would like to experience life as most locals do, if you would like to contribute to your hosts, if you would like to establish contacts, acquire friends, we hope this book will help. Not everyone has space available to offer you. You will find the individuals listed here often have friends or relatives who could help you.

Romanians, like most people who live in Eastern and Central Europe, survive by their wits, by barter, by having relatives or friends abroad. The average monthly wage is $30 (150 French francs, 50DM) or what one spends for one meal in an inexpensive restaurant in New York, London or Paris. As someone noted : "They pretend to pay us; we pretend to work". It goes without saying that all of you who purchase this book and travel to Romania, no matter how poor you might consider yourself, are (in comparison with the local population) very rich.

Tourists and travellers can always survive in Romania, can always find something to eat and a place to sleep. But it is not so easy for locals. It is helpful and considerate to arrive with something, a gift the host or hostess might need or enjoy. Food is appreciated. So, too, are books, magazines, audio and video cassettes, and clothes, shoes and medicines.

With their average monthly wage, it is almost impossible for a Romanian to travel outside the country. But not impossible. Just very difficult. After years of not being able to have a passport, now they can get one. One hurdle overcome only to meet another. Now a visa to Britain, France, Germany, USA etc. is very difficult to obtain. Plus the costs of the travel : transportation, hotels, food, etc. One can reciprocate. They host you, you invite them back to your country.

DISCLAIMER
The publishers and editors have done their best to ensure the accuracy and currency of the information in People to People: Romania; however, they can accept no responsibility for any loss, injury, or inconvenience sustained by any traveler as a result of information or advice contained in this guide.

FEEDBACK

We solicit your feedback. Let us know how this book contributed to your trip. For future editions, we need your suggestions. If you would like to be included in a People to People book, please fill in the form at the back of the book post it to:

>Jim Haynes
>Atelier A2
>83 rue de la Tombe Issoire
>75014 Paris, France

Symbols and Layout

Each entry in the book has several symbols highlighting specific information:

- ☎ city telephone prefix code
- ✆ telephone numbers
- ✂ collectables
- ☞ city region
- ✉ mailing address
- 📣 languages
- ♥ passions
- H housing

Entries are classified alphabetically by city, followed by an alphabetic list of individuals from that city. Many cities are followed by notes of interest for that city, which are condensed from personal information compiled. Each individual entry has the person's name, the name of their spouse or child, birthdate, occupation followed by a brief biographical note, and then contact information.

The names in Romanian should be pronounced phonetically, like in Italian. However there are some diacritical marks which alter the pronounciation of a,i,s and t, which are not printed. This will not affect writing though, and your letters will certainly reach their addressees.

For people who live in houses and villas, only the name of the street and number are given. Fore those who live in blocks of flats, the complete address comprises all the details, starting with "Bl." (from "Bloc"). The addresses must be written exactely as given in book, adding the town's name and code (if any) at the end.

In order to locate a small town or village on a Romanian map, you should look for the name of the county (placed after "Jud." in the address - from "Judet", Romanian for "county"). All other towns or cities are usually on map. The name of a county may often be the same as the name of the biggest city in it (its so called "capital").

While every effort has been made to assure the accuracy of the information in this book, it happens even in Romania that people move and change their residences. We would appreciate feedback to ensure that future editions contain as few errors as possible.

AGIGEA

BAICOIANU, Diana b.03/17/74 Pupil
"My mother's name is Georgeta and my father's Mircea. I have a 14 year old brother named Costin."
✉ Jud. Constanta, Agigea, 8711 ✆ (917) 43031
✍ English, French ♥ reading ∎ yes

AIUD

" ... my town is not big but it is placed in a nice landscape ..."

TAT, Ecaterina b. 11/19/51 Medical assistant
"I was born and I work in Aiud. I was engaged with an Italian. I wanted to marry him but I lost him. He drowned in the Black Sea. I lived a great tragedy. Since I lost him I stopped thinking of marriage and dedicated my life to ill people"
✉ Str.Sergent Hategan,Bl.H4,Ap.6,Jud.Alba, Aiud, 3325 ✆ (968) 63058 ✍ Italian, French, Rusasian ♥ tourism, music, painting, dance, reading ∎ yes ☆ board

TOMOIAG, Liviu b.07/27/59 Mechanical engineer
"I work in a research institute. I am divorcing my wife. The special situation I am in because of a train accident (both legs amputated) does not prevent me from travelling by car and even by foot."
✉ Str.Sg.Hateganu,Bl.7B,Ap.9,Jud.Alba, Aiud, 3325 ✆ (968) 63155 ✍ French, English ♥ football, car racing, music, folklore, literature, trips ∎ yes

ALBA-IULIA

IUGA, Bianca Iulia b.08/14/74 Pupil
"I have a brother, Nini. He is 14. My mother is a teacher and my father is a veterinarian doctor. I want to become a journalist."
✉ Str.1 Decembrie 1918 nr.26,Bl.11B,Ap.26, Alba-Iulia, 2400 ✆ (968) 20084 ✍ French ♥ literature, voyages ∎ yes ☆ breakfast

POPA, Danil b. 02/28/50 Engineer
"I am married to an architect. I work as designer. We have two daughters."
✉ Str.Ulmului 3A,Bl.E10,Ap.4, Alba-Iulia, 2500
✆ (968) 22813 ✍ German, French ♥ fishing, beekeeping, archaeology ✂ stamps ⌂ yes ☆ board

ALEXANDRIA

IVAN, Valeriu b. 06/17/51 Chemist operator
✉ Str.Dunarii,Bl.L2,Sc.C,Ap.43,Jud.Teleorman, Alexandria, 0700 ✍ English ♥ tourism ⌂ yes
☆ breakfast

ARAD

" ... is considered the guardian at the Western gates of Romania, just like Timisoara. It has many vestiges of culture and architecture and the recent "traces of the Revolution". One can see them all together ... or a tourist can see what 45 years of communism has done ... but it is beautiful enough, still!"

CAPATINA, Marius b.03/29/57 Doctor
"I was born in Arad. I graduated from the Medical Faculty in Timisoara in 1982. I got married just 20 days before the Revolution. My wife is a teacher of Physics in a highschool. My father is a doctor gynecologist and my mother a clerk (both retired)."
✉ Str.Banu Maracine 1,Ap.5, Arad, 2900 ✆ (966) 30535 ✍ French, German, English ♥ tourism, mountain climbing (I am member of alpin club in Arad), tennis, films, books, all that is new ⌂ yes ☆ board

GHERANESCU, Nicolae b.12/16/47 Chemistry Engineer
"Born in Timisoara, graduated in Chemistry Enginering in 1970, being married the same year with a highschool colleague.I occupied several positions in a large chemi-

cal fertilizers complex in Arad. Since 1978 I am Plant Manager in the same Company."
✉ Pta.Sporturilor 3,Bl.45,Ap.15, Arad, 2900
✆ (966) 33136 ✍ English, French, German ♥ touring, some painting, some photographing, history of arts ⌂ yes, in Arad or summer house 23 Km from Arad. ☆ board

ILEA, Delia b. 11/20/55 Teaching computers
"I was born in a family of intellectuals. I graduated the University in Timisoara. I work as a teacher for 12 years in a secondary school 200 Km from Arad. I am not married."
✉ Str.Marasesti 36, Arad, 2900 ✆ (966) 34523
✍ French, English, Spanish ♥ computers, cinema, music, reading, sports, politics ⌂ yes ☆ bed and breakfast

BACAU

> " ... not a big town, but with a splendid environment ... the Moldavian monasteries are near, as is the resort Slanic Moldova, and Durau ... museums, parks, an island with boats ... "

BADIC, Virginia b.07/18/57 Physician, specializing in patologic anatomy
✉ Str.Mioritei,Bl.68,Sc.B,Ap.11, Bacau, 5500
✆ (931) 46941 ✍ French, English ♥ cinema, literature, hand working (tailor work) ⌂ yes ☆ breakfast

BRUMA, Vasile b. 02/14/60 Engineer
"Height : 1.75m. Weight : 67kg. I have brown eyes and brown hair. I am not married. I like women to be intelligent, sensible, beautiful and men to have a good character."
✉ Str.9 Mai Nr.5,Sc.A,Ap.6, Bacau, 5500 ✆ (931) 44296 ✍ French, English ♥ friends, skating, tennis, basketball, swimming, music (hard rock, progressive and symphonic), literature, movies, car driving, trips in the mountains ⌂ yes

BACAU

CIUHODARU, Atena - Irina   b.07/18/42   Physician gynecologist

"My husband is also a doctor. He is born 06.03.40. We have 2 children, a son, studying medicine, and a daughter, pupil."

✉ Str.Aleea Parcului 46,Et.2,Ap.11, Bacau ✆ (931) 23344   ✍ French   ♥ my profession, tourism, children   **H** yes

COSMESCU, Marin   Teacher (retired)

"I studied philology. I was a teacher for 35 years. My wife is a schoolmaster. We have a son, engineer, who lives in Bacau."

✉ Str.Petru Rares 5,Sc.C,Ap.4, Bacau, 5500   ✆ (931) 34110   ✍ French, English   ♥ reading and writing, tourism, rebus, philately   **H** yes, at my son's house too

DOSPINESCU, Gabriela   b.08/01/58   Industrial chemist

"I have been working in my profession for eight years and I can say that I am quite well paid. My sons are nine years old; they are twins."

✉ Str.Ana Ipatescu,Bl.6,Sc.A,Ap.12, Bacau, 5500   ✆ (931) 47510   ✍ French, English   ♥ tennis, classical music   **H** yes (I live in a 4-room flat)

FITA, Monica-Maricela   b.11/16/74   Pupil

"I am studying in the secondary school in Bacau. My father is a professor at the University in Bacau. My mother is a nurse. My sister is 13. I like mathematics, physics, drawing. I practice winsurfing. I like skiing, skating, swimming and tennis."

✉ Str.Fagului 2, Bacau, 5500   ✆ (931) 31517   ✍ English, French   ♥ fashion, dancing, gardening   **H** yes

GRIGORE, Livia   b.09/21/49   Teacher

"I am a B.A. of Iasi "Al.Cuza" University where I took my degree in English and French in 1972. I teach English and French in a middle school in Bacau. My

husband is an engineer. He speaks German. We have 2 daughters, Roxana, aged 17 and Anca, aged 12."
✉ Str.Soimului 13,Bl.D,Sc.A,Ap.1, Bacau ✆ (931) 23814 ✎ English, French, Italian (a little) ♥ tennis, swimming, volleyball, chess; music (opera, operetta, concertos, vocal music - Pavarotti, Maria Callas, Edith Piaff, Tina Turner, etc); film, theatre, literature, dance ⌂ yes ☆ board

MARGINEANU, Rodica b.06/12/55 Engineer
"I am married and I have two daughters: Gina, aged 12, and Ana-Maria, aged 5. My husband is 35 and works in a design group. We live on a 3 rooms flat in Bacau, a big industrial, cultural and commercial centre; population: 800,000"
✉ Str.Marasesti,Bl.197,Sc.B.Ap.25, Bacau, 5500
✆ (931) 70339 ✎ French ♥ reading, travelling
⌂ yes

MIHALACHE, Maria b.03/20/35 Pediatre
"I spent my childhood in Botosani and Suceava. I have been working in Suceava and Bacau. I am married. We have no children."
✉ Str.Garofitei,Bl.9,Sc.B,Ap.19, Bacau, 5500
✆ (931) 57879 ✎ French ♥ reading, travelling
⌂ yes ☆ board

MOISA, Petrut b. 05/25/38 Engineer
"I am working in the field of high voltage transmission lines. I worked a lot abroad. My wife, Emilia, (44) is an electromechanical engineer and speaks German. We have two daughters: Laura (17), learning English and German and Flavia (10), learning English."
✉ Al.Armoniei 7,Ap.9, Bacau, 5500 ✆ (931) 14412
✎ English, Farsi(Iran-no write) ♥ aviation, wrestling, theatre, cinema ⌂ yes, up to 4 pers. in the centre of the town ☆ board, 2 cars

NASTASE, Liviu b.07/16/67 Electrician
"I learned 3 years at a special school to make sculptures (Romanian popular art in wood). I carve lime wood,

cherry wood, nut wood, sycamore wood. This is my hobby. I work as an electrician in a factory."
✉ Str.9 Mai,Bl.78,Sc.B, Ap.30, Bacau, 5500
✆ (931) 25073 ✍ English ♥ wood carving ⌂ yes

BAIA MARE

" ... *the Old Town, with Steven's tower, mineral collections, Ethnographical Museum ... sports - swimming, skiing ...* "

BRAN, Hajnalka b.03/28/53 Engineer
"I have been married for 14 years to Claude, who is an engineer too. We have two children : a 13 years old daughter, Claudia, and a 9 years old son - Claudiu."
✉ Str.P.Rares 20/11,Bl.20,Sc.A,Ap.11,Jud.Maramures, Baia Mare, 4800 ✆ (994) 25838 ✍ French, Hungarian
♥ mathematics, computers, naturist medicine, tourism
⌂ yes

CELCAN, Dorin b.11/24/63 Engineer (metalurgy)
"I was born in Triteni, county Cluj. I finished secondary school in Cimia Turzii - Cluj. I graduated the Metallurgy Institute in Timisoara. I work in a small plant in Baia Mare. Now I try to set up a private association of recording video creations."
✉ Str.Cuza Voda 9A/67,Jud.Maramures, Baia Mare
✍ English ♥ sport (karate), film (I make short films), artistic photography, the Japanese style of life
⌂ yes ☆ breakfast

DRUG, Vasile-Liviu b.03/29/65 Student
"I graduated from high school in 1983. At the end of the year, I hope to become a physician."
✉ Bd.Bucuresti,Bl.8,Ap.25, Baia Mare, 4800
✆ (994) 36512 ✍ English, French, Hungarian
♥ music, dancing, making excursions ⌂ yes ☆ breakfast

MATYIKU, Adriana b.12/26/58 Economist
"I graduated from high school in Baia Mare. I graduated in 1981 from the Faculty of Cybernetics in Bucharest and since work as an analyst at the Comput-

ing Centre in Baia Mare. I am not married. I live together with my father in a house with a garden."
✉ Str.Aleea Noua 5, Baia Mare, 4800 ℂ (994) 20368 ✍ French, Hungarian, English ♥ going to the theatre, concerts, plastic arts, mountain climbing, sports, literature, music, travelling, dancing ♂ yes ☆ guide

OTOIU, Adrian   b.04/30/58   English teacher
"I was born in Rimnicu Sarat, in the South. I studied in an Arts secondary school then at the University. During these years I made more films on ethnography. For 6 years I taught in Oradea, then in Baia Mare. I am not married."
✉ Str.Iza 1A/10, Baia Mare, 4800 ℂ (994) 20493 ✍ English, French, German ♥ photography and amateur cinema, mountain climbing, mountain flowers ♂ yes ☆ board and transportation by car.

BAICOI

" 40km away from my town, Sinaia, a nice resort, and 90kkm away, Bucharest."

ADET, Elena Alice   b.07/12/64   Student
✉ Str.Republicii 79 ,Jud.Prahova, Baicoi, 2064 ℂ (972) 60406 ✍ English, French, German ♥ music, travelling, motorcars ♂ yes

ADET, Marius Alin   b.08/30/69   Student
✉ Str.Republicii 79 ,Jud.Prahova, Baicoi, 2064 ℂ (972) 60406 ✍ English, French ♥ music, travelling ♂ yes

IRIMESCU, Dragos   b.07/12/61   Mechanical Engineer
"I was born in Constanta. I am an engineer specialized in machine building. Now I am attending the courses of the Academy of Economic Studies because I started working in a little enterprise of which I share action."
✉ Str.Toamnei 27 ,Jud.Prahova, Baicoi, 2064 ℂ (972) 60427 ✍ French, English ♥ sports, travelling, Impressionist painters (Monet, Gaugan, Pissaro) ♂ yes

BALS

NASTASE, Florin   b.05/01/74   Pupil
"*I have dark hair, green eyes, 1,80m height and 64 kg weight.*"
✉ Str.N.Balcescu 207,Bl.P2,Sc.6,Ap.118,Jud.Olt, Bals, 575 ✍ Italian, French (a little), English (a little) ♥ tourism, tennis, music, reading ⌂ yes

BIRLAD

> " ... not a tourist town ... the "Vasile Pirvan" museum ... in the east of the coutry, in Moldavia, close to Iasi ... the monasteries, Sucevita, Moldovita, Agapia ... "

ASULTANEI, Eugen   b.12/04/23   Retired
"*I was educated as a military man (captain). After 1954 I worked in the technical service of the post. I am a widower. I live in a house that I own with my daughter, 39,music teacher, my son in law, 40, doctor, and my grand-children, 10 and 2.*"
✉ Str.K.Marx,29, Birlad, 6400 ✆ (984) 12997
✍ French ♥ gardening, fishing, life in clear air, watching TV, reading ⌂ yes

BUDESCU, Octavian   b.05/23/61   Engineer
"*I am a mechanic engineer and I work in a factory in my town. My wife is an economist and we have a kid 3 months old.*"
✉ Str.Orizontului 35, Birlad, 6400 ✆ (984) 12192
✍ French ♥ tourism, tennis, beekeeping, gardening (flowers) ⌂ yes, in a villa

COSTACHE, Ioan   b.09/23/46   Mechanic
"*Both me and my wife do not hear well, so, although we do not speak any foreign language, we could communi-*

cate using the deaf-mute alphabet, we use with each other. We have a child."
- Str.Sterian Dumbrava 70,Bl.Z2,Sc.B,Ap.47,Jud.Vaslui, Birlad, 6400
♥ history ■ yes ✯ breakfast

MARCU, Eugen   b.06/01/53   Engineer
"I studied in Bucharest. I am not married."
- Str.Karl Marx 27, Birlad, 6400 ✆ (984) 11323
✍ French, English ♥ tennis, opera, ballet, cinema, theatre, painting ■ no

PASCANU, Catalin   b.05/17/69   Medical assistent
"My parents are intellectuals. I finished school in Murgeni and then graduated from the Sanitary College in Iasi. I am married since June 1990 to Georgette, nurse at the Children Hospital of Birlad. I am also a qualified guide for two tourist agencies."
- Str.Cerbului 112, Birlad, 6400 ✍ French
♥ tourism, tennis, fishing ■ yes

PECHEANU, Danut Iustinian   Engineer
"I was born in Birlad. I studied in Iasi. I am married. My wife is a physician. We have a seven year old child."
- Str.Energiei 43,Jud.Vaslui, Birlad, 6400 ✆ (984) 11956 ✍ French ♥ literature, directing, cinema, theatre, psychology, travelling, chess, bridge, philately
■ yes

SAVESCU-RADUCU, Rodica   b.10/08/51   Teacher of psychology
"I graduated from the faculty of Psychology. I work as a translator in a plant. My husband is an engineer. We have a 12 year old child."
- Str.Maraseşti 5,Jud.Vaslui, Birlad, 6400 ✆ (984) 13968 ✍ French ♥ literature, art, music, gymnastics, gardening, film, travelling ■ yes, in two houses
✯ board, traditional food

BISTRITA

> " In Bistrita one can visit medaeval buildings, the Evangelic Church, the architectural ensemble Sugalete, Dogarilor Tower, Argintarului House. "

SABIE, Bogdan-Victor b.03/20/56 Electromechanic technician
"I am married and I have a little boy of 2 years and a half."
✉ Str.Pacii 5, Bistrita, 4400 ✆ (990) 11177
✍ Italian, English, French ♥ fishing, gardening, electronics, philately, cars ⌂ yes ☆ board; transport by car to touristic spots.

BLAJ

> " ... is an old historical and cultural centre, and also the centre of the Greek Orthodox church in Romania. The Alba district is famous for its wines ... Timave wine could be a startingpoint for trips to Cluj, Tg. Mures, Sibiu, and Brasov ..."

PASCU, Lucian b.01/27/69 Student
"I study medicine. My mother is a teacher, my father is a physician, retired now."
✉ Str.I.M.Clain 16.,Jud.Alba, Blaj, 3175 ✆ (967) 11924 ✍ English, German ♥ tennis, gardening ✂ stamps ⌂ yes ☆ board

POPA, Emil Enea b.02/04/32 Surgeon
"I studied in Iasi and Cluj. I work as a surgeon since 1961. I am chief physician at the town's hospital. My wife is a physician too. We have two sons; one of them is studying medicine, the other has just graduated from high school."
✉ Aleea Viitorului 2A.,Jud.Alba, Blaj, 3175 ✆ (967) 11690 ✍ German, English (a little), French (a little) ♥ hunting, walking ⌂ yes

BLEJOI

> " ... *starting point for trips to Ploiesti,*
> *Valenii de Munte, Drajna, Cheia, Sinaia ...*"

ANGELESCU, Nicolae   b.03/07/57   Engineer
"In 1981 I graduated from the Polytechnical Institute in Bucharest. I am the chief of the Design department in a factory in Ploiesti. I founded a rock group."
✉ Str.Cimitirului 608 ,Jud.Prahova, Blejoi, 2047
✆ (972) 12105 ✍ French ♥ music (I play guitar)
🏠 yes ☆ board, trips by car

BOCSA II

GYURIS, Adalbert   b.08/23/53   Electrician
✉ Str.Victoriei,Bl.1,Ap.4,Jud.Caras-Severin, Bocsa II, 1726 ✆ (965) 51716 ✍ Hungarian ♥ photography, film, painting, sculpture ✂ old coins and foreign money 🏠 no ☆ I would like to help

BOTOSANI

ALUPOAIEI, Ioan   b.09/05/62   Worker
"I work in a textile industry. I am not rich. I have a small flat with one room, bathroom and kitchen. I like visitors."
✉ Str.Rotunda,Bl.64,Sc.A,Ap.33, Botosani, 6800
✍ French ♥ literature, cinema, music, travelling
🏠 yes

DRON, Dorin-Cezar   b.04/01/63   Engineer
"I was born in Trutesti, a small village in Botosani county. I studied in Botosani, where I moved with my parents when I was 3, and I graduated from the University of Iasi."
✉ Str.Aleea Viilor 3,Bl.S5,Ap.8,Jud.Botosani, Botosani, 6800 ✆ (985) 12253 ✍ French
♥ good music (rock, rap, pop, disco, but also Ravel, Saint-Saens, Tchaikovsky, Bach), dancing, cinema
🏠 yes ☆ breakfast; tours by car to the monasteries.

MINDRILA, Fanel-Cezar b.09/29/61 Mechanical engineer

"I was born in Voronet, a place known because of the monastery built by Steven the Great. I graduated from faculty in Suceava. My wife is an engineer too. We have a six year old daughter."

✉ Str.Rondului 5,Bl.G2,Sc.A,Ap.9, Botosani, 6800
✍ English ♥ automobiles, films (Charles Bronson), (wife) cooking (cakes) and tailoring for children
♦ yes, in Botosani and Voronet ☆ bord, driving

BRAILA

" ... *is a big town and a harbor on the Danube. The Danube forms a nice delta, a real monument to the power of nature.*"

CIUNAE, Mandita b.09/18/68 Chief of a working party

"I was born in Braila. My father is a driver, my mother is retired. I have a 21 year old sister who is married and has two children. I hope to be able to become a student in the future. I attended a course of bookkeeping and hope to work in tourism."

✉ Str.Plevna 128, Braila, 6100 ✆ (946) 72253
✍ French ♥ nature, music, fashion, travelling, curiosities, sports ♦ yes

DAICER, Marian b.08/01/52 Electronist

"I first qualified as a printer, but I was fired because I was a dissident. I requalified and became an electronicist. I married in 1982, but then divorced."

✉ Str.Hipodrom,Bl.N2,Ap.24, Braila, 6100 ✆ (946) 32374 ✍ French (a little) ♥ theatre, music, philately, numismatics, electronics ♦ no

GHEORGHIU, Cristina b.10/16/54 Engineer

"My husband died in an accident. I have two children : a 12-year-old daughter and a 9-year-old son"

✉ Str.Hristo Botev,Bl.B1,Sc.A,Ap.8, Braila, 6100
✍ French, English ♥ operetta, voyages, sports, music, books ♦ yes

BRAILA

GRIGORESCU, Tinca b.12/19/55 Office worker

"I was born in Braila. I have no brothers or sisters. I am married since 1978 and my son was born in 1980. We live in a nice house with 4 rooms and garden. We are a happy family and we like very much to drive our car."

✉ Str.Flacara Rosie 31,cart.Radu Negru, Braila, 6100 ✆ (946) 35953 ✍ English ♥ tourism
H yes ☆ bed and breakfast

NEMTANU, Valentin b.12/17/52 Mechanic engineer

"I am married to a doctor and we live in the centre of the city. We love to travel and to make new friends. I was a referee for car-races championships of Romania."

✉ Str.Eliberarii 21, Braila, 6100 ✆ (946) 14371
✍ French, German, English ♥ car-racing, a bit of philately H yes ☆ breakfast

RUNCEANU, Paula Liliana b.02/13/58 Laboratory Assistant

"I was born in Otopeni-Bucharest, I am 32, I am 1.63 m tall and I weigh 58 Kg, I have black hair and green eyes. I am married to a professor of Mathematics, 39 years old. I have a boy 7 years old and a little girl three months old."

✉ Str.Franceza Bl.20A,Sc.1,Ap.6, Braila ✆ (946) 33515 ✍ French ♥ dance, (husband) tennis
H yes

VODA TRAIAN, b.07/29/36 Physician internal diseases

"I graduated from the Faculty of Medicine in 1960. Since then I passed all the exams in my profession, so that now, I am a primary doctor, chief of section in the hospital no 1 in Braila. My wife is an architect and my daughter - a pupil."

✉ Str.Eliberarii,Bl.I,Ap.6, Braila, 6100 ✆ (946) 14949 ✍ English, French ♥ travelling, photography (color slides) H yes ☆ breakfast

BRASOV

> " ... the Brasov fortress (1395), the first Romanian School (1597), the Saint Bartholomeu church, the Black Church, a Franciscan Monastery (1500) Poiana Brasov resort (skiing) ... surrounded by mountains with resorts ... see Bran Castle - which belonged to Dracula!"

ANTIMIR, Ioan and - wife   b.11/19/50   Engineer; Medical assistant (wife)

"I was born in Brasov. I am married since 1976. We have no children. I am a tourist guide. I work in the wood industry. I visited the countries in Eastern Europe and also Lybia."

✉ Str.Sitarului 19,Sc.B,Ap.2, Brasov, 2200 ✆ (921) 85305 ✍ French, German (a little) ♥ chess, tourism ■ yes

BADARAU, Ciprian   b.07/27/60   Mechanical engineer

"Beginning with July 1990, I established in Brasov a private tourism agency "CLUB '90". I am not married. I enjoy working in tourism, journalism (I collaborated with two of the Brasov's magazines), publicity and public relations."

✉ Str.Sirul Livezii 22,Ap.1, Brasov, 2200 ✆ (921) 19473 / 72829 ✍ English, French, Spanish
♥ literature, music, sports, cinema ■ yes ☆ breakfast

BADEA, Sorin   b. 01/18/66   Electrical Engineer

"I work in a plant that produces electric equipement for cars. I am not married. I don't have children."

✉ Str.Harmanului 17,Bl.30,Ap.69, Brasov, 2200 ✆ (921) 37208 ✍ English, French ♥ I love nature, especially mountains, skiing, mountain climbing, swimming, logic problems ■ yes

BANICA, Anca-Mihaela   b.11/14/51

"I was born in Brasov, where I graduated from school and University. I work in an office together with my husband."

✉ Str.Colonel Buzoianu 29, Brasov ✆ (921) 14619
✍ French, English ♥ literature, trips ⌂ exceptional conditions(2 room flat,garden;center) ☆ breakfast (maybe)

CONSTANTIN, Florin   b.04/09/60   Technician

"In 1979 I graduated from high school; then, I worked as worker at the trucks factory "The Red Flag" on SIP machines. Since 1983 I work as a technician."

✉ Str.Rindunicii 8,Bl.18,Sc.A,Ap.17, Brasov, 2200 ✆ (921) 81451 ✍ English ♥ literature, theatre, films, music, driving the car ⌂ yes, I have a nice chalet in a forest near Brasov ☆ breakfast

COSTACHE, Ilie   b.02/12/32   Engineer and Economist

"I finished the Polytechnic in Iasi (1955) and Bucharest (1970). I worked as a fashion designer (8 years), chief engineer (8 years), managing director (11 years), in the Textile Enterprize in Brasov. I am married and have a daughter and a son."

✉ Str.Simion Barnutiu 25, Brasov, 2200 ✆ (921) 11290 ✍ German, English, French ♥ music, literature, philately, chess, bibliophily ⌂ yes, up to 4 persons. ☆ breakfast

CRACIUN, Aurora   b.07/22/37   Prompter at the Drama Theatre

"My parents were victims of the Stalinist era, their goods confiscated and they themselves deported in 1952. After some years we were permitted to live in Brasov again, but having nothing, I could hardly finish highschool and find a job."

✉ Bd.Grivitei 69,Bl.49,Sc.B,Ap.28, Brasov, 2200
✍ French ♥ Gobelins, lace "Frivolite", theatre, trips, jazz ⌂ yes

BRASOV

DANCU, Rodica b.02/10/47 Teacher of geography
"I was married, but my husband died and I am alone now. I would very much like to exchange accomodation."
✉ Str.Saturn 41,Bl.25,Sc.D,Ap.28, Brasov, 2200
✆ (921) 30704 ✍ Italian, French (learning) ♥ trips
⌂ yes

DIACONU, Andorra b.02/05/59 Engineer
"I live together with my husband - Valentin. He teaches at the University and I work in a plant. We are very happy to meet persons who want to know other countries."
✉ Str.Popa Sapca 8,Bl.46,Sc.A,Ap.9, Brasov, 2200
✆ (921) 84523 ✍ French, English ♥ travelling, sports, books, music ⌂ yes

DRAGUSIN, Nicolae b.02/25/58 Aircraft engineer
"I graduated from the Polytechnical Institute in Bucharest in 1982. I work in an helicopter factory in Brasov since 1982."
✉ Str.Mercur 3A,Ap.19, Brasov, 2200 ✆ (921) 26354 ✍ English, French ♥ tourism, basketball, bridge game ⌂ yes ☆ breakfast

FILIP, Alexandru-Catalin b.03/04/67 Student
"I was born in Brasov and lived here since. My parents are engineers.I would like to make friends all over the world."
✉ Str.Maior Cranta 2B, Brasov, 2200 ✆ (921) 11631 ✍ English, French ♥ trips in the mountains, reading books of adventures, meeting people, knowing places ⌂ yes

GAVRILIU, Maria b.06/18/58 Engineer
"I don't like to speak about myself. I am an ordinary woman. I was born and studied in Brasov. While a student I married my husband and we have a 10 year old son. His name is Alexander and he wants to make a lot of friends all over the world."
✉ Str.Dealul de jos 18, Brasov, 2200 ✆ (921) 18456 ✍ German, English, French ♥ theater, listening to music, dancing ⌂ yes

JIPA, Jorjean   b.   07/06/49   Cinema operator

"I attended the courses of the Art School (sculpture) for 3 years. In 1988 I was rewarded a special prize for one of my sculptures. I have a 17 years old daughter. I am a member of the Ecologist movement."

✉ Str.Constantin Lacea 25, Brasov, 2200 ✆ (921) 16831 ✎ Italian ♥ sculpture ⛨ yes

LAZAR, Daniel   b. 07/14/46   Worker

"I am an anonymous worker, with many children, secretly animated by a great desire: the tour of the world "per pedes", after being retired having the appropriate age. I love life and nature: the bright sun in the blue sky, the fresh air, the flowers..."

✉ Str.Linii 30,Bl.I24,Sc.B,Ap.2, Brasov, 2200 ✆ (921) 61360 ✎ French ♥ gardening, literature ⛨ yes ☆ bed and breakfast

OPREAN, Roxana-Cristina   b.04/21/65   Librarian

"I have a 1 year old son."

✉ Str.I.L.Caragiale 6,Bl.19,Sc.A,Ap.8, Brasov, 2200 ✎ English, German ♥ photography, filming ⛨ yes ☆ bed and breakfast

PACIOGLU, Dorin   b.08/07/49   Building engineer

"I graduated from high school in 1967 and from the Building Institute in Bucharest in 1972. I have been working in a company in Brasov for 18 years. I am married. We have two sons. We own a 4 rooms flat. I also worked abroad, in Iraq and Maroc for 2 years"

✉ Str.Harmanului 15 A,Sc.B/6, Brasov ✆ (921) 26279 ✎ French, English, Esperanto ♥ opera, symphonic music, history, agriculture, buildings ⛨ yes ☆ breakfast

RACOSSY, Anemarie   b.03/19/50   Electrotechnic engineer

"I was born in Arad : my father was German, my mother is Hungarian. I studied in Timisoara. I am married. I

have a son (8) and a daughter (6). My husband (45) is technician. We have a house with a little garden."
✉ Str.Ucenicilor 35, Brasov, 2200 ☏ (921) 80480
✍ French, English, German ♥ foreign languages, literature, (Kafka, Dostoievski, Balzac), symphonic music (Beethoven, Mozart, etc.), opera (Verdi, Rossini, Puccini), agriculture ⌂ yes ☆ board

REIT, Radu   b.   09/18/53   Engineer
"I was born in Brasov in a family of magistrates. I am half German after my father, but I am an Orthodox Christian after my mother. In school I studied violin, but however I decided to become an engineer and graduated Polytechnic. I am married."
✉ Str.Memorandului 13/7, Brasov, 2200 ☏ (921) 15168 ✍ English, French, German ♥ ski, tennis, swimming, playing violin. I am a ski instructor at Poiana Brasov, working with foreign tourist agencies ⌂ yes ☆ board, guide

RUCAREAN, Antoinette - Denise   b.09/09/55
    Economist
"I was born in Bucharest, where I also graduated from faculty. I have been living in Brasov since 1981, when I came here to work as an economist. I am married."
✉ Bd.Victoriei 11,Bl.35,Sc.B,Ap.61, Brasov, 2200
✍ French, English ♥ gardening, sports ⌂ yes

SAPLACAN, Arcadius Damian   b.01/18/53
    Economist
"I was born in Bucharest. I studied in Brasov and in Bucharest. I work with the department of statistics in Brasov. I am not married. I own a big flat in a villa situated in a very picturesque part of the town."
✉ Str.Alexandru Petofi 19,Ap.1, Brasov, 2200
☏ (921) 41785 ✍ French, English ♥ fishing, philately, books, movies on video ⌂ yes ☆ breakfast

STUPARU, Ion   b. 12/07/29   Economist
"I am not yet retired. Hope I'll be soon. My wife is a wonderful lady 56 years old. We have a son 38 years old. He is a Karate master and engineer. We have a

beautiful two rooms flat in the centre. We are all very friendly."

✉ Bd.Grivitei 76,Ap.5, Brasov, 2200 ✆ (921) 17980 ✍ Italian, French (a little) ♥ tourism, music, tennis ■ yes ☆ board

TICU, Ion   b.03/16/32   Engineer

"I was born in a small town on the Black Sea coast. I graduated from the University in Brasov in 1957. Since, I have been working at the tractor building plant in Brasov. My wife, Florina, is aged 49. WE have a daughter(25,engineer) and a son(22,student)."

✉ Bd.Grivitei 62,Ap.7, Brasov, 2200 ✆ (921) 61738 ✍ French, English ♥ classical music, tourism ■ yes

UDROIU, Razvan   b.03/04/72   Student

"I study airships at the University in Brasov. Height : 1.85m. Weight : 78kg. I am dark haired. My parents are engineers. We live together in a comfortable three rooms flat in the centre of the town."

✉ Str.13 Decembrie Nr.13,Bl.7,Ap.5,Cartier Grivita, Brasov, 2200 ✍ French ♥ handball, swimming, tourism in the mountains, reading good books, modern music, art albums ■ yes ☆ board, guide

URS, Alina Mariela   Medical assistent

"I was born 19 years ago in Brasov. After 8 years of elementary school was accepted at "Sanitar Lyceum" and after two years I had another exam at Chemistry and Anatomy. I finished the 12th form this year and I passed the final exam."

✉ Str.Republicii 16,Ap.1, Brasov ✆ (921) 43288 ✍ English, French ♥ riding (I love horses and I'd like to have my own stud or just my own horse, but this is just a dream.), reading, listening to music (all kinds, except hard rock), dancing, writing poems ■ yes ☆ bed and breakfast

VIOREL, Angela   b.12/13/47   Teacher of French in a highschool
"I was born in Deva. I studied in Sibiu, then I graduated the Faculty of Philology. I am not married. I have a daughter aged 19."
✉ Str.Saturn 12,Sc.C,Ap.6, Brasov, 2200 ☏ (921) 32752 ✍ French ♥ reading (French literature), films (Oscar winners), children, music, paintings, voyages ⌂ yes. Send letter in advance. I like letterwriting.

VIOREL BULENCEA, George   b.09/19/55
Zootechnician Engineer
"I am the chief of a research animal farm in Sercaia, near Brasov. My wife, Anne-Helene, aged 29, is a scientific researcher in the same farm. I have two children, Oana-Luise aged 6 and Paul aged 2. I have an apartment in Brasov and a house in Sercaia."
✉ Str.13 Decembrie,Nr.111,Ap.33, Brasov, 2200 ☏ (921) 64125 ✍ French, English ♥ ski, mountains, horse riding, music ⌂ yes ☆ breakfast

VIRCEOROVEANU, Teodora   b.10/11/63   Jurist (solicitor)
"I live together with my mother. I have no brothers or sisters. I am not married. I studied law in Cluj."
✉ Str.Traian 1,Bl.33,Sc.D,Ap.44, Brasov, 2200 ☏ (921) 82833 ✍ English, French ♥ sports (swimming, skating, sledging), music and dance, animals, nature ⌂ yes, in Brasov and in Codlea

BREAZA

TUDOR, Marian   b.05/06/53   Engineer in metals
"I studied at the Technical Faculty of the University of Brasov. I am married and my wife Constanta is also an engineer. We have a little girl, Laura, aged 10."
✉ Str.Republicii 33,Jud.Prahova, Breaza, 2165 ☏ (973) 41307 ✍ French ♥ football, tennis, history literature (WW2) ⌂ yes, in a privat house at Comarnic, at 5 Km. ☆ board, transport by car.

BUCURESTI

> *"... hospitality ... a city left to hazard, with abandoned buildings, weeds, a black market ... a palace in ruins, the university, and wonderful people in the streets ... "The People's House", Ceausescu's folly ... Bucharest was once "The Little Paris" before the dictator ... The literary cafe (Fundatei street, Nr.4 near Piata Romana)"*

AILINCA, Dragos   b.10/31/69   Student at the Polytechnical Institute in Bucharest
"I graduated from the "Spiru Haret" highschool in Bucharest. I am now studying Materials and Semiconductors."
✉ Drumul Taberei 120,Bl.OD1,Ap.223,sector 6, Bucuresti ✆ (90) 266821 ✍ French ♨ yes ☆ breakfast

ALEXANDRESCU, Florin - Grigore   b.09/18/52   Building engineer
"I am married. I have no children. I work in building industry."
✉ Str.Sandu Aldea 31-33,sector 1, Bucuresti, 7000 ✆ (90) 218439 or 654494 ✍ English, French, Italian ♥ professional photography for exibitions and magazines, listening to good music ♨ yes ☆ board

AMARITA, Adrian   b.08/26/56   Economist
"I am married and my wife, aged 30, teaches foreign languages (English, French, Bulgarian). We have a 3 years old boy. I work at the enterprise "Underground"."
✉ Bd.1 Mai 148,Bl.8,Ap.28,sector 1, Bucuresti, 78302 ✆ (90) 659201 ✍ English ♥ travelling ♨ yes

ANASTASIADE, Anca   b.04/27/44   Public relations
"I come from a family with a long standing tradition in law practice. Have studied foreign languages. Expelled for my family's bourgeois origins and their staunch

democratic ideals, but still finished studies. I translate and work with the movie industry."
✉ Str.Toamnei 38,sector 2, Bucuresti, 70264
✆ (90) 104311 ✍ English, French, Italian ♥ opera, ballet, movies, reading, dancing, knitting ⌂ yes
☆ breakfast

ANDREIESCU, Luiza
and Liviu (husband)   b.06/06/59   (she) Chemical Engineer/ (he) Mechanical Engineer

"We met in high school and later married. We have a three month old daughter. My husband works in an institute for fine mechanics."
✉ Str.Miraslau 8,sector 3 or Str.Mihai Bravu 126,Bl.D25,Sc.A,Ap.10,sector 2, Bucuresti
✆ (90) 216540 or 426560 ✍ French, English
♥ arts, nature, cars, animals (we have three dogs and three cats) ⌂ yes

ANDRONOVICI, Liviu   b.06/30/56   Engineer
"I work in a research institute in Bucharest. I am a bachelor. I have a flat with two rooms and a car. I am 1.75 m tall, weigh 75 Kg, I have brown hair and brown eyes."
✉ Alea Istru 7,Bl.A3,Sc.B,Ap.23,Sector 6, Bucuresti
✆ (90) 788371 ✍ French, English, Italian ♥ judo, karate (five years of practice), tennis, travelling, car-mechanics, carraces ⌂ yes ☆ board

ANGHEL, Dan and Mariana (wife)   b.03/30/52
Mechanical engineer (he)/Teacher (she)

"I have been working in different places as a mechanical engineer. I am the inventor of two inventions and one innovation. My wife works as a translator in a big plant. We have been married since 1978. We have an eight year old son named Pintea-Catalin."
✉ Str.Teiul Doamnei 14,Bl.8,Sc.B,Ap.42,sector 2, Bucuresti, 72243 ✆ (90) 871597 ✍ French (both), English (both), Spanish (she) ♥ trips, bridge, motorcars (he), tailoring (she) ⌂ yes, while our son is on vacation ☆ board

BUCURESTI

ANTON, Doru b. 08/23/47 Electric engineer
"I work in the Technical Medical Industry factory. Post university studies in: computer programming, maintenance of electrotechnical plants, power plants. My wife is an engineer in textiles. We have two sons: Radu, aged 17 and Daniel, aged 2."
✉ Bd.Armata Poporului 14,Bl.13,Sc.B,Ap.96,sector 6, Bucuresti ✆ (90) 719866 ✍ English, French ♥ travels ♓ yes ☆ conviniences for accomodation in any town.

ANTONESCU, Cristina b.08/17/67 Student
"My parents and my brother, who is 32, are engineers. I study medicine and love my profession a lot. I travelled little."
✉ Str.Eugen Botez 38,sector 2, Bucuresti ✆ (90) 106882 ✍ English, French ♥ medicine and biology, classical music, cinema, skiing, tennis ♓ yes, in a 6 rooms villa; also in a villa in Sinaia ☆ we have two cars

ARDELEANU, Cornel - Daniel b.07/04/61 Aviation mechanic
"I was born in Onesti, Moldova. In 1980 I graduated from the secondary school of aviation in Bucharest and now I work in a factory for planes and helicopters motors. I am married and have 2 children, a girl aged 7 and a boy aged 3."
✉ Str.Poiana Muntelui 2,Bl.OD3,Ap.189,sector 6, Bucuresti, 77386 ✆ (90) 451330 ✍ French, English ♥ photography, fishing, aviation, literature ♓ yes

ASLAN, Corina b.09/20/30 Architect
"I have a 33 years old son, architect, married. My second husband died of cancer in 1982. I travelled before and would like to travel more."
✉ Calea Victoriei 100, Bucuresti ✆ (90) 158867 ✍ French, German, Spanish ♥ arts and everything connected to visual arts, travelling ♓ yes, in the center ☆ breakfast, car

BUCURESTI

ATANASIU, Ioana b.12/17/47 Architect
"I represent all my family. I live with my parents and my daughter aged 18. They are all very nice people. My father is a well known painter, my mother is a doctor, my daughter is a pupil. I have a house in the centre. I am a good cook and so is mother."
✉ Str.Ion Slavici 3,sector 1, Bucuresti, 70769
✆ (90) 156722 ✍ French, English ♥ tennis, swimming, dance, bridge, all arts, tourism, etc ⌂ yes, for one or two middle aged persons. ☆ board

AVRAMESCU, Mihai b.11/22/58 Electromechanical Engineer
"I was born in Craiova and I also studied there. I live in Bucharest together with my wife, who is teaching mathematics. I work in a design institute."
✉ Str.Mieilor 22,Bl.224,Sc.1,Ap.58,sector 2, Bucuresti, 73208 ✍ French ♥ sports (tennis, football, chess), aphorisms and thoughts about men, humor, music, trips ⌂ yes, a bed only ☆ breakfast

BACALUM, Dan b.10/28/69 Student
"I was born in Constanta at the seaside, I graduated high school and now I am a student at the Polytechnical Institute, Electronics, in Bucharest."
✉ Str.Maior Coravu 1-7,Bl.C4,Sc.B,Ap.57,sector 2, Bucuresti ✆ (90) 201336 ✍ English ♥ tennis, ski, music, parties, picture ⌂ yes ☆ I offer everything for my guests.

BALACEANU, Sanda b.03/16/60 Secretary
"I graduated from high school in Bucharest. I tried to pass the entry exam at the Institute of Theatre and Cinema but I failed. I had played in various amateur theatrical performances since the age of 17. I was married. I have a 4 year old son."
✉ Str.Robanesti 39,sector 1, Bucuresti, 78449
✆ (90) 671801 ✍ French, English (a little) ♥ theatre, music, dance ⌂ yes ☆ board

BALASOIU, Florea b.07/20/50 Electronic Engineer
"I was born in Mozaceni, a village in the Arges district. My parents are peasants. I graduated the Polytechnical

Institute in Bucharest. I am married. My wife is an engineer. I have an 11 years old son."
✉ Str.Lotrioara 5,Bl.V31,Ap.75, Bucuresti, 74601
℃ (90) 741119 ✍ French, English ♥ voyages, mountain climbing, literature, cultural and technical information, gardening ∎ yes ☆ board; tour by car, guide, good company.

BANCEANU, Patricia   b.04/20/62   Economist
"I studied finances and work at the Romanian Banque for Foreign Trade. I am not married. I live in a two rooms flat next to my parents."
✉ Str.Odobesti 4,Bl.Z3,Sc.6,Ap.79,sector 3, Bucuresti, 74576 ℃ (90) 739778 ✍ English, French ♥ English language, music, dancing, cinema, theatre, bridge ∎ yes ☆ breakfast

BANU, Cristian   b.08/17/62   Oil engineer and Computers engineer
"I hate communism and I love freedom, human dignity, I like very much western democracy, except violence. I believe in God. I like very much to travel, to see the world."
✉ Str.Burdujeni 18,Bl.N-15,Sc.A,Ap.4,sector 3, Bucuresti, 74634 ℃ (90) 441572 ✍ English, Spanish ♥ music (British, but also Italian and French), tennis, football, automobiles, friendship ∎ yes ☆ board; tours by car

BARBU, Gabriel   b.07/05/67   Student
"I am a calm man, a little shy, but with much energy and love of life. I have dark hair, I am tall enough and slim. I am tidy. I study energetics. I have a 22 year old brother."
✉ Str.Firidei 3,Bl.H-19,Sc.4,Ap.64,sector 3, Bucuresti, 74603 ℃ (90) 743959 ✍ Italian ♥ disco music, dancing, sports, watching TV, movies ✂ postcards, old coins ∎ yes

BARNA, Emil   b. 02/06/24   Chemic engineer
"I was born in Blaj, a small town in Transylvania. I studied in Blaj, Cernauti and Iasi. I worked in the field of glass and ceramics; I retired. My wife, Ariana (52),

works as a technician and speaks Hungarian and English. My son lives in Brazil."

✉ Str.Maior Coravu 9-15,Bl.C5,Sc.A,Ap.31, Bucuresti, 73291 ✆ (90) 212956 ✍ French, German (a little) ♥ tourism, literature, shows ⌂ yes, in other parts of the country too ☆ board

BARNA, Peter b. 10/05/57 Computer engineer

"I am 33 years old. I was born in Bucharest; I am married; I graduated the Polytechnical Institute of Bucharest."

✉ Soseaua Stefan cel Mare 5, Bl.6 Dinamo,Sc.C,Ap.88,sector 2, Bucuresti, 71421 ✆ (90) 100495 ✍ English, French ♥ computer software, history, literature, geography, theater, opera, sports (tennis, football, swimming) ⌂ yes ☆ board

BARONCEA, Alexandrina b.04/23/45
Mathematician

"My husband Eugeniu is a physicist and an amateur painter. He is 45. My daughter, Olga Antoneta is 22 and a student at the Faculty of Metallurgy in Bucharest."

✉ Str.Moghioros 32,Bl.A11,Ap.7,sector 6, Bucuresti, 75822 ✆ (90) 454523 ✍ French, English
⌂ yes ☆ board

BATI, Olivia b. 05/26/59 Mechanic engineer

"I am divorced. I live together with my parents in a 4 room flat."

✉ Calea Dorobanti 61-63,Ap.25,sector 1, Bucuresti ✆ (90) 115566 ✍ French, English ♥ tennis, skating, swimming, walking, trips, shows (theatre) ⌂ yes
☆ breakfast

BICLEANU, Dan and Olimpia (wife) b.09/16/25
Physician (retired); Physician (wife)

"I was born in Tirgu Neamt, in Northern Moldova. I am a specialist in nuclear medicine. Now I am retired. I live with my wife in a flat in the centre of the city."

✉ Bd.Gheorghe Magheru 27,Ap.49,sector 1, Bucuresti ✆ (90) 596597 ✍ French, German (a little), French (wife) ♥ bridge, football, reading (thrillers)
⌂ yes ☆ board

BICLEANU, Dima - Florin b.04/14/57 Physicist & writer; Computer programmer (wife).

"I am trying to be happy with myself and enjoy living. I am happily married with the same woman for 12 years (her name is Roxana), a wonderful creature."

✉ Bd.1848 nr.20,Sc.B,Ap.21,sector 3, Bucuresti
✆ (90) 148448 ✍ English, French, German (wife)
♥ blue eyed girls (especially blondes), computer games, history of religions, folklore, music (Genesis, Gentle Giant, Jethro Tull, Sting, Beatles, Bach, Pachelbel, Grieg), pornography of good quality (Penthouse magazine like..), American culture, Cinema (Oscar and Cannes winners) ✂ Beatles records (originals). ⌂ yes, with pleasure! ☆ board, and much more...

BIRCMAN, Silvia Manuela b.09/11/65 Energetic Engineer

"I am married to Jacob, aged 28. We both speak English. My husband works in high electronics. I have no brothers or sisters. We have a new apartment, that we are now decorating. We have no children, though I'd like to."

✉ Str.Lunca Bradului 1,Bl.H1,Sc.3,Ap.50,sector 3, Bucuresti, 74624 ✆ (90) 431213 ✍ English, French ♥ reading, music (jazz), knitting, travelling ⌂ yes ☆ breakfast

BIRLEAZA, Florentina and Nicolae (husband) b.04/20/51 Mechanical engineer (both)

"We have big possibilities for travelling (a car and enough money), we have open characters, we are glad to meet and receive other persons."

✉ Bd.Pacii 1,Bl.22B,Sc.A,Ap.19,sector 6, Bucuresti, 77531 ✆ (90) 715225 ✍ French, English
♥ (she) cinema, fashion, the life of great men; (he) tennis, sports (cars, motorcycles), cinema ⌂ yes

BUCURESTI

BLINOF, Jeanina   b.06/18/50   Technician

"I am married and have no children. In my free time I work as a guide. I live in the centre of the city. My husband speaks English."

✉ Str.Franklin 7, Bucuresti, 70149 ✆ (90) 158515
✍ French, German ♥ travelling, music, dance
🏠 yes ☆ breakfast

BOBOC, Adriana   b.07/17/55   Bookkeeper

"I was born in Ardeal (Transylvania) and moved to Bucharest in 1957. I am married and I have a daughter, Laura, aged 13. My husband is highschool master. We traveled in East Germany, Hungary, Tchechoslovakya."

✉ Sos.Alexandriei 17,Bl.26,Sc.2,Ap.24,sector 5,
   Bucuresti ✆ (90) 769272 ✍ French, English
♥ I love French culture and civilization and I like a lot to read books in French and English. My dream: to see Paris, since the revolution, I am very interested in politics and read all the independent newspapers in Bucharest, I like to read, to travel, the flowers, the children 🏠 yes ☆ breakfast

BOERESCU, Dorin   b.03/24/73   Pupil at the high school
   of Informatics

"Height : 1.78m. Weight : 65kg. My eyes are green-hazel, my hair is black. My father works at the ministry of National Economy, my mother is a worker at the Cigarettes Enterprise. I like fair-haired girls."

✉ Str.Porumbacu 72,Bl.89,Ap.28,sector 6, Bucuresti, 77731 ✆ (90) 174795 ✍ English, French
♥ tennis, swimming, dancing, music, reading, karate
🏠 yes

BOLDICI, Dolores Amalia Carina   b.07/22/70
   Schoolmaster

"I was born and spent my childhood in Bucharest. I am the only child in my family. I graduated the Pedagogic high school in 1989 and now I am teaching in a school

in Bucharest. In autumn I intend to attend a course of decorative art."

✉ Str.Aleea Arinis 2,Bl.A40,Sc.A,Ap.15,sector 6, Bucuresti, 77414 ✆ (90) 780744 ✍ French, English ♥ reading (Zola, Cronin, Maugham, Hardy, Hemingway, Mann, Steinbeck), music (disco, new wave, rapp, heavy-metal, jazz, clasic), painting (I paint myself), fashion, travelling, sports ♂ yes

BORCOMAN, Ioan Student

"I study physics at the University in Bucharest."

✉ Bd.Dimitrov 176, Bucuresti, 73339 ✍ English ♂ yes

BRADEANU, Dan Engineer, scientific researcher

"Born in 1930"

✉ Calea Dorobanti 111-131,Bl.9B,Sc.F,Ap.194, Bucuresti ✆ (90) 330441 ✍ French

BRATOSIN, Aurelian
and Claudia (sister) b.06/26/67 Computer operator; School girl (sister)

"I am 1.88 m tall, dark haired, good-looking. I work in an electronic research institute of satellite telecomunications. I have a very pretty sister born 03.22.72 who speaks Italian and English. We want very much to meet people."

✉ Str.Drumul Taberei 25,Bl.Z48,Ap.22,sector 6, Bucuresti, 77331 ✆ (90) 467994 ✍ Italian, English, French, Spanish ♥ travels, foreign languages, nature, music, jewelry, fashion ♂ yes ☆ breakfast

BREAHNA, Alexandru
and Madlena (wife) b.05/21/26 Engineer (retired); wife: Teacher of Romanian language and literature

"I am liberal, social democrat in politics, Christian Orthodox but very moderate in religious life, open to dialogue. We have a son Radu, student at the Polytech-

nic Institute. He speaks English, French, Russian, and a married daughter in Piatra Neamt."

✉ Calea Giulesti 109, Ap.39, Bucuresti, 77725 ✆ (90) 176656 ✍ French, English, and French, Russian, (wife) ♥ sports (mountains climbing, volleyball, tennis, chess, swimming), reading, music (I studied violin), travelling, wife: reading, tourism, family life, son: chess (master category, rated elo 2360), tennis, skiing (instructor), mountain climbing ⌂ Yes. 3 rooms flats very comfortable. ☆ Board, guide-interpreter, tours over Romania.

BUSUIOC, Irina b.09/17/71 Student at the Academy of Economic Studies, faculty of trade, section of marketing.

"My father is a mathematician and my mother is a dress creator at the Art Galleries. I finished the Cybernetic highschool this year and then passed the exam and was admitted by the faculty. I have hazel eyes and I am dark haired. I am 1.70 m high."

✉ Str.Tirgu Neamt 11, Bl.M4, Sc.A, Ap.5, sector 6, Bucuresti, 77481 ✆ (90) 266476 ✍ English, French ♥ music, dancing, skiing, table tennis, climbing mountains, learning foreign languages ⌂ yes

BUTA, Daniela b. 06/22/69 Student

"I am 21. My height is 1.65 m. My weight - 50 Kg. I have green eyes and blond hair. I am a nice and very sentimental girl. I am studying cybernetics."

✉ Str.Dealul Tugulea 46-50, Bl.12, Ap.96, sector 6, Bucuresti, 77572 ✆ (90) 715159 ✍ English ♥ art. I like to write poems, and why not, letters, good music, new music, to know a man, his feelings, what he loves, what he thinks of life, fashion design, I am a good dress maker ⌂ yes

BUXAR, Valentina   b.03/03/56   Scientific researcher
"My husband is a pilot. We would like to know people from other countries, with their hobbies and their way of living, their ideas and dreams."
✉ Sos.Colentina 62A,Bl.113,Sc.C,Ap.143,sector 2, Bucuresti, 72446 ✆ (work: 505880) ✍ English, French ♥ literature (classics, SF), music, movies, travelling ∐ yes

BUZDEA, Anda Mihaela   b.03/24/56   Dentist
"Knocking and drilling people's teeth is not always entertaining, but that is my job and I like it. I have been married for eleven years. We have a three years old baby whom I love very much."
✉ Bd.Constructorilor 31,Bl.31,Sc.C,Ap.48,sector 6, Bucuresti ✆ (90) 189906 ✍ French, English
♥ travelling, reading, listening to opera and symphonic music, playing bridge, visiting museums, making embroidery ∐ yes ☆ board

CALIN, Doina Florica and Liviu   b.01/09/61   Scientific Researcher at the Institute for Life Quality; Liviu: Electronics Engineer at "Microelectronica" enterprise.
"We offer to work for a French society of tourism, foreign trade, electronics, in Romania or France. We have two girls (twins)."
✉ Str.Bibescu Voda 2,Bl.P5,Sc.4,Ap.51,sector 4, Bucuresti ✆ (90) 231673 ✍ French, English
♥ promenades, playing: tennis, basketball, chess
∐ yes ☆ board

CALOTA, Lucia Emanuela   b.09/18/63   Engineer
"I am a blond girl, with hazel eyes and my height is 1.65m. I am pretty. I am not married. I graduated from the faculty of Constructions last year and now I work in site. I think I have an interesting job."
✉ Str.Cricovul Dulce 2-4,Bl.17-18,Sc.H,Ap.112,sector 4, Bucuresti ✆ (90) 827514 ✍ English, German ♥ sports, dancing, literature, travels, people, children ∐ yes ☆ breakfast

CAMULEA, Lambert   b.04/10/25   Engineer
"I graduated from the Polytechnic in Bucharest and worked in geology and building materials. I am married.

My wife is 57. We have no children. I own a villa with a garden in the centre of Bucharest. After I retired I was sometimes guide interpreter."
✉ Str.Caderea Bastiliei 48, sector 1, Bucuresti
✆ (90) 592109 ✍ French, German, English ♥ music (opera, operetta, philarmonic) ⌂ yes ☆ breakfast

CARP, Jeannette b.09/08/67 Student

"I learned German in a private kindergarten. Now, I study Romanian as a main subject and German as a secondary subject. My main professional interest is translation. I have nice friends. I am interested in astrology and magical thought of any kind."
✉ Calea Giulesti 109,Bl.6,Sc.B,Ap.43,sector 6, Bucuresti, 77725 ✆ (90) 170847 ✍ English, German ♥ reading books, music, learning languages, talking ⌂ yes

CARSTEA, Stelian b.05/04/25 Engineer

"Scientist, Specialist in environment protection - soil pollution control, awarded the Romanian Academy Prize."
✉ Str.Elena 2,Bl.OD7c,Ap.9,sector 2, Bucuresti, 72271 ✆ (90) 879853 ✍ English, French, Italian ♥ opera, tourism, ballet, concerts, ecology, social and economical problems ⌂ yes

CERNAIANU, Liviu b.10/18/27 Journalist

"I studied law. My wife, Olivia, is an artist, my son,Calin, is a painter, sculptor and writer, my daughter in law, Ioana, is a laboratory assistant,my grandson, Liviu,is the king of our family. Although retired, I still work as an independent journalist."
✉ Str.Drumul Taberei 64,Bl.F4,Sc.V,Ap.91,sector 6, Bucuresti, 77381 ✆ (90) 450417 ✍ French, German ♥ making my guests feel at home, Romanian civilization, ancient popular work ⌂ yes (also at my son's and outside Bucharest-20km)

CHELARU, Ion and Rodica b.11/16/50 Engineer / Editor

"I work in a design institute in charge of the huge "House of the Republic". My wife works for a weekly

private magazine : "Expres Magazin". We have no children, but still hope."

✉ Str.13 Septembrie Nr.83,Bl.77,Sc.B,Ap.47,sector 5, Bucuresti, 76117 ✆ (90) 812606 ✍ French, English, Italian ♥ literature, music, ballet, dancing, bridge, voyages ♦ yes ☆ board

CINCA, Liviu   b.   01/11/65   Folk dancer

"I am married, no kids yet. We have a beautiful flat, located near a park. I like travelling."

✉ Str.Tohani 9,Bl.29,Sc.C,Ap.97,sector 4, Bucuresti, 75128 ✆ (90) 753583 ✍ English, French, Italian ♥ travel, dance, business, science fiction ♦ yes ☆ board

CIUBOTARU, Ernest   b.03/09/33   Economist

"I was born in the Neamt county, in Moldavia. I worked as an economist in industry. I am retired now. I own a two room flat in the centre of the city, a mountain chalet and a new car, by which we could visit all the country."

✉ Str.Cercului 6,Bl.5/7,Ap.50,sector 2, Bucuresti, 70266 ✆ (90) 198678 ✍ French ♥ tourism, dancing, gardening, gastronomy ♦ yes ☆ anything

CIUCA, Mihail - Eugen   b.07/28/53   Economist and Engineer

"I was born in Bucharest. I graduated from the Polytechnic Institute of Bucharest and after 11 years I graduated also the Academy of Economic Studies. I am married and have no children."

✉ Str.9 Mai,Nr.7,Bl.24,Sc.B,Ap.97, Bucuresti ✆ (90) 501474 ✍ French, English ♥ tennis (old player), football, music (Beatles, Pink Floyd, Jethro Tull), history of WW2, economic problems ♦ yes ☆ board

CIUREA, Gabriela   b.07/02/70   Student

"I study veterinary medicine. I have a sister named Adina,21. My mother, Marina, is a teacher, my father, Peter, is a doctor. I have a big house in Bucharest with

a big garden. I want to meet young people from all over the world."

✉ Str.Singerului 8, Bucuresti, 77288 ✆ (90) 577213 ✍ French ♥ dance, animals, performances, books, voyages ♠ yes

COARA, Doina Liliana   b.08/27/53   Teacher

"I graduated from the faculty of Classical philology (Latin and Greek); I am married to a chemist; we have two children"

✉ Bd.N.Titulescu 12,Bl.21A,Sc.B,Ap.104,sector 1, Bucuresti, 78152 ✆ (90) 598289 ✍ Italian, French, English (not good) ♥ pictures, theatre, TV, reading, music, trips, fashion ♠ yes

COCAN, Artemiza   b.02/06/51   Computer operator

"I had a happy childhood. I used to read the French "Pif" children magazine and correspond with kids from France. Later that was forbidden by the communists. I live in a 3 rooms flat near the centre. I have two children aged 9 and 11."

✉ Str.Aleea Cetatuia 10,Bl.25,Sc.B,Ap.47,sector 6, Bucuresti ✆ (90) 713323 ✍ French, English, Italian ♥ music, literature, foreign languages, trips ♠ yes ☆ breakfast

CODRU, Neculai   b.03/11/66   Student

"I've always lived in Bucharest. My father died in a car accident in 1970. My mother was an engineer, but she is retired now. I have no brothers. In 1985 I got a job at the Airplane Factory, then I worked in a small enterprise as locksmith. Student 1988."

✉ Str.Valeriu Braniste 56,Bl.A,Sc.A,Ap.1,sector 3, Bucuresti, 74136 ✆ (90) 208136 ✍ English, French, Spanish ♥ travelling, history, geography, mountain climbing, football, badminton, athletics, tennis, human anatomy, painting, politics ♠ yes ☆ breakfast

CONSTANTIN, Adrian   b.09/24/56   Engineer

"My parents divorced when I was born. I grew up with my mother. I studied Constructions Engineering. During holidays I worked as a tourist guide on the littoral. My

wife is a physician. We have a little girl, Anca Ioana, aged 3. We live in a big house."

✉ Str.Maria Rosetti 16A, Bucuresti, 70232 ✆ (90) 112642 ✍ French, English ♥ tennis, card collecting. I have a collection of over 12,000 B/W and colour starting from 1890 ⌂ yes; we also own a weekend house in the country.

CONSTANTIN, Amelia (Amy) b.06/13/73 Pupil

"I was born and spent my childhood in Bucharest. I am a high school pupil in the last year. I want to study trade."

✉ Str.Aleea Arinis 2,Bl.A40,Sc.A,Ap.1,sector 6, Bucuresti, 77414 ✆ (90) 780103 ✍ French, English ♥ reading (Zola, Cronin, Galsworthy), all music, painting, travelling, sports, fashion ⌂ yes

CONSTANTINESCU, Cornelie b.08/25/19 Retired

"In spite of the age, I am in a very good physical condition; I still work in Bucharest and through Europe as an interpreter (French & English) for the distinguished guests of our authorities. I have a daughter living in Paris and a son in Bucharest."

✉ Str.W.A.Mozart 2A,Bl.A,Sc.A,Ap.5, Bucuresti, 71457 ✆ (90) 332536 ✍ French, English ♥ music (preclassic, classic, opera). I play the piano ⌂ yes ☆ breakfast ·

CONSTANTINESCU, Gheorghe b.04/11/41
    Economist

"I studied economics. I am married and have three children. After the Revolution in December 1989, I became an independent businessman."

✉ Str.Bozieni 2,Bl.833,Sc.C,Ap.133,sector 6, Bucuresti ✆ (90) 267424 ✍ Russian, German ♥ bridge, horoscopes, racers ⌂ yes, but in Olanesti

CONSTANTINESCU, Monika b.01/26/40 Chemist

"I was born in Bucharest in a family with a passion for chemistry. I am married and we have a daughter."

✉ Bd.Magheru 43,Ap.16,sector 1, Bucuresti ✆ (90) 592132 ✍ French, English, Italian ♥ good music, voyages ⌂ yes

BUCURESTI

CONSTANTINESCU, Teodor Lucian b.05/15/46
   Engineer

"I am married. I graduated in 1969. I have been working at projects in the field of hydrology."

✉ Str.M.Kogalniceanu 95,Ap.9, Bucuresti ✆ (90) 162591 ✍ French, English, German ♥ electronics, sports, music ⌂ yes

COSTEA, Adrian - Cosmin b.05/09/68 Student at the Faculty of Computers of the Polytechnical Institute of Bucharest.

"I was born in Bucharest. I am not married. I'd like to travel abroad and meet many people."

✉ Str.Dr.Lister 44A,Sc.B,Ap.7, Bucuresti ✆ (90) 134174 ✍ French, English, German (a little) ♥ sports (especially tennis), listening to good music (opera, symphonic), dance, voyages ⌂ yes; I can rent a comfortable flat in centre. ☆ transport by car, etc.

COSTINER, Elmano and Maria Physician / Teacher of philisophy (retired)

"I was born in 1927 in Cernauti. I am a Jew, and was in a concentration camp; after the war I finished my medical studies. I have been married since 1955. My wife was born in 1930. She is Romanian. We have a son. Until 15 years ago I beleved in communism."

✉ Str.Izvorul Muresului 7,Ap.14,sector 4, Bucuresti, 75385 ✆ (90) 869803 ✍ German, French, English (a little) ♥ classical music, literature, walking, travelling ⌂ yes, in a little wooden house in Transilvania too

COZMIUC, Marian b.05/31/70 Student

✉ Str.Barajul Sadului 7C,Bl.M4A3,Sc.B,Ap.75,sector 3, Bucuresti ✍ English ♥ dance, basketball, swimming, body-building, music ⌂ yes ☆ board

CRACIUN, Viorel Mircea b.11/23/44 Chemistry engineer

"I live in a big flat. I can offer house and meal for a family. I was born in Oravita, near the Yugoslavian

border. I live in Bucharest since the age of 15. I have two children. They are both 10. My wife died recently."
✉ Str.Galati 18,Et.2,Ap.17,sector 2, Bucuresti, 70212 ✆ (90) 153972 🖉 English, French
♥ sports (volleyball, judo in my youth; tennis, swimming now), travel (I visited East Europe, Denmark, Sweden, Nigeria), I practise yoga, philately ✂ stamps
🏠 yes ☆ board

CRACIUNOIU, Victor and Lucia (wife) b.07/13/54
    Electronics engineer
"I am working in Bucharest in microelectronics. I am married since 1985 and I have a little boy. My wife was born in 1955, March 13, and she is also an electronics engineer. I studied also in Italy at SGS-ATES and visited a lot of it."
✉ Sos.Stefan cel Mare 230,Bl.46,Sc.B,Ap.53, Bucuresti, 72201 🖉 English, Italian, French (wife)
♥ mountain climbing, tennis, bridge, chess 🏠 yes; a whole appartament; holiday house too. ☆ board; tours by car

CREOSTEANU, Ileana b.06/09/60 Engineer
"Since 1989 I teach technical disciplines at "Gheorghe Lazar" high school in Bucharest. I am married and have two children : Ruxandra (5) and Radu (3). My husband is an electronic engineer also. He is very fond of history, politics and fishing."
✉ Str.Dorneasca 11,Bl.P79,Sc.2,Ap.59,sector 5, Bucuresti 🖉 English, French, German ♥ swimming, skiing, dancing, theatre, cinema, automobiles
🏠 yes ☆ car, guide

CRETU, Toma-Dan b.06/30/58 Engineer
"I was born in Calarasi; graduated the Polytechnical Institute in 1986; I am a bachelor; I attended a course in tourism and worked for 10 years as a guide; I'll soon be the owner of a little enterprise. I am going to found a tourism agency."
✉ Str.Rucar 26A,sector 1, Bucuresti, 78349
✆ (90) 664998 🖉 French, English (medium), Russian
♥ chess, karate, SF literature ☆ soon, housing and breakfast through my agency

BUCURESTI

CRISTESCU, Florin
and Gavrila Eugenia (mother) b.08/26/82 Pupil / Clerk
(mother)
"I am eight years old and my mother is 34. I live in Bucharest with my mother and my grand-mother. I have a nice street."
✉ Str.Durau 147, sector 1, Bucuresti, 7000 ☏ (90) 680707 ✍ French ♥ to write and receive letters from children in France, tourism, gardening, cartoons, hand working ♨ yes ☆ breakfast

CRISTESCU, Virgil b.08/23/26 Economist (retired)
"I am married. I am retired since 06.01.90."
✉ Str.Bibicescu Ion 6, sector 1, Bucuresti, 70758 ☏ (90) 135099 ✍ French ♥ opera, football ♨ yes, for a Parisian family of intelectuals.

CROITORU, Valeriu b.10/04/56 Drilling Engineer
"I was born in a town between hills, Slanic-Prahova. I have a sister. I am married to Liliana and we have a son Tiberiu, aged 13. My wife is 34 and we work together in the same company. We like to have friends."
✉ Str.Bradului 19, Bl.C2, Sc.4, Ap.128, sector 1, Bucuresti, 78136 ☏ (90) 501829 ✍ English, French ♥ football, music (hard, heavy), theatre, scrabble, thrillers ♨ yes ☆ board

CRUCEANU, Mircea b.07/01/30 Actor
"I am an actor at the Giulesti Theatre in Bucharest. I will soon be retired. In 1975 I worked in the Netherlands as a Professor at the Theatre Academy of Maastricht "Tonelakademie" - drama professor and stage director. I live in a villa with my wife."
✉ Aleea Zinelor 10, Bucuresti ☏ (90) 753913 ✍ French, English ♥ performances (at the French library in Bucharest, I staged music, ballet and theatre performances), tourist guiding (5 times with tourist groups to Istanbul) ♨ yes ☆ trips by car

CURELARU, Marian b.04/09/55 Teacher
"I studied philosophy and history at the University in Bucharest, and my wife (Mihaela) too. We have a 13-year-old son - Mihai. I taught history 8 years in a

village in the Prahova county. In the last 3 years I have been working as an inspector."

✉ Al. Giurgeni 4, Bl.F13, Sc.4, Ap.41, sector 3, Bucuresti, 74724 ✆ (90) 300719 ✍ French
❚ yes

DAN, Marguerite Marianne   b.12/06/30   Mathematician, computers expert (retired)

"I was born in Paris. I translated books of SF literature from English into Romanian (13 published). I am a widow and have a son age 31. I am in very good health and I have a joyful, impulsive temperament. Physique: 1.59/53, brown eyes. Politic: centre"

✉ Str.Lt.D.Lemnea 14, Ap.25, Bucuresti, 78122 ✆ (90) 505706 ✍ French, English, German ♥ reading, music (opera, symphonic, but also Jean Michel Jarre!), animals, flowers, swimming, cooking ❚ yes ☆ board; I also offer boarding for dog.

DAN, Rodica   b. 10/09/52   Xerox operator

"I was born in Bucharest. I studied at "George Calinecscu" school in Bucharest. Now I am not married and I have no children. I visited USSR, East Germany and other near countries."

✉ Str.Albotei 15-19, Bl.IX/3, Sc.1, Ap.4, sector 1, Bucuresti, 7000 ✆ (90) 663925 ✍ English
♥ I like very much to paint landscapes and flowers. I have some exibitions with my paintings and drawings in Bucharest, opera, especially Verdi; modern music (M.Jackson, Stevie Wonder, Ray Charles)

DIACENCO, Elena   b.03/04/50   Economist

"I work in a research institute. I am very interested in knowing the economic activity of the enterprises in the free world. I am divorced and have a daughter aged 15. I am feminine but courageous."

✉ Str. Blajel 2, Bl.V4, Ap.20, Bucuresti ✍ French, English, German ♥ literature (Dostoievski, Faulkner, Fr.Mauriac), dance, swimming, mountain trips, music (opera, jazz) ❚ yes ☆ board

DIACONESCU, Mariana   b.08/12/45   Physician

"I graduated from faculty in 1969 and married in 1970. My husband teaches mathematics in a college. We

have two daughters : the first is 19 and studies mathematics, the second is 15 and a pupil at the high school specialized in informatics."

✉ Str.Galati 60 ,sector 2 , Bucuresti ✆ (90) 117495
✍ French ♥ travelling ⌂ yes ☆ breakfast

DIMA, Dimitrie   Retired

"I am 65 and live in the very centre of Bucharest. I am alone. I was a cavalry officer and after the war I was obliged to retire. I worked as an unqualified worker, driver, mechanic, electrician. Meanwhile I graduated from the Theological Institute."

✉ Calea Mosilor 256 ,Bl.2 ,Ap.26 , Bucuresti, 73252 ✆ (90) 350472 ✍ French, German (a little) ♥ music, animals (horses), cars ⌂ yes

DIMITRIU, Maria-Ruxandra   b.05/16/66   Engineer

"I am a building engineer, but I work as editor with the Technic Editing House."

✉ Intr.Badeni 10,Bl.T5,Ap.10 ,sector 3 , Bucuresti, 74408 ✆ (90) 439051/437779 ✍ French, German (a little) ♥ trips, architecture, arts, history, the orient, the Macedonian people and language ⌂ yes, a whole 3 rooms flat ☆ guide

DIMO, Aimee   b. 11/16/56   Teacher of English in a High School

"I was born in Bucharest. I belong to an old family. My father was an architect and he died when I was 7. My mother was a teacher of Geography and now she has retired. We live in a large house in the centre of Bucharest. I am not married."

✉ Str.Tunari 32 ,sector 2 , Bucuresti ✆ (90) 106423
✍ English, French ♥ literature, gardening ⌂ yes
☆ house and breakfast

DINESCU HOLTEA, Daniela   b.11/21/56   Teacher (foregn languages)

"In 1979 I graduated from faculty and since then I've been teaching English and French in a middle-school in Bucharest. I am married to a wise, calm, vegetarian

Aquarius. We have a sweet girl, born in 1988, November the 9th. I am an 'official' guide."

✉ Str.Agrisielor 11,Ap.13,sector 3, Bucuresti ✆ (90) 207279 ✍ English, French, German (a little)
♥ my baby, literature, music, travelling, Sahaja Yoga
H yes

DINU, Maria-Ileana   b.09/11/41   Mathematician
"I studied in Bucharest. I have a PhD degree in mathematics. I worked for 15 years as a scientific researcher. For 10 years I have been teaching at the Polytechnical Institute. I have been married for 20 years. We have no children."

✉ Str.Romancierilor 5,Bl.C14,Sc.C,Ap.85,sector 6, Bucuresti, 77395 ✆ (90) 783155 ✍ French, English ♥ arts, architecture, music, foreign languages, travelling H yes

DOBRESCU, Mircea-Aurelian   b.10/18/60   Engineer, scientific researcher
"I did my secondary studies in Bucharest and in Abidjan, Ivory Coast (College Jean Mermoj). Then I graduated from the Faculty of Chemical Technologies in Bucharest. Since 1984 I work at the Institute of Research for Constructions and Buildings, Bucharest."

✉ Str.Firidei 1,Bl.H 15,Sc.1,Ap.17,sector 3, Bucuresti, 74603 ✆ (90) 744082 ✍ English, French
♥ electronics. I am a radio-amateur (my code is YO3FGF) and of course I work with a personal computer H yes

DOCIU, Igor   b. 04/01/25   Physician at the Institute for Medical Expertise and Work Capacity
"I spent my childhood in Basarabia, Romanian teritory occupied by the Soviet Union in 1940. In the years 1940-1941 I learned Russian, which my parents also spoke. In 1941 when the Soviets came back I left for Romania."

✉ Str.Gradina cu Cai 7,sector 5, Bucuresti, 70623
✆ (work: 277580 exten. 3) ✍ Russian, French
♥ Soviet literature H no, because I have only one room. ☆ I can be a good companion for tourists

BUCURESTI

DODESCU, Elidor and Nadejda (wife)   b.10/10/22
    Mechanical Engineer/Teacher of psychology and pedagogy
"I worked as an officer for 11 years (I fought in World War 2), then as an engineer in a machine building factory and in a research institute. We have no children. We live in a big two room flat in the centre of the town."
✉ Str.Gradina cu cai 4,Ap.13,sector 5, Bucuresti
✆ (90) 134240 ✍ French, German ⌂ yes, for two persons

DOMAINSCHI, Daniela
Adriana Carmen   b.06/28/56   Computer programmer
"I was curious, sociable and jolly as a child. In 1971 I passed the admission exam at the English High School. In 1980 I graduated from the Polytechnic Institute and started working as a computer programmer. I am married. Our daughter, Ana-Maria, is 6."
✉ Bd.Dimitrov 97,Bl.P17,Sc.C,Ap.75, Bucuresti, 73336 ✆ (90) 428801 ✍ English, French, Italian
♥ music (I studied piano), nature, flowers (ikebana), cinema, reading, travelling, making friends ⌂ yes
☆ breakfast

DRAGHICI, Andreea   Pupil
"I am 13. My parents would like to participate in this interesting dialogue you propose to us with great pleasure. I have a sister, Raluca, 10 years old. We have a lot of things to show to a traveller in the country and in my home town."
✉ Str.Albinelor 32,Bl.32,Sc.2,Ap.22, Bucuresti
✆ (90) 757313 ✍ English ♥ sports (handball, tennis), modern dance, music (slow rock), films, video
⌂ yes

DRAGONEI, Dumitru   b.05/29/31   Technician (retired)
"I was born in Bucharest, of Romanian origin, orthodox. I own a house and two cars (without drivers). I love people of crazy joy and who drink all the glass..."
✉ Str.Soveja 78,sector 1, Bucuresti, 78356 ✆ (90) 685463 ✍ French ♥ philately on: sports, cosmos, animals, flowers, Romanian painters etc.; I have a vegetable garden ✂ stamps ⌂ yes ☆ board

DRAGOS, Marius Bazil b.09/19/52 Electric engineer

"I graduated from the Polytechnical Institute in 1976. I am working in a foreign trade company. My wife (we are both the same age) is also an engineer, but in automation. We have no children."

✉ Str.Panduri 60,Bl.A,Sc.2,Ap.86,sector 5, Bucuresti ✆ (90) 316027 ✍ English, French, Russian ♥ skiing, tennis, Chinese art, the mountains, travelling ⌂ yes, also in the mountains and at the seaside

DRAGUSIN, Emil Adrian b.06/07/59 Teacher of English and French

"I was born in Tirgoviste. I studied music and arts in the grammar school, learning to play the violin, which I gave up after my father died in a tragic accident."

✉ Str.Dr.Burghelea 12 A,sector 2, Bucuresti, 73102 ✆ (90) 431578 ✍ English, French, German ♥ foreign languages, opera, gardening, reading, travelling, knowing new places and new people ⌂ yes, in Tirgoviste and Bucharest. ☆ board; trips by car.

DRAGUT, Tudor b.02/22/64 Economist

"I am an economist and my wife is also an economist. She is 25. We have no children. We have a 3 rooms apartment in the centre of the city."

✉ Calea 13 Septembrie 128,Bl.P35,Sc.1,Ap.35,sector 5, Bucuresti ✆ (90) 811324 ✍ English, French ♥ tennis, football, music, trips ⌂ yes ☆ board

DUMITRACHE, Marian b.10/02/55 Engineer

"I am married. My wife is an engineer. We have two children - aged 6 and 5. I am working at the Nuclear Power Plant in Cernavoda."

✉ Str.Latea Gh. 14,Bl.C35,Ap.54,sector 6, Bucuresti ✆ (90) 819209 ✍ English, French ♥ travelling, spelacology, fishing, sports (basketball) ⌂ yes ☆ breakfast

DUMITRESCU, Constantin b.06/09/21 Chemist

"I was born in Oltenia. My wife is also a chemist. We like to travel, we've been to Italy, Switzerland, Poland,

Hungary, Tchechoslovakya, Bulgaria, USSR. We are retired now."

✉ Str.Popa Nan 63,sector 2, Bucuresti ✆ (90) 213782 ✍ French, German, Italian ♥ history, classic music, voyages ⌂ yes ☆ beakfast

DUMITRESCU, Tamara   b.08/31/16   Engineer

"*I was born in a region that no longer belongs to Romaia. I studied in Bucharest : first philology, then I graduated from the Oil Institute. My husband studied law. We have no children. Although old, we are healthy and agreeable persons.*"

✉ Str.Apusului 34,Bl.M-6,Sc.B,Ap.69, Bucuresti, 77569 ✆ (90) 698838 ✍ French, English, Russian ♥ tennis, cycling, cars ⌂ yes

DUTESCO, George   b.02/24/26   Economist

"*My wife's name is Lucille and we have been married since 1948.*"

✉ Bd.L.Salajan 5,Bl.M4,Sc.2,Ap.26, Bucuresti, 74421 ✆ (90) 440041 ✍ French ♥ gardening, opera ⌂ yes ☆ we can offer you an unforgettable vacation

ERENA, Cristian   Engineer

"*Height-1,78, Weight-81, Eyes-hazel, Hair-brown. I am very fond of motorcycles. I would do everything to get in touch with people having the same hobby, from all over.*"

✉ Bd.1848 44,Sc.B,Ap.63,sector 3, Bucuresti, 70458 ✆ (90) 150142 ✍ English, Italian (a little), French (a little) ♥ motorcycles, music (George Benson, Al Jarreau, Billy Joel, Paco de Lucia, Al Dimeola) ⌂ I will accomodate anyone eager to take a ride. ☆ guide

FELDMAN, Maria   b.08/21/21   Social assistent

"*I was born in Ibanesti, Vaslui county. I studied in Birlad and Bucharest. After 1945 I practiced my job at the service for adopting children, at the Diabet Centre. I have no children. My husband died in 1986.*"

✉ Str.Cavafii vechi 3,Sc.A,Ap.4, Bucuresti, 70456 ✆ (90) 138572 ✍ French ♥ arts (music, theatre, opera), nature, philosophy ⌂ yes (for a woman)

FLOREA, Cristian   b.02/23/66   Student

"I study medicine. I live together with my parents. I have a younger brother. I think I am a little old fashioned. Although I am 24, I feel as a newborn child who has just opened his eyes to the world. I think that is a general feeling in Romania."

✉ Bd.Armata Poporului 11A,Bl.D3,Sc.2,Ap.20,sector 6, Bucureşti, 77202 ✆ (90) 810414 ✍ English ♥ flowers, dancing, tennis, movies, theatres, symphonic music ♓ yes

FLORU, Cristian   b.10/16/49   Engineer

"I graduated in 1972 from the Polytechnical Institute and in 1981 from the Academy of Economic Studies. I am divorced. I have a son born in 1981. I work at the Institute of Atomic Physics. I have a 3 room house with a small garden."

✉ Str.Precupetii Vechi 30, Bucuresti, 72154 ✆ (90) 101905 ✍ French, English ♥ tourism, reading, watching the political life ♓ yes

FRUNZA, Ana-Maria   b.12/01/52   Engineer

"I was born in Bucharest, I am married, I have two children : Laura-Daniela (11) and Alexandru (10). My husband is an electronic engineer. We live together with my parents and my grandmother."

✉ Str.Amiral Murgescu 22, sector 2, Bucuresti ✆ (90) 533393 ✍ French, English ♥ reading, cinema ♓ yes ☆ breakfast

GABRIELESCU BERCEANU, Aspazia   Ph.D. in Medicine - endocrinologist; Retired.

"We are an old couple, the wife is 72 and the husband 79, the former has a Ph.D. in medicine, the latter a Ph.D. in law (Faculty of Law in Paris)."

✉ Str.Judetului 15,Bl.17,Sc.A,Ap.6, Bucuresti, 72226 ✆ (90) 191201 ✍ French, Italian ♥ opera

GAGEA, Gloria Constanta   b.01/15/49   Engineer and Economist

"My 17 years old daughter, Laura - Isabela wants to correspond with persons her age in French. My husband, Nicolae, is 41, an engineer, and interested in

corresponding with persons working in the field of energetics, climatisation, preserving by cold."

✉ Aleea Cimpul cu flori 1,Bl.OD2,Sc.B,Ap.81,sector 6, Bucuresti, 77408 ✆ (90) 773147 ✍ French ♥ painting, poetry (I write poems), opera, ballet, travelling ⌂ yes

GEORGESCU, Alexandru b.11/18/53 Air traffic controller

"Married - no children; I'm working in Bucharest International Airport."

✉ Str.Cupolei 1,Bl.106,Sc.3,Ap.107,sector 6, Bucuresti, 71893 ✆ (90) 718193 ✍ English, French ♥ photography, motorcycles, travelling and music ⌂ yes

GEORGESCU, Alexandru b.11/18/53 Controler of Air Traffic

"I am married. I never had children. I work at the radar centre in the International Airport of Bucharest - Otopeni."

✉ Str.Cupolei 1,Bl.106,Sc.3,Ap.107,sector 6, Bucuresti, 77507 ✆ (90) 718193 ✍ French, English ♥ photography, music, cars, sports ⌂ yes

GEORGESCU, Alin b.07/26/24 Engineer

"My family is composed by myself and my wife. We are both retired. I am a civil engineer. We both can speak English, French, a little German and my wife, Italian. We have a two storied house in an old and green district of Bucharest - Cotroceni."

✉ Str.Carol Davila 70, Bucuresti, 76249 ✆ (90) 144510 ✍ French, English ♥ classical music, geography, history, politics ⌂ yes ☆ breakfast

GEORGESCU, Cristian b.06/10/54 Mechanical engineer

"I graduated the Polytechnic Institute in Bucharest and I am specialist in heat engines. I worked in testing engines and in foreign trade. I am married and have two children, a 9 years old boy and a 2 years old girl."

✉ Aleea Istru 7,Bl.A3,Sc.D,Ap.52,sector 6, Bucuresti, 77456 ✆ (90) 770739 ✍ English, German (a little), French (a little) ♥ engines and cars, tourism by car, mountain trips ⌂ no

BUCURESTI

GHELBANOIU, Gheorghe b.11/08/61 Engineer
"I was born in Bucharest and graduated the Polytechnical Institute in 1986. I work in the field of car transport. I am married. My wife teaches physics in a high school."
✉ Str.Calea Grivitei 228,Bl.4,Sc.E,Ap.16,sector 1, Bucuresti ✆ (90) 666936 ✍ Italian, English
♥ sports, travelling, reading ⌂ yes

GHEORGHE, Elena b.11/01/53 Teacher
"I graduated the Faculty of Foreign Languages in Bucharest and I've become a teacher of English and French."
✉ Sos.Stefan cel Mare 33, Bucuresti ✆ (90) 114170
✍ English, French ♥ Precolumbian civilizations of South America, South American literature, sports, music ⌂ no ☆ I can accompany tourists and show them places.

GHEORGHIADE, Mariana b.12/23/32 Economist
"I am retired. No children. My husband died 5 years ago. I live alone in a small apartment with a garden. I have relatives in Belgium where I travelled 2 times and also in France and Holland. I also travelled for business in Eastern Europe."
✉ Str.Caporal Buligea 7,sector 2, Bucuresti ✆ (90) 168983 ✍ French, Russian, German ♥ reading, history of the Middle Ages, geography, voyages, gardening, symphonic music ⌂ yes ☆ breakfast

GHERGHEA, Doinita b.02/27/59 Computer programmer
"I have been married to Nicu since 1985 and have a two year old son - Eugeniu-Marian. We live together with my mother and with my son's best friend - the dog Jerry, in a three room flat. I enjoy housekeeping."
✉ Str.Latea Gh. 14,Bl.C35,Sc.A,Ap.8,sector 6, Bucuresti ✍ French, English ♥ tailoring, knitting, flowers and gardening, films, theatre, reading, music

GHIRAN, Mariana b.03/31/51 Bookkeeper
"I was born in Bucharest; I graduated from high school."
✉ Str.Alex.Moghioros 19,Bl.OD5,Sc.1,Ap.4, Bucuresti ✆ (90) 463111 ✍ French, Italian ♥ nature

BUCURESTI

GHITA, Elisabeta   b.09/20/44   Computer programer - Computing Centre of the Enterprise of Geological Surveys and Geophysics for Hydrocarburs
"I am a widow and have two children: a son, studying at the Polytechnical Institute - Aeronautics, and a daughter, 16, highschool student. I love literature, music and paintings."
✉ Str.Alex.Moghioros 13,Bl.E10,Ap.27,sector 6, Bucuresti, 77369 ✆ (90) 458965 ✍ French
♥ voyages, reading, gardening; I have a little piece of land that I cultivate for domestic needs ⌂ yes
☆ board

GHITA, Simona Constanta   b.10/03/72   Pupil
"I go each week to the French library in Bucharest. I like to write and read. I want to study physics."
✉ Str.Drumul Taberei 53,Bl.R6,Sc.B,Ap.68,sector 6, Bucuresti ✆ (90) 457776 ✍ French, English (a little), Italian (a little) ♥ sports, music, arts, flowers, philately, walks, voyages ✂ stamps ⌂ yes

GIUGELA, George   b.02/19/72   Student
"I graduated highschool in Bucharest (chemistry profile). I am now student. I study law."
✉ Str.Copaceni 47,Bl.W3,Sc.A,Ap.2,sector 3, Bucuresti, 74414 ✆ (90) 212056 ✍ French, English (a little) ♥ tennis, skiing, horse races, astrology ⌂ yes

GIUSCA, Maria   b.12/18/41   Engineer
"I have been working for 10 years as a translator and guide for sportsmen and meet interesting people. I love this job. I have an 18 year old daughter who speaks French and English."
✉ Str.Ciucea 5,Bl.L19,Sc.6,Ap.218,sector 3, Bucuresti, 74696 ✆ (90) 302111 ✍ French, Spanish, English ♥ sports (skiing, swimming), dancing, music, theatre, cinema, gardening ⌂ yes in Bucharest, Herculane, Danube Delta ☆ telephone, car, guide

GLANGER, Isabella   b.02/17/61   Translator

"I work as a translator in an embassy. I graduated from the University of Bucharest. I studied music for 12 years and I play the piano."

✉ Intr.Crisul Alb 37,Bl.5,Sc.B,Ap.20,sector 4, Bucuresti, 75356 ✆ (90) 232227 ✍ English, French, Spanish (a little) ♥ opera, literature, theatre ⓗ yes ☆ bed and breakfast

GOIA, Alexandru   b.10/05/29   Engineer

"I graduated from the Polytechnical Institute and worked as an engineer. I retired a year ago. I am married. My wife is also a retired engineer. I have an appartment and a car."

✉ Str.Grigore Alexandrescu 105,Bl.12B,Sc.E,Ap.127, Bucuresti, 71129 ✆ (90) 116838 ✍ French, Russian (my wife) ♥ philately, travelling ⓗ yes ☆ board

GOLDSTEIN, Hansi Ioana   b.05/18/32   Retired

"I was born in Cernauti. My father was a lawyer. Being Jews, we were deported between 1942 and 1944 and my health was affected for life. My husband died. I have no children and am all alone."

✉ Str.Eufr. Popescu 54,Bl.37,Sc.D,Ap.142, Bucuresti, 74536 ✆ (90) 470831 ✍ German, English, Russian ♥ opera, theatre, antics, knitting ⓗ yes

GRECU, Hortensia Otilia   b.03/17/36   Engineer

"I am a university teacher."

✉ Str.13 Decembrie 27,Sc.1,Ap.30, Bucuresti, 70707 ✆ (90) 143108 ✍ French, English

GROHOLSCHI-MICLESCO, Sergiu Grigorie   b.02/19/24   Physician

"I studied medicine in Iasi and Bucharest. I am member of the French Society of ORL."

✉ Str.Pravat 4,Bl.Z-34,Ap.41, Bucuresti, 77324 ✆ (90) 463004 ✍ French ♥ history of music ⓗ yes, also all over the country ☆ board

GUGU, Florin   b. 02/14/62   Designing Engineer at Electric Power Designing Institute in Bucharest

"I was born in Bucharest. During 1973-1975 I lived in Egypt (my father was working there). In 1986 I con-

cluded my studies at the Polytechnical Institute. During 1986-1989 I worked at a company producing beer and brandy as chief of the power plant."

✉ Bd.Miciurin 13,Bl.7,Sc.A,Ap.17,sector 1, Bucuresti, 71314 ✆ (90) 660558 ✍ English, French (a little) ♥ ski, tennis, travelling, dogs ⌂ yes, in Bucharest and Busteni (mountain resort) ☆ I have a villa in Busteni; can accomodate 10 pers.

GURAN, Vasile   b. 01/01/44   Building engineer

"I am working in a Projection Institute. I am married and have a daughter."

✉ Str.13 Septembrie 108,Bl.52-54,Sc.A,Ap.10,sector 5, Bucuresti ✆ (90) 816557 ✍ English ♥ yachting, hunting, travelling ⌂ yes

HALMAGYI, Stefan and Constantina (wife)   Retired

"I was born 1928 in the Mures county. My father was Hungarian, my mother Romanian. I have a brother in Hungary and three sisters in Romania. My wife is born in 1935. I have a son and 2 grand-children. I live with my wife in a modest house."

✉ Str.Bailesti 16,sector 4, Bucuresti, 75374 ✆ (90) 290761 ✍ Hungarian ♥ chess, backgammon, pool ⌂ yes, a lot of space but little comfort.

HALUNGA, Dionisie - Dorin   b.09/16/30   Engineer

"I was born in the village Hantesti, Suceava county. I graduated from highschool in Suceava and Faculty in Iasi (engineering) and Bucharest (economic sciences). Since 1964 I traveled in 56 countries for business, including directing building of embassies."

✉ Str.Cpt.Vasilescu Mircea 27,sector 4, Bucuresti, 70529 ✆ (90) 137279 ✍ French, English, German (a little) ♥ tourism, swimming, beekeeping, gardening ⌂ yes

HANGU, Radu - Michael b.07/26/57 Jurist
"After finishing my law studies, I worked as a jurist for an enterprise in Bucharest. I am a bachelor, with no obligations to anybody."
✉ Calea Dorobanti 135-145,Bl.10,Sc.A-2,Ap.19,sector 1, Bucuresti ✆ (90) 331782 ✍ French
♥ corresponding with people from all the world, voyages, reading, listening to classic and modern music, defending justice, philosophy, religion, all that culture, civilisation, humanity represents ⌂ yes
☆ breakfast

HARTENIS, Panait b.03/04/12 Economist (retreated)
"I worked in foreign trade, dealing with books. I am a bachelor. I travelled a lot inside the country and outside. I am still in good shape and have a camera."
✉ Str.Podul Giurgiului 5,Bl.12,Ap.14, Bucuresti
✆ (90) 850346 ✍ French, English, German ♥ trips to admire the landscape ⌂ yes, after knowing the person

HARTULARI, Stefan b.10/12/43 Electronics engineer
"I am married. My wife Carmen is 43, a computer engineer. We have a son, Stefan, student. We live in a nice house near the TV studio. This caused a lot of trouble in December 22nd when Securitate attacked TV and shot around, setting fire to our flat."
✉ Calea Dorobantilor 236, Bucuresti ✆ (90) 799991
✍ French, German, English ♥ skiing, mechanic handwork, symphonic music ⌂ yes ☆ breakfast

HURLOIU, Manuela b.12/19/63 Engineer
"I was born in Baicoi. I'm living in Bucharest together with my aunt, but soon I'll have my own flat in the centre of the town. I work in a big plant."
✉ Str.Valea Rosie 7,Bl.Z6, Bucuresti ✆ (90) 265153
✍ French ♥ voyages, the sea, sports (football), music
⌂ yes, in Baicoi too

IACOBAI, Andrei b.03/22/49 Engineer
"I graduated from two faculties. I am married. I have a 17 year old son. My father and I have never joined

the Communist Party. The political opinions of the whole family are liberal."

✉ Bd.Dimitrov 26, Bucuresti, 70313 ✆ (90) 355042 ✍ French, German, English ♥ exchanging ideas, phylately, collections, photography, tourism, cars, books, biology, any other problem ⌂ yes ☆ board

IAMANDI, Darmina Cristina b.02/12/54 Computer programmer

"*I am married and have a 12 year old boy named Daniel. I think friendship is the most wonderful thing in the world. I am confident in my country's future and I must say that the Romanians are indeed very friendly and deserve a better life.*"

✉ Str.Sachelarie Visarion 4,Bl.112A,Sc.A,Ap.32,sector 2, Bucuresti ✆ (90) 422721 ✍ English, French ♥ writing ⌂ yes

IERCAN, Eugen b.12/01/25 Physician

"*I am a hematologist physician, principal researcher at the Hematology centre in Bucharest, chief of works (conference master) at the faculty of medicine in Bucharest. I travelled for studies to USSR, Hungary, France, etc. Married, no children.*"

✉ Intrarea Drumul Taberei 4,Bl.K,Sc.2,Ap.16, Bucuresti, 77303 ✆ (90) 462824 ✍ French, Italian, Hungarian ♥ history, archeology, museology, linguistic, Romanian folklore, architecture, opera ⌂ yes ☆ breakfast; tours with my car

IFTODE, Georgeta b.08/26/45 Bookkeeper

"*I work in a big electronic factory. I love nature and have many friends. I am member of a tourism club. We spend our weekends and our holidays on the peaks.*"

✉ Str.Patriotilor 4,Bl.PM14,Sc.A,Ap.23,sector 3, Bucuresti, 74594 ✆ (90) 742960 ✍ French ♥ literature, theatre, cinema, tourism in the mountains, photography (slides) ⌂ yes ☆ breakfast

ILIESCU, Delia b.12/21/33 Engineer

"*After studying mechanics and technologies, I specialized in informatics. My husband, Romulus is a specialist in power stations. We are both retreated now. We have a 29 years old son who is an engineer, not married."*

✉ Bd.Republicii 86,Ap.31,sector 2, Bucuresti, 70312 ✆ (90) 155004 ✍ French, German, English ♥ reading, tourism, music ♖ yes ☆ board, transport by car

IONESCO, Liviu   b.02/07/60   Engineer

"I am not, I was not and I will not be a member of the communist party."

✉ Bd.I.B.Tito 57A,Bl.Y2B,Sc.1,Ap.19,sector 3, Bucuresti ✆ (90) 740755 ✍ French, English
♥ cybernetics

IONESCU, Adriana   b.06/01/50   Engineer

"I am a joyful, thrifty and lovely wife, a good mother, civil engineer, I am 40 years old, I have a clever daughter and a good husband. We are a happy family."

✉ Sos.Colentina 26,Bl.64,Ap.85, Bucuresti, 72444 ✆ (90) 887732 ✍ English, French ♥ music, dancing, trips, coresponding with people who love English or French ♖ yes

IONESCU, Ana-Maria   b.03/24/50   Geologic engineer

"I work in a research institute for hydro-electric stations. I have a 17 year old son and a 13 year old daughter. My husband is 45 and an electromechanical engineer."

✉ Bd.1 Mai Nr.93,Bl.14,Sc.II,Ap.77,sector 1, Bucuresti ✆ (90) 662405 ✍ German, French (a little) ♥ music (jazz and symphonic), philately, tailoring, swimming, walks in the mountains ♖ yes

IONESCU, Calin-Radu   b.03/04/55   Architect

"I was born in Bucharest where I also studied. I am married. I have two children : a daughter born in 1984 and a son born in 1989."

✉ Str.Eforiei 8,Ap.5,sector 5, Bucuresti, 70623 ✆ (90) 140646 ✍ French, English, German (a little)
♥ skiing, working with wood ♖ yes, 2-4 pers, in the center ☆ breakfast

BUCURESTI

IONESCU, Diana   Typist

"I live together with my mother in a three room flat in a quiet place. I am 23 years old; height : 1.68m, weight : 50kg."

✉ Str.Burdujeni 10,Bl.N13,Sc.C,Ap.42,sector 2, Bucuresti, 74500 ✆ (90) 432950 (work: 355000 / 1302) ✍ English, Spanish (a little), French (a little) ♥ travelling, reading ✂ stamps ⌂ yes

IONESCU, Mery   b.09/07/39   Medical assistent

"I was born in Craiova. I graduated highschool in Craiova then I followed the medical school. I work as medical assistant since 1962. Now I live in Bucharest, I have no children. Not married."

✉ Str.Brasov 15,Bl.E9, Ap.38,sector 6, Bucuresti, 77369 ✆ (90) 453037 ✍ Italian ♥ painting, reading, skating, gymnastics, dance ⌂ no

IONESCU, Mihaela Ottilia   b.07/23/54   Economic scientific researcher

"I graduated the Academy of Economic Studies. I am fond of sun, water and mountains and I usually make trips in summer and go skiing in winter. I am interested in contacting people from outside my country."

✉ Bd.Pacii 1,Bl.22B,Sc.C,Ap.159,sector 6, Bucuresti ✆ (90) 712307 ✍ English, French, Italian ♥ literature, philosophy, sociology, theatre and film, tailoring, travelling ⌂ yes ☆ guide

IONESCU, Viorel   b.10/11/29   Engineer

"I am married. My wife is also engineer. We have no children. We are both retired. We have a 2 rooms flat and a car."

✉ Str.Aviator Iliescu 7,etaj 1,Ap.10, Bucuresti, 71238 ✆ (90) 794527 ✍ French ♥ philately, arts ⌂ yes. Non-smokers, two persons, aged 50 -60.

IONITA, George   b.02/18/27   Economist (retired)

"I worked in film production at the Buftea studios as a production director. I had the chance to work also with Gaumont, Technisonor, etc. I was in Paris in

1970,1972,1979,1988. I love Paris. I live alone in the centre of Bucharest."

✉ Str.Finlanda 12,sector 1, Bucuresti ✆ (90) 338004
✍ French, English (a little), German (a little) ♥ voyages, working in open air, sports, walking, working in the country-side **H** yes

IONITA, Mihaela   b.06/06/74   Pupil

"(1,63m/43kg) I am an agreeable, sociable person, I have chestnut-brown hair and brown eyes. I love travelling. My favorite country is France. I intend to study medicine. I have a 9 year old brother (Daniel)."

✉ Str.Viorele 28,Bl.20B,Sc.B,Ap.63,sector 4, Bucuresti ✆ (90) 633162 ✍ French, English (a little) ♥ sports (cycling,volleyball,skating), dancing ✂ stamps,postcards **H** yes, in town and outside, in the countryside

IORDACHE, Liliana   b.04/04/53   Economist

"I am married, I have two children, boys, aged 5, respectively 10. My husband is also economist and his hobby is the football. He likes climbing mountains and history books."

✉ Bd.Dacia 1,Ap.6,sector 1, Bucuresti ✆ (90) 114222 ✍ English, French ♥ Egyptian culture, foreign languages (films, books), travelling **H** yes ☆ bed and breakfast

IOSEP, Orest Octavian   b.07/12/30   Engineer and Economist

"I worked 25 years in foreign trade as director of "Mecanoexportimport" company. Now I am retired and own a small company of import-export. I am married, my wife is an engineer. I have a daughter, student in the 4th year. She speaks French and English."

✉ Str.Armeneasca 20,sector 2, Bucuresti, 70288 ✆ (90) 112454 ✍ German, French, Russian ♥ sports (dumbbells) **H** yes ☆ board

ISACESCU, Ileana b.03/29/40 Medical assistent
"I was not a member of the Romanian Communist Party."
✉ Str.Capitan Nicolae Licaret
10,Bl.PM41,Sc.B,Ap.45, Bucuresti ✆ (90) 473538 ✍ Italian ♥ I do not have time for it
⌂ yes

IUORAS, Monica b.09/27/42 Biologist-researcher
"I was born in Blaj. I graduated from the University in Cluj in 1965. In 1979 I moved to Bucharest. I am working in the field of genetics. I am not married. I have a sister living in Cluj, a brother living in Bucharest and another one living in Canada."
✉ Str.Sachelarie Visarion 18,Bl.119,Ap.7,sector 2, Bucuresti, 73331 ✆ (90) 534161 ✍ English, French, Russian (a little) ♥ classical music, opera, dancing, skiing, swimming, reading, travelling, ice-cream ⌂ yes ☆ guide

IUROV, Alexandre b.05/19/69 Student
"I was born in Bucharest. I was in kindergarten, grammar school, highschool, always in Bucharest (!!!). Now I am a student at the Faculty of Architecture, 2nd year."
✉ Str.Poet Buzdugan 15,Et.2,Ap.5,sector 1, Bucuresti, 78304 ✆ (90) 650528 ✍ French, Italian
♥ architecture, painting, design, music (especially jazz, but not only), sports (ski, rugby, football), theatre, mountains ⌂ yes

**IVANOVICI, Magda
and Angela (mother)** b.12/07/68 Student/Teacher
"I don't like adventures, vulgarity, I hate telling lies. I want to correspond with people who are brave and sensitive. I live together with my mother, who is also my best friend. She was born in 1948."
✉ Str.Drumul Taberei,Bl.OD4,Sc.4,Ap.118,sector 6, Bucuresti, 77334 ✆ (90) 256894 ✍ French, English ♥ arts, travelling ⌂ no

JUDE, Aurel b. 05/31/29 Engineer

"Both, my wife and me, we worked in the mining industry. We have no children."

✉ Str.Fr. Chopin 42,Ap.3,sector 2, Bucuresti
✆ (90) 794410 ✍ French, English ♥ travelling
🏠 yes max 4 people(a family of intellectuals) ☆ board, transport, guide

JUGARU, Anca-Cristina   b.09/11/57 Analyst (informatics)

"I was born in Bucharest, where I am still living. I am married since 1986. My husband studied Mathematics and Philosophy. We are expecting a baby (we found out it is a BOY !)."

✉ Str.Calea Mosilor 201,Bl.9,Sc.A,Ap.10,sector 2, Bucuresti ✆ (90) 108357 ✍ English, French, German ♥ vestimentary design, cinema, orientalism
🏠 yes ☆ breakfast, guide

JUGARU, Gheorghe   b.12/06/25 Economist

"Starting the first of June I retired and my wife too. Our daughter, Anca (33) is a specialist in informatics and her husband, Vlad (36) studied mathematics and philosophy. They have a three months old son. I worked more than 42 years in foreign trade."

✉ Bd.N. Balcescu 24,Sc.A,Ap.3,sector 1, Bucuresti, 70122 ✆ (90) 149872 ✍ French, English, Spanish
♥ tourism, swimming, opera shows 🏠 yes, I live in the centre of the town

KORMUS, Marian   b.11/03/29 Electrician

"I am retired now and my wife too. I don't smoke, I don't drink. We would like to exchange accommodation with a family with no children."

✉ Str.Valea Viilor 7,Bl.M40,Ap.17, Bucuresti, 77409 ✆ (90) 775860 ✍ German, Russian (a little) ♥ tourism 🏠 yes ☆ breakfast

LADARU, Costel   b.07/31/55 Chemical engineer

"I graduated from the Polytechnic Institute in Bucharest in 1980. Now, I work as a scientific re-

searcher in a toxicology laboratory. I live in a nice, two rooms flat."

✉ Sos.Oltenitei 250,Bl.148 bis,Sc.1,Ap.30, Bucuresti, 75652 ✆ (90) 349502 ✍ French, English
♥ music, literature ⌂ yes ☆ breakfast

LAZARESCU, Radu Victor b.04/28/32 Mechanic engineer

"I graduated from high school Gh. Lazar and from the Polytechnical Institute in Bucharest. I took part in the Revolution in December. My wife is a beautiful, 46 year old woman. She can cook very well and has a wonderful voice."

✉ Str.Ghiulamila 3,sector 5, Bucuresti ✆ (90) 316522 ✍ German, French, English (a little)
♥ tennis (champion in 1950); volleyball (between 1950 and 1957 I played several times in the national team);, trips in the mountains, dancing ⌂ yes, in a villa and in Busteni too ☆ music, TV, video, breakfast

LAZARESCU, Sorin b.10/26/57 Engineer

"With 14 I started studying everything alone. I read Greek philosophy, history of physics, ...I have been married for eight years and have two children. I was abroad only once : one day in Bulgaria."

✉ Calea Ferentari 8,Bl.117,Sc.2,Ap.63,sector 5, Bucuresti ✆ (90) 819245 ✍ French, English, German ♥ swimming, physics, music, special traits of the matter, the connection between music and the theory of sound, politics, the efficiency of scientific education ⌂ yes

LAZEA, Valentin b.04/26/58 Economist

"I was born in Huedin, Cluj county. Soon my parents moved to Bucharest. I graduated from the Academy of Economic Studies in 1982. Now I work in the Institute of Industrial Economy. I am married since june 1985 with Mihaela. We have a son, Victor, aged 2."

✉ Str.Carol Davila 93, Bucuresti ✆ (90) 377901
✍ English, French, Russian ♥ painting (as a painter and viewer); football, which I used to practise in my teens; bridge, cinema, pop music, reading and writing books; travelling ⌂ yes

LUNGU, Alexandru-Viorel   b.06/09/63
   Mathematician

"I graduated in 1982 from the German high school. I studied mathematics and , since 1988, work in a research institute for informatics. In my free time I work as a translator and as a beekeeper. I have a sister, who studies medicine."

✉ Str Londra 17,sector 1, Bucuresti, 71217
☎ (90) 333481 ✍ German, English, Italian ♥ sports (swimming, basketball, skiing, walking), films, theatre, music ⌂ yes, we have two comfortable flats and 2 cars ☆ I can be a guide and translater in any season

LUNGU, Cameliu - Florinel   b.03/21/68   Student

"I graduated from the "Matei Basarab" secondary school. Now I am a student at the Polytechnical Institute, Car Technology Construction. Very clever, sincere, ambitious, serious. I am not a spoiled child, don't drink, don't smoke. I am a sentimentalist."

✉ Str.Tg.Neamt 19,Bl.TS-10,Ap.36,sector 6,
   Bucuresti ☎ (90) 261396 ✍ English ♥ I play football and make athletics; I like beautiful clothes; I like beautiful girls ⌂ yes ☆ breakfast

MANCAS, Christian   b.12/02/53   Engineer

"I am a computer engineer. I was born in Bucharest. I graduated the Polytechnical Institute in Bucharest in 1977. In 1980 I had a 6 weeks technical training at CII-Honeywell Bull of Paris. I am married and I have two kids, aged 4 and 7."

✉ Str.Mecet 2 bis,Ap.1, Bucuresti, 73113 ☎ (90) 214460 ✍ French, English ♥ history, geography, philosophy, music, painting, photography, the mountains ⌂ yes

MANU, Andrei   b. 04/04/63   Physician

"I am sometimes contemplative and sometimes very active. I wish I could be active most of the time. I am not married now, but no convinced bachelor either."

✉ Str.Ion Maiorescu 37,sector 2, Bucuresti, 73256
☎ (90) 190117 ✍ French, English ♥ sports, films, swimming, languages ⌂ yes

MARASESCU, Adrian b.01/12/50 Computers engineer
"I was born in Ploiesti. I graduated the Faculty of Electronics in Bucharest. Now I work in research (on IBM-PC's). I am married and have two children."
✉ Str.Serdarului 7, Bucuresti ✆ (90) 656506
✍ French, English ♥ bridge (I won several international competitions), football ■ yes ☆ I have a car that can be used.

MARCULETIU, Alexandru Gabriel b.03/07/53
Metalurgical engineer
"I am 37 years old. I work in a great state enterprise."
✉ Str.Pecineaga 5,Bl.29C,Ap.42,sector 5, Bucuresti
✆ (90) 841020/781 ✍ French, English ♥ literature, arts ■ yes ☆ breakfast

MARIN, Daniel b. 04/26/70 Student at the Politechnic Institute Bucharest, technology of machines construction
"I have a brother, Gabriel, age 15, and a sister, Andreea-Elena, age 15 (twins). In 1988 I graduated secondary school. On December 22nd 1989, our sacred day, I was at the Intercontinental Hotel with my girl friend to demonstrate against Nicolae Ceausesc"
✉ Sos.Colentina 38,Bl.70,Ap.8,sector 2, Bucuresti, 72445 ✆ (90) 555274 ✍ French, English (a little), German (a little) ♥ football, skiing, dancing, disco music, funk, rap, blues, opera, car racing, motorcycles, volleyball, handball, surfing ■ yes ☆ bed and breakfast

MARINESCU, Aida b.01/29/64 Computer programmer
"I am tall (171), fair, blue eyed."
✉ Bd.Leontin Salajan 47,Bl.C2,Sc.8,Ap.100,sector 3, Bucuresti, 74641 ✆ (90) 735765 ✍ Italian, English, Slovach ♥ little dogs, sports ■ yes

MARINESCU, Catalin b.05/14/33 Geological engineer
"A life of work for trying to understand the aim of life."
✉ Intrarea Legendei 1, Bucuresti ✆ (90) 119890
✍ French, English ♥ the beautiful connected with a terrible curiosity ■ yes

MARINESCU, Codruta b.05/07/67 Student

"I study mechanics at the Polytechnical Institute in Bucharest. I have been married for two years. My husband is an engineer. My knowledge of French is poor, but my desire to communicate is big."

✉ Bd.I.B.Tito 35, Bl.N5, Sc.5, Ap.194, sector 3, Bucuresti, 74572 ✆ (90) 745055 ✍ French, English, German (a little) ♥ the connection between mechanics and medicine, books, I love horses and dogs, theatre, film, everything that is nice ♅ no

MEHEDINCU, Sanda Stanca b.11/13/35
Architect; stage-painter

"I have been working in the design department of the Architecture Institute. I have a Ph.D degree in architecture. I am a member of the Academy in Romania. I was awarded several prizes from the Romanian Union of Architects."

✉ Str.Mozart 7, Sc.C, Ap.47, sector 2, Bucuresti ✆ (90) 335873 ✍ German, French ♥ illustrating books for children, opera, trips, nature, gardening ♅ yes

MICU, Ecaterina b.05/20/49 Philologist, Romanian language and literature, poet, texts for musical performances

"I am the daughter of Eugeniu Micu, a great Romanian musician (composer and orchestra director), who died 10 years ago. I fought all my life for the spreading of my father's music. I didn't encounter the Great Love yet."

✉ Str.Intr.Sold.Mina Gh. 5, sector 2, Bucuresti, 73278 ✍ French ♥ symphonic music, poetry, but also housekeeping and my never ending love for my mother ♅ No. ☆ I can be an excelent guide and musical advicer.

MICU, Lucretia b.07/20/50 Teacher of French
"I was born in the country, I finished highschool in 1969, then graduated from the University in Bucharest in 1974. Now I work at the Central of Bookshops."
✉ Str.Poarta Alba 2-4,Bl.109A,Sc.A,Ap.39,sector 6, Bucuresti ✆ (90) 714586 or 676535 ✍ French, English ♥ universal literature, gardening ⌂ yes ☆ breakfast; trips with my car.

MIHAI, Eugen b. 08/18/69 Photoreporter
"I graduated secondary school in Bucharest and then became a photoreporter. I am fair-haired, I have green eyes, I am 1.85 m tall and weigh 75 Kg. I am not married."
✉ Sos.Alexandriei 80,Bl.L21,Ap.9,sector 5, Bucuresti, 76525 ✆ (90) 762385 ✍ English ♥ art of photography, football, jogging, science-fiction, classic music ⌂ yes ☆ breakfast

MIHAIL, Cristian and Ira b.10/26/33
"(he) 51-56 Mining Institute; 56-90 senior geophysicist;1981 Pg.D in geophysics. (she) 66-71 Geological Faculty; 71-90 geological engineer."
✉ Aleea Topoloveni,Bl.TD4,Ap.64, Bucuresti, 77435 ✆ (90) 261021 ✍ French, English ♥ linguistics, swimming (he), picture, dance (she) ⌂ yes

MIHAIL, George-Paul b.05/31/41 Painter (teacher)
"I have been teaching painting at the Art School in Bucharest since 1968. I had exhibitions in Romania in : 1970, 1974, 1980, 1983, 1988 and abroad in 1980 (Munich) and 1983 (Rome). My paintings are to be found in many state and private collections."
✉ Str.Iuliu Theodori 3,sector 5, Bucuresti, 76246 ✆ (90) 159901 ✍ French, English, Italian ♥ painting, literature, art albums, records, skiing, swimming ⌂ yes ☆ breakfast

MIHALACHE, Sorin and George b.08/09/62
Economist / Forest researcher (George)
"George is born in 10.11.36"
✉ Cl.Dorobanti 172,Sc.A,Ap.71, Bucuresti, 71232 ✆ (90) 331280 ✍ English, French ♥ trips, English, jazz, mountain trips

BUCURESTI

IHUT, Octavian Stefan b.08/01/44 Engineer
"In 1969 I graduated from the University in Brasov. I worked in tourism and transports. Since 1982 I have been working in the researching field. My wife is a dentist. We have an eight years old son. We are members of the National Liberal Party."
✉ Bd.Uverturii 87,Bl.014A,Sc.A,Ap.7,sector 6, Bucuresti, 77545 ✆ (90) 722573 ✍ English, French ♥ sports ♅ yes ☆ breakfast

INDRU, Alexandru b.10/25/42 Mechanic engineer for building equipments
"I was born in Bucharest. I live in a 3 rooms flat. I am married to Mindru Mihaela, aged 47. She is a geologist. I have a 17 years old son, student."
✉ Str.Dr.Felix 61,Bl.B1,Ap.16,sector 1, Bucuresti ✆ (90) 594655 ✍ French ♥ the life of bees ♅ yes

IRICA, Anca-Daniela b.02/13/62 Engineer
"I was born in this city and spent most of my life here. I have never had the opportunity to travel."
✉ Sos.Giurgiului 127,Bl.2B,Sc.5,Ap.182,sector 4, Bucuresti, 75387 ✆ (90) 866518 ✍ English, French (a little) ♥ peoples, habits, customs, reading, drawing, cartoons, travelling - knowing people and places ♅ yes ☆ bed and breakfast for 1-2 persons

IRONESCU, Valeriu b.02/23/60 Mechanic designer
"I was born in Botosani. I lived in Craiova between 1962 and 1985. In 1985 I graduated the Faculty. In 1987 I moved to Bucharest and got married."
✉ Sos.Stefan cel Mare 234,Bl.77,Ap.22, Bucuresti ✆ (90) 191532 ✍ English ♥ sports (volleyball, badminton, table tennis, football), tourism, music, computers, affairs, entomology ♅ yes

ITRICA, Dumitru b.07/03/68 Student
"I am a student at the Polytechnical Institute in Bucharest. I intend to study psychology too. My father died when I was 18 and now I live together with my mother and my brothers."
✉ Str.Ing.Zablovschi 1,Ap.18,sector 1, Bucuresti ✆ (90) 669089 ✍ English, Italian ♥ psychology, sports, chess, bridge ♅ yes

MIU, Sever and - wife General practitioner; dentist (wife)

"I am 49. We have 4 children, three of them are students at the University (one girl and two boys). The youngest is a boy aged 9 and the only one who lives with us. My wife is 44."

✉ Bd.Aviatorilor 66,Ap.1,sector 1, Bucuresti, 71279
✆ (90) 338888 ✍ French ♥ arts, opera, ballet, literature, music, history, theatre, cinema. I paint. I had many exibitions ⌂ yes; we own a big house with 5 rooms. ☆ breakfast

MLADIN, Petru - Eugen   b.06/22/21   Officer in the Romanian Army (1944-1954), Football trainor (1954-1982); retired

"Nobody in my family ever dealt in politics. I am married since 1949 with Arestia Mladin, 61, philosophy teacher, now retired. We have a daughter, Mladin Mirela-Maiana, 37, physicist."

✉ Str.Ezareni 1,sector 1, Bucuresti, 70759 ✆ (90) 145343 ✍ Hungarian, German, French ♥ the cat of the family, film, opera, philately ⌂ yes, for two persons. ☆ breakfast

MOGA, Gheorghe   b.04/17/35   lawyer

"I graduated from college in 1967, in Bucharest. I worked as a jurist until 1985, when I retreated. My wife, (45), studied geology-geography. We have a 19 years old son. We have a house in the countryside: Augustin 176,Jud.Brasov,cod 3016."

✉ Str.Obcina Mare 4,Bl.O.S.2,Sc.5,Ap.190, Bucuresti ✆ (90) 463824 ✍ Italian, Spanish, French ♥ literature, arts, music, gardening, travelling ⌂ yes, exchange or payment in hard currency ☆ all kind of

MOGOSEANU, Catalin   b.07/30/68   Aircraft Lease and Charter Flights Manager

"When I was three years old I left Romania, together with my parents (my father is a diplomat) for Skandinavia.All together I spent 10 years there, in Finland,

Sweden, Norway. I am now a part time student at the Academy of Economical Studies."

✉ Str.Glinka 5, Bucuresti ✆ (90) 792639 (work: 333761) ✍ Finnish, English, French (a little)
♥ traveling around Europe and making new friends; learning foreign languages; studying international politics;, European integration; aviation ⌂ yes
☆ tours around the country.

MOISE, Marian　　b.04/19/50　Driving teacher and Manager of the private company (2nd job).

"My parents were divorced, so I grew up almost alone since my mother was working during the day; I was always choosing friends older than I. After highschool I became a student in law but could not finish as I had to earn a living. Married 2nd time."

✉ Str.Voronet 11,Bl.D6,Sc.3,Ap.39,sector 3, Bucuresti, 74122 ✍ English, French ♥ reading (history, philosophy, fiction), travelling ⌂ yes
☆ organize vacations (I have 62 days vacation/year).

MOLDOVAN, Augustin　　b.10/29/24　Chemisty - Ph.D. in pharmacy, scientific researcher

"I work since 25 years as a researcher in controlling antibiotics. I am married. I have a daughter who studies industrial chemistry."

✉ Bd.Lacul Tei 126-128,Bl.17-18,Sc.C,Ap.93, Bucuresti ✆ (90) 873289 ✍ French, German, Italian ♥ restoring old Charles Boulle style French furniture ⌂ yes

MORARETI, Liviu　　b.01/14/60　Engineer

"I graduated from high school "Sf. Sava" and from the Polytechnical Institute (1985)."

✉ Str.Sandulesti 5,Bl.Z13,Ap.30, Bucuresti, 77391 ✆ (90) 460174 ✍ French, English ♥ photography, electronics, voyages, mountains ⌂ yes ☆ breakfast

MOSCOVICI, Mina　　b.12/29/20　Lawyer (retreated)

"I graduated from Sapienza (Roma). I had two brothers, physicians, who died. My husband, who was an engineer, also died. Now, I have a pension, my own

flat and can offer accommodation to a nonsmoking person."

✉ Str.Drumul Taberei 91,Bl.R2,Sc.B,Ap.75,sector 6, Bucuresti ✆ (90) 263026 ✍ French, Italian, German ♥ reading ⌂ yes ☆ breakfast

MUNTEANU, Ovidiu   b.01/19/48   Coach

"Married, my wife is an economist. I have two daughters (Diana, 9, and Lavinia, 7)."

✉ Bd.T.Vladimirescu 57,Bl.T4,Sc.2,Ap.42,sector 5, Bucuresti ✆ (90) 813853 ✍ French ♥ sports (boxing, tennis, swimming), fishing, trips ✂ stamps ⌂ yes ☆ board and transportation by car

MURESAN, Mihaela   b.01/10/55   Computer programmer

"I live for the curiosity and for the pleasure to enjoy life."

✉ Bd.Nicolae Titulescu 39-49,Sc.A,Ap.27,sector 1, Bucuresti, 78151 ✆ (90) 597144 ✍ French, English, German ♥ travelling, pictures and books ⌂ yes ☆ breakfast, guiding

MUSATESCU, Virgil and Doina (wife)   b.09/23/45
Professor dr.eng. at the Polytechnical Institute of Bucharest; wife:Highschool Teacher

"I am an engineer in Thermoenergetics; Ph.D. in 1983; My wife is a physicist, electronic microscopy, now a teacher."

✉ Str.Volga 39,sector 1, Bucuresti ✆ (90) 300350 or 655771 ✍ English, French, +German (wife) ♥ chess, bridge, tennis, music (opera, symphonic, rock, jazz); wife: music, good books, german language, nature ⌂ yes; we have a beautiful house in Sinaia.

NACEV-BADESCU, Alexandru   b.09/29/28
Tradesman

"I worked in foreign trade, in Romania and abroad (Berlin, Hanoi, Havana). Since 1989 I retired. My wife, Margareta, also worked in foreign trade and retired.

We have no children. We own a four rooms flat and a car."

✉ Bd.Metalurgiei 31,Bl.I-5,Sc.2, Ap.58, Bucuresti, 75574 ✆ (90) 823411 ✍ German, French
♥ travelling, making lantern slides, talking about our adventures, collecting mushrooms, visiting museums
🏠 yes, in summer, 2 pers ☆ breakfast, trips by car

NAFORNITA, Eliza b.03/21/59 University teacher (assistent) at the Polytechnical Institute.

"We are a family composed of a chemistry engineer, a university teacher and two children, a boy aged 10, very good chess player, and a girl aged 7, who plays chess and tennis."

✉ Str.Domnita Ruxandra 15, sector 2, Bucuresti, 72129 ✆ (90) 105519 ✍ French, English, German ♥ voyages, music (opera) 🏠 jes ☆ board

NASTASIA, Ion b.04/27/42 Biologist

"Married, no children. My wife is a Mathematics teacher."

✉ Str.Plut.Petre Ionescu 9, sector 3, Bucuresti, 74692 ✆ (90) 300563 ✍ French, English, Russian
♥ ecology, philately ✂ stamps (flowers, animals, energy saving, painters, gymnastics) 🏠 yes ☆ board . Also car tours.

NEAGU, Vera-Maria b.07/29/43 Journalist

"I have been working with ROMPRES since 1966. I have four children, aged between 11 and 26. I translated books from Romanian into French and from French into Romanian. I am interested in living one year in France together with my three younger children."

✉ Str.Voronet 7,Bl.D5,Sc.A,Ap.14,sector 3, Bucuresti
✆ (90) 201903 ✍ French, English, Spanish ♥ books
🏠 yes, a 4 room flat ☆ good library, piano

NECULAE, Zaharia b.06/26/35 Engineer (civil works)

"I was born in a large family. I started to work in a Designing Institute and had interesting activities during about 27 years. My wife is 50 years old and works in

a Chemical Laboratory. My son is 23, not married and works in a big factory."

✉ Str.Drumul Taberei 37,Bl.Z43,Ap.11, Bucuresti, 77334 ✆ (90) 461088 ✍ English, French, Russian ♥ electronics, mechanics, music, motoring, travelling ⌂ yes, in 2 flats of 3 rooms each

NEGREA, Florin b.05/10/33 Electrotechnic engineer

"After graduating from the Polytechnical Institute in Bucharest I started working in the domain of electric powered locomotives. I am married, no children. I live with my wife Octavia, aged 51. In my spare time I work as a guide-interpreter."

✉ Sos.N.Titulescu 78,Ap.41, Bucuresti, 78161 ✆ (90) 182650 ✍ French, German, English ♥ mountain climbing in all seasons (I am member of the Alpin club in Bucharest); music, paintings, radio, foreign languages (I started studying Russian, Serbian, Swedish, Spanish) ⌂ yes, in Bucharest or in Predeal (mountain town). ☆ board

NEGUT, Adrian b.09/01/58 Engineer

"Born in Bucharest. Height : 1.80m. Weight : 80kg. Unmarried."

✉ Calea Floreasca 150,sector 1, Bucuresti ✆ (90) 338306 ✍ English ♥ mountains, trips, music, nature, travelling ⌂ yes

NETEA, Liliana b.05/12/70 Draughtsman

"I was born in Tirgoviste, but I live in Bucharest since 1978. I attended a highschool for math and physics."

✉ Sos.Giurgiului 125,Bl.4A,Ap.10, Bucuresti, 75387 ✆ (90) 864114 ✍ English, French ♥ ballet, animals, listening to music (preclassic - Vivaldi), the Beatles ⌂ yes, in Bucharest and in Bucovina region. ☆ breakfast

NICODINESCU, Laurentia b.07/01/55 Engineer

"I graduated in 1980 from the University in Bucharest (Geology). While student I worked as a guide. I now work in a research institute in Bucharest. I have a seven

year old daughter - Ramona-Alice. I live in a little flat close to the Herastrau Park."
✉ Str.Capilna 22,Bl.15L,Sc.2,Ap.21,sector 1, Bucuresti, 71507 ✍ French, English, Italian ♥ literature, travelling by car, music, sports (swimming, gymnastics, tennis, badminton) ∺ yes ☆ board

NICOLAE, Pastorel b.10/15/59 Engineer
"I was born in Moldova, where I did the grammar school, getting acquainted with the beautiful Bucovina. After living in Constanta for 3 years, we moved to Bucharest. I graduated from Faculty in Brasov. I am married and have a 1 1/2 year son."
✉ Bd.R.S.R. 17, S.A.I. Otopeni; / or: Str.Popa Nicolae 12,Bl.50,Sc.1,Ap.17,sector 2, Bucuresti, 71911 ✆ (90) 143581 ✍ English, French, Italian (a little) ♥ mountain trips, driving, swimming, tennis, moving in clean air, even dancing, I like to create around me an atmosphere of joy and goodwill ∺ yes; I own two flats, one near Otopeni. ☆ trips (eventually by car), guide.

NICOLESCU, Cristian Horia b.06/04/62
  Designing engineer
"I am not married. I graduated last year. I live alone in my apartment in a beautiful district of Bucharest. I love to write letters and correspondence."
✉ Bd.Nicolae Grigorescu 23,Bl.Y9A,Ap.22, Bucuresti ✆ (90) 434190 ✍ English, French ♥ yachting, trips ∺ yes ☆ board

NICOLESCU, George b.01/30/25 Engineer
"I studied Construction Engineering. I worked in an institute for studies till 1985. I am retired now. I am married; my wife, also engineer, retired in 1990."
✉ Aleea Pajurei 1 - Vila 30 - Sc.A,Ap.2, Bucuresti, 78416 ✆ (90) 682751 ✍ French, Italian ♥ history, geography, tourism ∺ yes ☆ breakfast, dinner; tours by car.

NICOLESCU, Tiberiu b.10/09/69 Student
"There is nothing special about my biography. I graduated from high school, I worked, I quit my job,

now I am a student. I study medicine. I visit the French library frequently."

✉ Str.Domnita Anastasia 17,Ap.3,sector 5, Bucuresti ✆ (90) 162425 ✍ French, English, Spanish ♥ psychology, botany, geography, cars, swimming, skiing, literature ⊞ yes

NICOLESCU, Vlad   b.05/22/59   Engineer

"I am married, my wife speaks French, she is 31 and a physician. I graduated from the Installations Faculty for Buildings and I used to work for some time with the National Travelling Office as a guide."

✉ Str.Bibescu Voda 1,Ap.45, Bucuresti ✆ (90) 235972 ✍ English ♥ read and discuss about strange phenomena (like UFO), tennis, occasionally to dance, travelling, swimming, my wife likes reading, swimming, travelling, driving, dancing ⊞ yes

NICULAE, Teodor   b.02/18/40   Engineer

"I live in the same house in Bucharest since I was born. The apartment is in a house 2 km from the centre and has 3 rooms. I studied constructions engineering in Bucharest. My wife teaches Physics in a highschool. We have two sons, aged 16 and 17."

✉ Str.Raditei 15, Bucuresti, 76138 ✆ (90) 230945 ✍ Russian, French ♥ bibliophilie, sports. I started now a matrimonial agency to help people know each other ⊞ yes

NISTOROIU, Gheorghe   b.02/23/60   Mechanical engineer

"I was born in Moscow. I graduated from faculty in 1985. I am working at a research institute. I am married to Mihaela, who is a mechanical engineer too. We have no children. We are very fond of travelling and hope to visit as many countries as possible."

✉ Str.Capitan Licaret 1,Bl.B33,Ap.245, Bucuresti, 74516 ✆ (90) 483926 ✍ French, English, Russian ♥ mountaineering, photographing ⊞ yes

NITULESCU RADU, Alexandru　　b.08/25/64
　　Electronics Engineer
"*I am not married - I live with my father. The apartment is quite big.*"
✉ Str.Clucerului 11-15,Bl.49,Ap.18,sector 1, Bucuresti, 71308 ✆ (90) 664208 ✍ French, English, German (a little) ♥ tennis, ski, the sea, tourism, photography, cybernetics, music ⌂ yes ☆ breakfast

NOURESCU, Andree　　b.07/29/71　　Student
✉ Str.Brasov 13,Bl.E10,Ap.50,sector 6, Bucuresti, 77369 ✆ (90) 460593 ✍ English, French (a little) ♥ tennis, football, tourism, music ⌂ yes ☆ board and transportation.

NOVEANU, Nicodim　　b.06/26/48　　Engineer (electronics)
"*I attended the German school. I work in a research institute. I married in 1976 and have two daughters aged 13 and 11. My wife died this year and I live together with my daughters.*"
✉ Sos.Nicolae Titulescu 117,Bl.4,Ap.52,sector 1, Bucuresti, 78161 ✆ (90) 170962 ✍ German, French, Italian (a little) ♥ cars ⌂ yes

OPREA, Radu Costin　　b.09/09/60　　Economist at the Institute of World Economy belonging to the Romanian Academy, scientific researcher in market studies.
"*In 1988 I graduated the Finance and Accounting evening classes of the Academy of Economic Studies in Bucharest. I am a member of the Romanian Marketing Association. I am married and have two children, girls, aged 6 and 1.*"
✉ Str.Anastasie Panu 1,Bl.A2,Sc.1,Ap.17, Bucuresti ✍ English ♥ animals and plants world (especially wild life), travelling (climbing mountains, trips across the country), rowing and fishing on a mountain lake or river, jazz music; my special hobby: Finland and Scandinavian countries ⌂ yes ☆ board

OPRESCU, Ana and Ioan (husband)　　Chemist engineer and Economist (husband).
"*I worked 30 years in a laboratory of mineralogic analysis. My husband worked 30 years in the Ministry*

for Agriculture. We are retired for the last 20 years. We live in a house in Bucharest, in a very nice place full of green. We have no children."

✉ Str.G.Puccini 9,Ap.4, Bucuresti, 71408 ℂ (90) 338437 ✍ German, French ♥ what is nice and noble, art, music, reading, things that make a pure and honourable life;, voyages, meeting intelligent, good, kind persons ∎ yes ☆ breakfast

OPRISAN, Valeriu   b.10/18/48   Engineer - professional fireman

"I graduated the Polytechnic Institute - hydrotechnic constructions in 1971. I worked in research till 1982 when I became an officer engineer in the Firemen's Department. I am married and have two children, aged 20 and 10."

✉ Str.Brebu 1,Bl.T9A,Ap.4,sector 2, Bucuresti, 72233 ℂ (90) 873226 ✍ French, English, Italian ♥ fishing, travelling, reading ∎ yes ☆ board

OSIAC, Dumitru   b.04/01/47   Constructions Engineer

"I am divorced."

✉ Str.Baba Novac 20,Bl.24A,Ap.118, Bucuresti ℂ (90) 484286 ✍ French, Italian, Spanish ♥ opera, literature ∎ yes ☆ breakfast

PALIFRON, Vasile   b.08/11/61   Forest Engineer

"I love nature, especially the mountains."

✉ Str.Elena Cuza 79,Bl.13,Sc.2,Ap.56, Bucuresti, 78168 ℂ (90) 230340 ✍ English, French ♥ cinema (I realised short films as an amateur), literature ∎ yes ☆ car

PANA, Corina Ileana   b.05/08/65   student,elestronics

"I was born in spring in a christian country, a poor country from the material point of view, but a rich one spiritualy. I work in a physics institute and I am a student at the faculty of physics."

✉ Bd.Iosip Broz Tito 13,Bl.58B,Ap.33,sector 3, Bucuresti, 74335 ℂ (90) 475076 ✍ French (a little) ♥ promenades, voyages, the beauty in general ∎ yes

PANDELE, Mariana b.08/03/24 Pensioner

"I was born in a family of intellectuals. I studied foreign languages. I am a widow. I have a daughter who studied chemistry."

✉ Calea Plevnei 58A, sector 1, Bucuresti, 77102
✆ (90) 138375 ✍ French, English, Italian ♥ philately, trips, literature, opera, the new ⌂ yes

PAPADOPOL, Carmen Liliana b.03/01/43 Mechanic engineer

"I am now a lecturer at the Polytechnical Institute in Bucharest. I am co-author of 22 books on engineering. I am not married."

✉ Bd.Dacia 1A, Ap.16, sector 1, Bucuresti, 70185
✆ (90) 119073 ✍ French, Russian, German (a little)
♥ my car and car driving; opera, classic music, tourism, dance, literature, videos ⌂ yes

PARASCHIVESCU, Gabriela b.03/24/50 Medical assistant

"I am married. We live together with my mother in a three room flat we own."

✉ Str.Apusului 33, Bl.D4, Sc.D, Ap.35, sector 6, Bucuresti ✆ (90) 696075 ✍ French ♥ I love my profession and opera music ⌂ yes ☆ breakfast

PARVULESCU - CODREA,
Doina Virginia Elena b.05/06/26 Economist - retired.

"I am married. My husband is an engineer, his name is Dumitru. We worked in foreign trade and traveled to all the countries in Europe."

✉ Str.Aviator Popisteanu 1, Ap.21, sector 1, Bucuresti
✆ (90) 653456 ✍ French, German, Italian ♥ travelling all over the world as a tourist ⌂ yes ☆ breakfast

PATAPIEVICI, Horia-Roman b.03/18/57 Physicist

"I was struck by my talents, by my father's death in A.D. 1985 and by the quest of AEQUANIMITAS."

✉ Str.Mosilor 189, Bl.1, Sc.A, Ap.17, sector 2, Bucuresti, 70314 ✆ (90) 115893 ✍ French, English
♥ history, philosophy, literature, arts ⌂ yes

PATRICHI, Mihaela Dora   b.03/24/54   Economist

"I started learning French and swimming since the age of 7. I graduated from the Academy of Economic Studies in 1977. I am married, I have a son aged 5. I like to do mountain trips with all the family."

✉ Bd.1 Mai,Nr.96,Bl.44B,Sc.A,Ap.9,sector 1, Bucuresti ✆ (90) 650832 ✍ French ♥ swimming (ex-national champion); I admire Claude Monet, J.Prevert, Vivaldi, Remarque, Hemingway, Cousteau, the Beatles, Rod Stewart ⌂ yes

PAVLENCO, Georgetta   b.04/18/27   Retired

"I have a daughter who is a teacher of piano at the George Enescu Highschool of music in Bucharest."

✉ Str.Drumul Murgului 4,Bl.C4,Sc.4,Ap.48, Bucuresti ✆ (90) 471915 ✍ Italian, French ♥ music, voyages (I visited East Germany, Czechoslovakia, Hungary, Bulgaria, USSR, Israel) ⌂ yes

PETCULESCU, Roxana Veronica   b.11/14/65
Economist

"I graduated from high school in 1984. I will graduate from the Academy of Economic Studies in September 1990. I studied commerce and tourism."

✉ Str.Zborului 8A, sector 3, Bucuresti, 70482 ✆ (90) 222791 ✍ English, French, German ♥ reading, modern music, theatre, cinema, dancing, gardening, badminton ⌂ housing, no breakfast

PETRESCU, Carmen   b.07/12/68   Student in the 4th year at the faculty: Technology of machines construction

"I was born in Cimpia Turzii, district Cluj. I went to a kindergarten with French language. I studied skating and drawing. I graduated a Maths-Physics highschool in Bucharest. My parents are engineers."

✉ Calea Dorobanti 111-131,Bl.9,Sc.A,Ap.24,sector 1, Bucuresti ✆ (90) 333174 ✍ French, English, German ♥ travelling, skiing, surfing, drawing ⌂ Yes. In Bucharest, Cluj, or cottage near Tirgovist ☆ board

PETRESCU, Ion b.11/02/51 Economist

"I studied economy and worked abroad in Iraq and Iran. I am married since 1980 and have no children. My wife's name is Geta."

✉ Str.Dumitrache Bahu 1,sector 2, Bucuresti
✆ (90) 192238 ✍ English, French, German (a little)
♥ reading, cinema,theatre,opera,listening to music, sports ⛉ 2 bedrooms in Bucharest, 3 bedrooms in Cimpulung ☆ breakfast or full board

PETRESCU, Ion b.03/06/17 Engineer - ex-pilot in military aviation; retired

"Ex-officer (colonel)-pilot, I fought on the Eastern front (U.S.S.R.). When I left the army, I worked with a company for foreign trade, dealing with aeronautics, then in an Institute. I have a great interest in the French culture (history, literature)."

✉ Bd.Uverturii 43,Bl.1,Sc.3,Ap.91, Bucuresti, 77546 ✆ (90) 714601 ✍ French, German, English (a little) ♥ voyages and literature; 50% of my library is in French, classical music ⛉ yes ☆ board

PODEA, Petre b. 07/30/32 Economist

"I was born in Domnesti, a village close to the mountains, where I still go almost every week. I graduated from the "Commercial Academy" in 1955. I married in 1962. My wife teaches mathematics in a high school in Bucharest. We have no children."

✉ Calea Dorobanti 111-113,Bl.9F,Sc.A,Ap.20, Bucuresti ✆ (90) 335902 ✍ French, English, German ♥ classical music, philately ⚔ stamps ⛉ yes, but I prefer the arrangements made in advance

POGACIANU, Dana b.06/21/68 Student at the University

"I was born in Bucharest. I moved to Timisoara with my parents in 1977 and after two years to Tirgu Mures. We returned to Bucharest in 1988. Now I study Mathematics. I like very much to travel but until December 1989 it was very difficult."

✉ Str.Banul Manta 26,Bl.19A,Ap.18,sector 1, Bucuresti ✆ (90) 502232 ✍ English, French
⛉ yes

POLOSAN, Radu Corneliu b.04/26/66 Electronics engineer

"My mother is an architect and a professor. My father is an engineer. I work in a factory that produces equipment for industrial automation."

✉ Bd.Lacul Tei 79,Bl.15A,Sc.III,Ap.124,sector 2, Bucuresti, 72301 ✆ (90) 870151 ✎ English, French ■ yes ☆ board; tours.

POP, Cornelia and Dan (husband) b.09/15/46
Engineer and Economist in foreign trade

"I am married to Dan, who is an engineer too and speaks English and French."

✉ Str.Viorele 34,Bl.15,Sc.1,Ap.18,sector 4, Bucuresti, 75168 ✆ (90) 414941 ✎ English, French ♥ (she) fashion, bright conversation, literature, theatre, music, arts, travelling, entertainment, (he) tennis and other sports, literature, theatre, music, arts, travelling, entertainment, a good drink, good food ■ yes, not only in Bucharest

POPESCU, Bogdan b.04/24/62 Engineer

"I am a constructions engineer. I work in Bucharest. I well finished the German school, so I can speak German as good as Romanian. I got married in 1988. My wife Dana is born on September 30th 1964 and she is a doctor."

✉ Str.Intrarea Detectorului 2,sector 2, Bucuresti ✆ (90) 425638 ✎ German, English, French (a little) ♥ sports, gardening, philatelie, foreign languages ■ yes

POPESCU, Constantin b.04/04/33 Retired

"I am married. My wife's name is Elena and she works as a clerk. I worked with a building company as a technician. I learned German by attending the courses of the Popular University. I have a driving license."

✉ Str.Emil Racovita 16-A,Bl.I-11,Sc.2,Ap.40,sector 4, Bucuresti, 75594 ✆ (90) 839825 ✎ German, French ♥ sports (rugby, football, tennis), theatre, cinema, opera, dande ■ yes ☆ board, guide all over the country.

POPESCU, Constantin b.05/02/43 Building engineer

"*I have been married to Natalia since 1965. We have two children : Elena (23) and Alexandru Ioan (21).*"

✉ Str.Bodesti 2,Bl.29B,Sc.A,Ap.42,sector 2, Bucuresti, 73516 ✆ (90) 277627 ✍ English, Russian
♥ tennis, skiing, symphonic music, opera ♨ yes
☆ board

POPESCU, Dana b.02/18/51 Electric Engineer

"*I work in a research institute in Bucharest. I like to travel and I went all over the country. I am a sociable woman but till now I had no possibility to be acquainted with foreigners.*"

✉ Str.Buturugeni 24,sector 5, Bucuresti ✆ (90) 819459 ✍ English, French, Italian (a little)
♥ skiing, mountain climbing ♨ Yes.In Bucharest and in a mountain cottage. ☆ bed and breakfast

POPESCU, Liviu b.07/15/58 Engineer

"*My mother teaches mathematics, my father works as a ship builder. I graduated from high school in Braila and from faculty in Galati, where the only Institute specialized in ship building is. I am married and have a nine months old child.*"

✉ Sos.Colentina 41,Bl.OD44,Ap.22, Bucuresti, 72245 ✆ (90) 875231 ✍ English, French
♥ tennis, trips in the mountains, dancing, swimming, skating ♨ yes, on Prahova Valley too (Poiana Tapului)

POPESCU, Mircea b.01/25/59 Engineer

"*I studied in Bucharest. I graduated as an engineer in 1985. Since then I work in the Electronica plants in Bucharest. I am married and I have one girl aged 8.*"

✉ Bd.1 Mai Nr. 333, Ap.41,sector 1, Bucuresti ✆ (90) 655947 ✍ French, English, Italian ♥ tennis, car racings, dance, long walks ♨ yes, in Bucharest and Constanta. ☆ board

POPESCU, Teodor b.03/08/30 Engineer

"*I was born in the village Traian, Braila, near the Danube Delta. I graduated from the Polytechnical Institute in Iasi in 1953. I worked as army engineer*" *officer, then in aeronautics industry for 20 years. My wife is a doctor; we have two children."*

✉ Str.Baneasa 14-16,sector 1, Bucuresti ✆ (90) 651695 ✍ French, Italian, Russian ♥ the unknown books ▉ yes ☆ breakfast

POPOVICI, Dorin Iulian b.06/25/59 Computer programmer

"I was born on a very hot summer day in Iasi. After a lot of schools and passions (motorcars, fishing, basket), I decided to enter the computer world."

✉ Intr.Dridu 5,Vila 28,Ap.15,sector 1, Bucuresti ✆ (90) 677362 ✍ English, French ♥ tennis (never practiced), music (never played), underwater fishing (never practiced), french cognac (never drank), flowers ▉ yes

POPOVICI, Mihai Daniel b.05/07/27 Engineer (retreated)

"I studied in Craiova and Timisoara. I worked for 30 years in a research institute. In 1968 I received a scholarship from the United Nations. Between 1970 and 1971 I worked in Iran. I retired in 1988 and became an international guide."

✉ Str.Cuza Voda 15C,Bl.27B,Sc.C,Ap.88,sector 4, Bucuresti, 75142 ✆ (90) 753591 ✍ English, French, Italian ♥ travelling ▉ yes ☆ breakfast, trips by my car

POPOVICI, Traian b.10/14/51 Dentist

"I am married since 1981. My wife has a Ph.D in electrotechnic engineering and teaches at the Polytechnic Institute in Bucharest. I have two children, Traian Gabriel - 8 years old, and Karina Diana - 1 year and a half."

✉ Str.Latea Gheorghe 12,Bl.C47,Ap.74, Bucuresti ✆ (90) 819884 , 772646 ✍ French, German, English ♥ sports (tennis), music, tourism, painting ▉ yes ☆ board

ORTEANU, Alexandru
and Rodica (wife)   b.01/11/34   Professor, historic researcher/Professor foreign languages
"Ph.D. in history. Main specialty: modern history. Research themes: history of Transylvania, Romanian - Hungarian relations, history of law, military history. Awarded prize of Romanian Academy. My wife has experience as a guide and interpreter."
✉ Bd. Nicolae Titulescu 14, Bl.21, Sc.B, Ap.79, Bucuresti, 78152 ✆ (90) 593851 ✍ French, (wife)English, (wife)French ♥ music, tourism (by car), (wife) art, literature, classic music, opera, ballet, art galleries, travelling, news magazines ⌂ yes ☆ board and lodging

UWAK, Iosif - Mihai   b.12/05/45   Building engineer
"I was born in Resita, but lived in Bucharest since 1949. I graduated in 1970 from the Building Institute. My wife has a Ph.D. in economic science. We have a 14 years old son and an 11 years old daughter."
✉ Soseaua Iancului 7, Bl.109B, Ap.80, sector 2, Bucuresti, 73371 ✆ (90) 539219 ✍ German, English ♥ walking in the mountains, theatre, opera ⌂ yes

ADU, George   b. 06/26/60   Engineer
"I graduated from the National Institute of Chemistry in 1986 and now I work in a laboratory of the Glass Factory in Bucharest."
✉ Bd. Muncii 208C, Bl.G7bis, Ap.10, sector 2, Bucuresti, 73427 ✆ (90) 433959 ✍ Hungarian, English ♥ travels, photography, home computers ⌂ yes, in a double room with kitchen in Brasov.

ADUCANU, Cezar   b.10/21/58   Teacher of sports
"Between 10 and 18 I practiced swimming (100m butterfly), then, between 18 and 27 - pentathlon; I took part in the Olympic Games."
✉ Str. Mihaila Radu 16, sector 2, Bucuresti ✆ (90) 193006 ✍ French, English ♥ theatre, travelling ⌂ yes, but only for 3-4 days

RADULESCU, Anca   b.03/20/46   English teacher and translator

"I graduated from the University of Bucharest, foreign languages, in 1969, then I worked as foreign trade translator. Since 1987 I have been appointed translator in the Ministry of Electrical Engineering. I live in Bucharest with my husband (engineer)."

✉ Intr.Pristolului 5,sector 3, Bucuresti ✆ (90) 212377 ✍ English, French ♥ opera, fresh air going ☗ yes ☆ breakfast

RADULESCU, Ermina   b.05/31/38   Engineer

"I am master engineer and am working as a researcher, but I intend to retire and begin a private activity, probably connected with tourism. I have no children, so that I have enough time to travel with my guests around the country."

✉ Str.Elena Cuza 70,Bl.29,Sc.A,Ap.18,sector 4, Bucuresti, 75168 ✆ (90) 755850 ✍ English, French ♥ swimming, skiing, all arts, books, opera, tourism ☗ yes ☆ board, car

RADULESCU, Horia   b.03/21/29   Engineer

"My wife and my son are physicians. In my life, I travelled a lot. I retired in 1989 and now I travel around my room, attend the French Library, go to exhibitions and wait for my future friends, to whom I am prepared to show the whole country."

✉ Bd.G. Dimitrov,Bl.T4,Ap.34, Bucuresti, 73339 ✆ (90) 424064 ✍ French, English (wife, son) ♥ reading (history of civilizations, geography, travels), travelling abroad ☗ yes ☆ breakfast

RADULESCU, Marian and Gabriela (wife)   b.07/03/59   Economist; Translator - interpreter - English - German (wife)

"I graduated the Trade Academy in 1983, being specialized in Tourism and Trade. I'm now working in one of the greatest shops in Bucharest as a teacher for the

professional improvement of the staff. I have no children."

✉ Str.Piscului 9,Bl.79,Sc.A,Ap.67,sector 4, Bucuresti, 75191 ✆ (90) 759561 ✍ English, German ♥ literature, films, music, politics, economy, sociology, psychology, philosophy, trips in the country and abroad, yoga, tennis, swimming, martial arts, astrology, religions, history, walking with friends and talking./wife: playing guitar, (American songs), literature (poetry), history of religions (Oriental and Christian), philosophy, making friends ⌂ yes

RADUTA, Romeo b.01/08/68 Waiter
"I am an amateur bodybuilder."

✉ Bd.Metalurgiei 50,Bl.R11,Ap.88,sector 4, Bucuresti ✍ English ♥ video, films, fashion, music ⌂ yes

RISTOIU, Marian b.10/12/63 Computer Engineer
"I attend the evening classes of the Polytechnical Institute. I'll graduate next year. I work in a factory as electronist worker. I am married. My wife, Dana, studies Energetics."

✉ Str.Rosia Montana 1,Bl.17,Sc.4,Ap.128,sector 6, Bucuresti, 77584 ✆ (90) 727589 ✍ English ♥ my wife, football, skiing, geography, history (ancient greece) ⌂ yes ☆ my wife cooks very well

ROMAN, Anca Editor
"I was born in 1935. I graduated Psychology and I worked as an editor at a publicity agency belonging to the artist's union."

✉ Str.Hramului 18,sector 2, Bucuresti ✆ (90) 217079 ✍ French, English ♥ voyages, mountain climbing, gymnastics, foreign languages, music ⌂ yes ☆ breakfast

ROMAN, Georgette b.07/16/38 Chemist
"I graduated from faculty in 1965 and worked as a biochemist. I am retreated now. I am married and have a son (28, mechanical engineer)."

✉ Bd.Eroilor sanitari 9,sector 5, Bucuresti, 76245 ✆ (90) 157647 ✍ French ♥ music, voyages ⌂ yes ☆ breakfast

BUCURESTI

ROMAN, Maria-Romana   b.04/28/67   Engineer (chemist)
"*I was born in Tirgu Mures. I am blond, 1.70 m and 55 Kg, blue eyes. I spent the first 7 years of my life in Piatra Neamt, a romantic town between 4 mountains. I followed school in Tirgu Mures, then highschool and faculty in Bucharest. I am not married.*"
✉ Str.Frigului 19, Bucuresti, 75206 ✍ French
♥ gymnastics, volleyball, horse riding ∎ yes

ROTARIU, Marina   b.05/07/56   Engineer
"*I studied informatics in Bucharest. I married in 1980 Marcel, who is a chemical engineer. He loves the mountains. We have two sons : 4 years old and 9 months old.*"
✉ Str.Dr.Draghiescu 12bis,sector 5, Bucuresti, 76224 ✆ (90) 816996 ✍ French, English
♥ tourism, skiing, climbing, theatre ∎ yes, also in Sibiu

ROTARU, Diana   b.05/08/55   Engineer
"*I am not married. I live alone in a big house with two floors and a nice garden. I like to travel and meet people. I have a brother who lives in Bucharest with his wife.*"
✉ Str.Maior Racoteanu Ion 9,sector 3, Bucuresti
✆ (90) 203212 ✍ English, French ♥ car driving, opera, symphonic music, gardening ∎ yes ☆ board; trips by car.

RUDEANU, Alexei   b.04/24/39   Head of "Literary Cafe" and bookshop "Citadel" in Bucharest; writer and journalist.
"*Born in Chisinau (now part of Soviet Moldavia), the Iron Curtain hindered me from knowing my native town. The nomadic childhood in houses and hotels abroad, the continuous dreaming for more than 20 years of journalism, made me respect work and a home.*"
✉ Str.Visarion 2,sector 1,P.O.BOX 333-1, Bucuresti, 71116 ✆ (90) 476901 or 594792 (work: 502251) ✍ Russian ♥ literature, of course! I have 12 volumes published, stories and novels

RUSU, Nicolae   b. 05/03/32   Engineer
"*I am an expert in automation and computers. I am married; my wife, Eteri, is an engineer too. I have two*

BUCURESTI

children, Dorian (25), an engineer and a daughter (22) studying computers. I have a 3 room flat in the centre and a car."

✉ Calea Dorobantilor 102-110,Bl.2,Sc.A,Ap.1,sector 1, Bucuresti ✆ (90) 790594 ✍ English, French, German ♥ gardening **H** yes (exchange) ☆ breakfast

SANDU, Octavian - Dan   b.02/12/69   Translator

"I myself think I'm a boy just like any boy of my age. I try to do all my best for my real FRIENDS, for all who are always beside me. I don't like lies, selfishness or hypocrisy. "BE WHAT YOU WANNA BE" is the life principle that I'm going for..."

✉ Bd.Muncii 78,Bl.36,Ap.77,sector 2., Bucuresti, 73404 ✆ (90) 483244 ✍ English, German,, French, Bulgarian, Spanish, Italian ♥ classic-pop-rock music, travelling, reading, skiing, art, video, film, windsurfing, concerts, discos, telefunken, correspondence, and much more **H** yes

SAVA, Lucian Florin   b.07/31/53   Diplomat Engineer

"After doing several unskilled jobs I became dissatisfied with my position and decided to follow the courses of the Politechnic Institute in Bucharest. I am married. My wife is 22, very pretty and we are expecting a baby."

✉ Str.Rm.Sarat 2,Bl.H7,Sc.1,Ap.16, Bucuresti, 74542 ✆ (90) 476818 ✍ English, German ♥ sports : tennis, skiing, swimming, martial arts, fishing, engines ✂ stamps **H** yes ☆ accomodation

SAVESCU, Camelia   b.07/18/27   Constructions engineer (retired since 1988)

"I graduated the Politechnical Institute in 1950. I worked 4 years on a big building site (the Bicaz dam), then in a design institute for hydropower constructions. I was never involved in politics. I live with my husband, Savescu Ioan, aged 70 in a villa"

✉ Str.Pictor Rozenthal 10,sector 1, Bucuresti, 71288 ✆ (90) 338685 ✍ French ♥ voyages, aesthetic activities **H** yes ☆ bed and breakfast; tours with our car.

SAVOIU, Alexandra Letitia b.04/25/43 Economist
"I worked for 20 years in a Foreign Trade Enterprise as a knitwear seller; after I divorced, I was forced to leave the enterprise and now I am working in a knitwear factory. I have a 22 years old son, who is a student in the Politechnic Institute."
✉ Str.Dr.Taberei 55,Bl.R5,Sc.A,Ap.19,sector 6, Bucuresti, 77381 ✆ (90) 462943 ✍ English ♥ travelling, knowing people, dogs ⌂ yes. 1-2 pers. ☆ breakfast

SCORTANU, Vasile b.06/01/53 Receptionist
"I own an apartment in the centre of the city, to house a family and for free! I am 1.85 m tall, slim and bearded; an agreeable face, an open personality."
✉ Str.Virgiliu 35, Bucuresti, 77106 ✆ (90) 376392 ✍ French, English ♥ literature, yoga, music ⌂ yes ☆ board

SDIREA, Romulus b.07/05/40 Chemist
"I have been working in the field of energetic chemistry for more than 20 years. I participated in four inventions. I am the president of a philatelic club."
✉ Str.Prevederii 26,Bl.G8,Ap.51, Bucuresti, 74592 ✆ (90) 308032 ✍ English, French, Spanish ♥ philately ✂ stamps ⌂ yes ☆ breakfast

SEGALL, Sava and Adriana b.03/13/50 Writer and Journalist
"Octavian: Enrolled in Medical College, earned a M.A. in Romanian language and literature from Bucharest University; joined Radio Bucharest in 1949; head of drama section since 1969. Adriana: born 03.13.50; graduated from Chemistry Faculty; journalist."
✉ Bd.1 Mai Nr.58, Bl.35A,Ap.23, Bucuresti ✆ (90) 666834 ✍ English, French, German ♥ Octavian: theatre, opera, dance, concerts, trips, swimming, stamp collecting, mugs collection, Adriana: photo picture, chess (national champion at 12), piano (I like to play piano - Chopin, Mozart, Beethoven), trips to the mountains ✂ stamps, mugs. ⌂ yes

SERBAN, Camelia Florenta b.04/03/76 Pupil

"I study in the "Spiru Haret" highschool, first year. I candidate for master at chess. I will become world champion and keep the title for all the rest of my life with the help of mathematics. No kidding! Height: 172 cm; eyes: blue; hair: chestnut"

✉ Str.Sblt.Cristescu Dima 5,Bl.220,Sc.A,Ap.4,sector 2, Bucuresti, 73324 ✆ (90) 538661 ✍ French, English ♥ chess, mathematics ♖ yes

SERBAN, Romeo b.08/08/64 Engineer

"I am not married and have no obligations. Height: 1.90m. Weight: 85kg. My greatest wish is to meet girls (20-28 year old) who are pretty, funny, loving sports, music, trips, exchange of visits. I work as a guide too."

✉ Sos.Pantelimon 256,Bl.53,Sc.D,Ap.216,sector 2, Bucuresti ✆ (90) 275361 ✍ French, English ♥ high level technique, sports (tennis, football, swimming), films, video, trips, cars, rock music ♖ yes

SICHITIU, Maria Mechanic engineer

"I was born and finished my studies in Bucharest. I am married. My husband is a juridical consultant. God gave us two children: a daughter - Alexandra (18) and a son - Horatiu (17). I am a Catholic."

✉ Str.Valea Ialomitei 13,Bl.A32,Sc.C,Ap.34,sector 6, Bucuresti, 77411 ✆ (90) 778570 ✍ French, German ♥ music, literature, tourism ♖ yes

SIMION, Marian Constantine b.05/28/35 Retired

"I worked as an officer in judicial police until 10 years ago, when my brother-in-law left Romania illegally and I had to retire. My wife is of Albanian nationality and manages a shop for fashion clothes in the centre of the city."

✉ Str.Rodul pamintului 2,Sc.B,Ap.17,sector 3, Bucuresti ✆ (90) 472609 ✍ Italian, English, Albanian ♥ folk dances, opera and operetta music, gardening ✂ stamps ♖ yes (we own a small in Snagov too) ☆ board, 2 cars

SIRBU, Traian b. 07/19/37 Engineer - retired

"I graduated as an electronics engineer. Then I attended the Civil Aviation School and graduated in 1960. I

worked in aviation till 1989 when I retired after having flown all over the world. My wife is an air hostess and I have two daughters."

✉ Bd.Bucurestii Noi 78,Bl.C1,Ap.48,sector 1,
   Bucuresti ✆ (90) 675066 ✍ English, Russian
♥ airplanes, fishing, hunting, chess, tourism, photography and film making ∎ yes

SOLOMON, Bella Bookkeepr (retired)

"I was born in 1905. Between 1969-1986 I travelled to Bulgaria, Israel, Hungary, Austria, West Germany (four times), France, Belgium, Holland, U.S.A., Canada."

✉ Str.Judetului 9, Bucuresti, 72226 ✆ (90) 875264
✍ French, German, Ydisch ♥ I have no exclusive passion, I am interested in learning in all fields ∎ yes. I offer lodging. ☆ kitchen to use

SPANU, Viorel b. 11/21/58 Metallurgy Engineer

"I was born in Brasov. I got married at the age of 22 and I have 2 daughters. I have a car and a color TV. I have a sister and my wife has two brothers. They all live in Bucharest."

✉ Str.Laborator 138,Bl.S 31 B,Ap.25,sector 3,
   Bucuresti, 74364 ✆ (90) 473105 ✍ English
♥ flowers, animals ∎ yes

SPINEI, Adrian b.11/18/50 Medical assistent

"I am not married. I am 1.86 m tall, weigh 92 Kg. I am blond I own a nice 3 rooms flat near the Arch of Triumph and Herastrau Park."

✉ Bd.1 Mai,nr.111,Bl.12A,Sc.B,Ap.54,sector 1,
   Bucuresti, 7000 ✆ (90) 664863 ✍ English,
French, German, Italian ♥ tennis, swimming ∎ yes

STAICU, Ana b. 12/21/35 Technician

"I worked in a chemistry institute. I own an apartment in Bucharest, I am not married."

✉ Str.Vasile Milea 9,Bl.A,Sc.D,Ap.41, Bucuresti,
   77303 ✆ (90) 451358 ✍ French ♥ history,
Romanian folklore, opera ∎ yes ☆ breakfast

STAMBOLI, Ioana b.09/05/68 Student

"I study vestimentary design at the faculty of Textile Industry. In the same time I study sociology. During vacations I work as a guide."

✉ Str.Visinilor 15,sector 2, Bucuresti, 73109
✆ (90) 212648 ✍ French, English, German ♥ foreign languages, sports, classical music, literature, guiding
H yes, in excellent conditions ☆ board

STANASILA, Laura b.04/13/71 Student

"I study biochemistry (second year). I graduated from high school the first, I attend a faculty that does not completely fit my taste. Maybe , I'll study physics, or philosophy; another project of mine is to edit a cultural magazine."

✉ Bd.1 Mai Nr.70-84,Bl.45,Ap.25,sector 1, Bucuresti, 71215 ✆ (90) 662828 ✍ French, English
♥ reading (especially French), France, music, travelling H yes

STANCIULESCU, Roxana b.06/28/63 Electronist

"I live with my parents in a 3 room apartment. I work in an enterprise for computers maintaining and repairing as secretary."

✉ Str.Serdarului 11,Bl.47,Ap.15, Bucuresti, 71308
✆ (90) 173298 ✍ English ♥ travelling, mountaineering, caving, reading, English, dancing H yes, only for one person.

STANCU, Marcela b.08/06/47 Technician

"Divorced. I have one daughter, Adriana, 20, a chemist and one son, Daniel, 17, who is in college. I am healthy, affectionate, radiating good will and I enjoy every moment of my life. I think life is an eternal recommencement."

✉ Str.Drumul taberei 30,Bl.OD3,Sc.4,Ap.143,sector 6, Bucuresti ✆ (90) 306338 ✍ French, English, Italian ♥ theatre, cinema, music, knitting, flowers, animals ✂ good moments H yes

STANCULESCU, Socrate   b.08/10/55   Mechanic engineer

"Both, me and my wife, graduated from Polytechnical Institutes. We have no children. We live in a three room flat."

✉ Str.Veronica Micle 22,Bl.M5,Sc.A,Ap.7,sector 1, Bucuresti ✆ (90) 594148 ✍ English, French
♥ sports, electronic music ♓ yes ☆ board, trips by car

STOIA, Paula Gabriela   b.07/05/27   Physician (rheumatism and physiotherapy)

"I worked as a researcher and then with Anna Aslan, in Otopeni, near Bucharest. At this point I have my own consulting room. I would like to exchange information with other physicians."

✉ Str.Drobeta 19,Ap.5,sector 2, Bucuresti ✆ (90) 192425 ✍ French, Italian, English (a little)
♥ travelling ♓ yes, on the Prahova Valley too
☆ trips by car

STOICA, Gabriela   b.03/30/44   Economist

"I was born in Bucharest. My family has been living in Bucharest for 400 years. My father and grandfather studied economy and law. Me too. My husband is an engineer. We have a son."

✉ Bd.Pacii 1,Bl.22B,Sc.A,Ap.16, Bucuresti, 77531 ✆ (90) 710827 ✍ French, English ♥ dance, flowers, music (symphonic and opera), painting, literature
♓ yes

STOICIU, Cristian and Gabriela (wife) Alexandru (son)   Physician / Chemist

"I am 39 year old, my wife is 34 year old. I work in a hospital as a physiotherapist, my wife works in a drugstore"

✉ Sos.Vergului 33,Bl.K2,Ap.14,sector 2, Bucuresti, 73512 ✍ French ♥ music, films, travelling
♓ yes

STURZOIU, Marius Teodor   b.09/27/55   Computer engineer

"I was born in Buzau, a small town; I studied in Bucharest, where now I live."

✉ Str.Fainari 6,Bl.69,Sc.A,Ap.21,sector 2, Bucuresti
✆ (90) 453163 ✍ French, English ♥ stamp collecting, opera, ballet ✄ stamps **H** yes

SUCIU, Adriana   b.06/27/57   Operator in a computer centre

"I was born in Bucharest. I studied piano, ballet, etc."

✉ Str.Peleaga 43,sector 5, Bucuresti, 76629
✆ (90) 235997 ✍ French, English ♥ correspondence, postcards, money, theatre, painting, music, ballet **H** yes

SUCIU ARAMA, Marilena   b.09/06/42   Physician

"I graduated from faculty in 1966. My husband is an engineer. I have a very beautiful daughter, who studies medicine. We live in the centre of Bucharest. We don't love communists. We have a little house next to the Snagov lake."

✉ Bd.Gheorghe Dimitrov 12,Ap.3,sector 3, Bucuresti, 70313 ✆ (90) 351576 ✍ French, English
♥ art, painting, music, travelling, art objects **H** yes
☆ breakfast

SZABADOS, Andrei   b.11/03/31   Engineer

"I was the first son in a wealthy family. I studied in Timisoara. I was married twice, but have no children. I inherited love for the Beautiful."

✉ Str.Pictor Verona 19, Bucuresti, 70153 ✆ (90) 115202 ✍ German, Hungarian ♥ great music, thoughts that help us in life **H** yes

TANASESCU, Radu-Gabriel   b.02/03/66   Locksmith

"I was born in Constanta. My parents moved to Bucharest when I was five. I graduated from a secondary mechanical type school in 1984. I have been

married since 1989. My wife, Nina, graduated from a guide school in 1988. We both love the mountains."
- ✉ Str.Cetatea Veche 5,Bl.III/5B,Ap.2,sector 4, Bucuresti, 75419 ✆ (90) 290528 ✍ English
- ♥ theatre, martial arts (Judo, Wu-Shu), music, films
- ⌂ yes ☆ breakfast or full board

TANCU, Mariana   b.05/31/54   Economist
"Since 1983 I work with the Independent Company of Tourism for the Youth. I intend to open my own agency. I am not married. I have a sister, Cornelia, who works in Lugoj - the town where I was born too."
- ✉ Bd.Dacia 88,Ap.88, Bucuresti, 70256 ✆ (90) 103978 ✍ French, English, German (a little)
- ♥ travelling, skiing, tennis, photography, swimming, dancing, listening to music, literature, theatre, sewing
- ✂ dolls, books, postcards, touristic guides and albums
- ⌂ yes (I live in a large room - 40 m) women, child
- ☆ breakfast

TEODORESCU, Olga   b.05/21/42   Teacher
"I have been teaching for twenty years and like my job. I can type in English better than in Romanian. I like doing any honest job. My psychic structure is an optimistic one."
- ✉ Str.Liviu Rebreanu 6,Bl.B1,Sc.5,Ap.193,sector 3, Bucuresti, 74623 ✆ (90) 430569 ✍ English, (son) French
- ♥ visiting foreign countries (but how?), reading, listening to music, walking in silent, remote villages
- ⌂ yes ☆ I am single and have time to be a good hostess.

TICOVSCHI, Vladimir Al.
and Cristina (daughter)   b.07/16/31   Engineer ; Student in cybernetics (daughter)
"I studied in Bucharest. I work now in a cybernetics research institute. I traveled in Eastern Europe, in France, West Germany, Italy, Spain, England, USA, etc. I have 60 books on cybernetics published. Cristina (daughter) is a student, not married."
- ✉ Str. Luterana 5,Sc.A,Ap.13, Bucuresti, 70741
- ✍ French, German, English ♥ tennis, daughter: tennis, skiing, classical music (Brahms), dancing ⌂ yes

TILICA, Mircea b.07/25/49 Engineer

"*I work with the Romanian Railroads. My wife, Gabriela, is an engineer too. Our daughter, Cristina, is 11 years old; she loves modern dancing.*"

✉ Str.Barbu Lautaru 8,Bl.24,Sc.1,Ap.30,sector 1, Bucuresti ✆ (90) 175478 ✍ French, German, English (a little) ♥ travelling abroad, music, literature, politics ♦ yes; previous corresponding necessary ☆ board, car

TIMUS, Clementina b.08/31/46 Physicist

"*I was born in a small village near Timisoara. My father was schoolmaster in a secondary school in Timisoara. I graduated University in Timisoara and then moved to Bucharest. I have a son of 17 and a daughter of 14. I am married.*"

✉ Str.Crisana 20-22,Ap.22,sector 1, Bucuresti, 70783 ✆ (90) 136907 ✍ English, French, Russian ♥ sports (aerobic gymnastics, skiing), classic music, philatelie ♦ My flat is too small for comfortable lodging.

TOMA, Elena b. 09/14/35 Astronomer

"*I studied mathematics at the University in Bucharest and then I worked for 32 years as an astronomer at the Observatory in Bucharest. My husband studied physics. I have two children, both married. We travelled a lot.*"

✉ Bd.C. Ressu 37,Bl.Z4,Ap.3, Bucuresti ✆ (90) 746337 ✍ French, English ♥ painting ♦ yes ☆ breakfast, guide

TOMESCU, Ioana b.06/14/69 Student

"*Since I was born, I have been living together with my parents. I have never been abroad, but I would like to see how people in other countries live. I study automation. I have a car and driving license.*"

✉ Str.Masina de Piine 3,Bl.2,Ap.15, Bucuresti ✆ (90) 426127 ✍ English ♥ swimming, skiing, skating, symphonic music, travelling, literature ♦ yes

TONCIU, Madalina   b.03/30/59   Teacher of Romanian
"I like a lot to travel and in 1985 I visited France with a folk group on a tour. I am joyful and have a lot of friends."
✉ Calea Cringasi 19,Bl.11B,Sc.1,Ap.7,sector 6, Bucuresti, 77732 ✍ French, English ♥ I like what is beautiful in art and life H yes ☆ breakfast

TOTAN, Mircea Cristian   b.12/18/56   Engineer
"I graduated from the Polytechnical Institute in Bucharest. I work in the computing centre of the Ministry of Tourism. While student I worked as a guide. I am married since 1987 and live together with my wife, Luciana and our two children in the centre."
✉ Str.Rezonantei 2,Bl.12,Ap.29,sector 4, Bucuresti, 75519 ℂ (90) 832289 ✍ French, English, Italian ♥ sports (tennis, skiing, swimming), classic music, voyages H yes, also on the Black Sea coast and in Transylv. ☆ board

TOUSSAINT, Gheorghe   b.05/20/20   Engineer (retired)
"I was born in Galati. My father, a general inspector, was of Belgian origin, a distinguished engineer. I graduated as an engineer in Bucharest in 1944. I worked as chief designer for many big plants in Romania. I am married - no children."
✉ Str.Baiculesti 15,Sc.B,Ap.62, Bucuresti, 78401 ℂ (90) 672762 ✍ French, Italian, English (a little) ♥ history of Romanian people, the touristic beauties of Romania H yes

TRANDAF, Maria   b.11/07/31   Engineer
"My husband, Mircea (62) and my son, Dan (25) are both engineers. I am retired. We live in a nice house in the most quiet and beautiful district of Bucharest."
✉ Str.Londra 48,sector 1, Bucuresti, 72425 ℂ (90) 334108 ✍ French, English ♥ nature, travelling, history, literature, bridge H yes ☆ car, guide

TRESTIANU, Eracle   b.04/28/21   Magistrate (retired)
"Born in Bucharest where I did my studies, Ph.D. included. Works in the international public law, criminology and criminalistic. In my youth I practised

sports as a professional (swimming, table tennis, horse riding). Married, 2 children."
✉ Str.Fr.Chopin 7,Sc.A,Ap.9,sector 2, Bucuresti, 71454 ✆ (90) 331083 ✍ French, Italian, English ♥ tennis (which I play regularily), bridge, listening to good music (symphonic, opera, jazz), tourism by car, esoterism (parapsychology, yoga, zen, chirology) ⌂ yes

TRIPA, Ioan b. 01/28/70   Student in Architecture
"I was born in Oradea. I went to school and secondary school in Bucharest. I visited Bulgaria, Libya, Yugoslavia and Italy. In December 1989 I took part in the revolution."
✉ Str.Duiliu Zamfirescu 8, Bucuresti ✆ (90) 593846 ✍ English, Italian ♥ tennis, basketball, swimming, skiing, art, cinema, theatre, music ⌂ yes

TRUICA, Tana Ionela   b.11/21/70   Student at the Music Academy in Bucharest - composition
"I was born in an intellectual family (my mother is a teacher of English, my father is a painter) and I was lucky to receive a serious education. So I attended the best and most famous school in Romania, where I studied piano thoroughly."
✉ Str.Poet Neculuta 70,sector 2, Bucuresti, 73304 ✆ (90) 539845 ✍ English, French ♥ sports, design, literature, music ⌂ Bucharest & Sinaia(large wooden house in a forest) ☆ breakfast and supper

TUDOR, Rigoleta and Mihai (husband)   b.11/21/61   Medical assistant
"I work in the hospital for students in Bucharest. I am married for 5 years but we have no children yet. My husband is born 08.23.58 and speaks Italian, French, English. He is a Mechanic engineer."
✉ Str.Albinelor 32,Bl.32,Sc.1,Ap.14,sector 4, Bucuresti ✆ (90) 758465 ✍ French, Italian (a little) ♥ opera, ballet, modern and Romanian popular dance, reading, politics. As a child I took ballet but couldn't continue, my husband loves music, nature, literature, films, SF, computers ⌂ yes

BUCURESTI

TUDOSE, Gabriela and Stana (mother) b.06/05/55 Biolog / Retired

"I am not married but I am looking for a husband. I have been living all my life in the communist prison, but my spirit is still alive and so are my hopes."

✉ Str.Nitu Vasile 58, Bl.10, Ap.37, sector 4, Bucuresti, 75522 ✆ (90) 844619 ✎ French, English
♥ knowing people, travelling ⌂ yes ☆ breakfast

TURLESCU, Ioan b.07/14/29 Teacher

"I studied lots of things and practiced many professions : pilot, journalist, chief editor. My wife died three years ago. My son, Ionut, is an analyst. He is 30. His wife, Florentina, is an analyst too."

✉ Str.Slatineanu 23-27, Ap.4, sector 1, Bucuresti, 71137 ✆ (90) 117389 ✎ French, Russian, Italian
♥ literature, music, photography, film, chess, trips, aviatic sports, philately, gardening, politic philosophy ⌂ yes ☆ board

TUROVSKI, Victor b.12/22/26 Chemist Engineer

"I was born in Tulcea (entrance gate to the Danube Delta). I graduated from high school in 1946. Then I graduated from the University and from the Polytechnical Institute. I have been working as a specialist in chemical materials. I am retired."

✉ Calea Plevnei 26, Ap.6, Bucuresti ✆ (90) 142067
✎ French, Italian (a little) ♥ photographing, piano playing ⌂ Yes ☆ I could rent the whole app. for a month or more

UNGUREANU, Mihai b.04/25/50 Teacher (Romanian language and literature)

"I am a free spirit, generally optimistic, lucid, I have friends everywhere because I can't live alone. I am married and have a 14 years old daughter. I worked as a guide and would be interested in a foreign partner for a tourism agency."

✉ Bd.Nicolae Grigorescu 36, Bl.S1D, Ap.76, sector 3, Bucuresti, 74628 ✆ (90) 747960 ✎ French, Italian ♥ reading, travelling, talking, exchanging opinions ⌂ yes

VARLAN, Anca b. 03/15/55 Economist

"During studying the Faculty of Trade I also worked in a fashion creation studio and also professional modeling. Now I work as an economist for nourishment trade in Bucharest. I have also graduated a school for guides-interpreters, international tourism."

✉ Int.Parfumului 10, Bucuresti ✆ (90) 214797
✍ French, Italian ♥ corresponding with people from all over the world, travelling to know past and present civilizations, classic and modern music, reading, fashion, dancing (I won many prizes...) **H** yes
☆ breakfast

VARLAN, Doru b. 07/27/50 Aviator

"I'm still an airline pilot working with Tarom (Romanian air transports), I'm the associate editor of the first Romanian independent private aerospace periodical. I'm married and we have three daughters aged 13, 8 and respectively 5."

✉ Str.Prometeu 29,Bl.16G,Sc.3,Ap.40,sector 1, Bucuresti, 71507 ✍ English ♥ flying and aerospace history, historic and geographical literature reading, meeting interesting people, correspondence **H** yes

VASILESCU, Dan b. 04/14/34 Engineer

"I spent my childhood in Giurgiu, once a very picturesque town, with Balcanic atmosphere, close to Russia and Bulgaria. My father, a priest, had to transfer to Bucharest in 1946. I am married. We have a son, student."

✉ Str.Dr.Mihai Ciuca 21,sector 5, Bucuresti, 76228
✆ (90) 132867 ✍ French, English (son) ♥ to know people and places abroad **H** yes, in our villa.
☆ board, tour by car, few days at Cimpulung.

VECSEY, Maria b. 12/02/41 Physician

"My father was a worker in the railway company. Now he is retired and lives in Canada. I graduated the University in Iasi. I lived 7 years in Onesti where I met

my husband Bela, of Hungarian origin. We've been married for 21 years and have a son aged 16."

✉ Bd.Timisoara 65,Bl.D44,Sc.B,Ap.25, Bucuresti, 77401 ✆ (90) 774515 🗬 French, English (a little), Italian (a little), Russian ♥ symphonic music, opera, light music, sports (football, gymnastics, volley, athletics), painting, literature, poetry, mountain trips, the sea ⌂ yes ☆ breakfast

VERSEHORA, Toma   b.12/12/29   Economist

"I was born near Cernautzi, which is now Soviet territory. Refugee in Romania in 1944-1945; I work as an economist in the Tourist department, chief of staff; my wife is also an economist."

✉ Aleea Sandulesti 5,Bl.E,Ap.49,sector 6, Bucuresti, 77391 ✆ (90) 459972 🗬 French, German, Russian ♥ tourism, literature ⌂ yes ☆ trips by car.

VISAN, Dan   b.07/23/44   Engineer

"We have two sons : Robert (born 1972, student, loves tennis, football, modern music, English) and Catalin (born 1974, pupil, loves physics, mathematics, computers, English)."

✉ Str.Doamna Ghica 1,Bl.1,Sc.1,Ap.20,sector 2, Bucuresti ✆ (90) 889971 🗬 English, Russian ♥ our children, bridge ⌂ yes ☆ board

VLAD, Cristian   b. 04/19/66   Worker and Student

"I work in an enterprise and study at the Polytechnical Institute in Bucharest. I'll finish studying next year. I am not married and live with my parents in the centre of Bucharest. I also have a little house near Tirgoviste."

✉ Bd.Schitu Magureanu 27-33,Sc.A,Ap.19,sector 1, Bucuresti, 70761 ✆ (90) 132652 🗬 French, English (a little) ♥ music (disco), sports, films ⌂ yes, only on agreement after two months notice.

VLAICU, Zeno Cornel   b.09/30/27   Mining engineer

"I have been working as a geologist and mining engineer in Romania and in South-American and African

countries. My wife is a geologist, now retired. My family is formed of four persons."

✉ Str.Dristor 5, Bl.A20, Ap.1, sector 3, Buceresti, 74321 ✆ (90) 202429 ✍ English, French, Spanish ♥ I am interested in visiting big European towns of architectural and cultural importance ⌂ yes, on the Prahova Valley too

VOICA, Dragos   b.01/05/69   Student
"Unmarried, goodlooking."

✉ P.O.BOX 74 - 41, Bucuresti ✆ (90) 774365 ✍ English, French, Italian ♥ nice girls, stamps (big collector) ✂ stamps

VOICESCU, Mihail   b.10/23/22   Economist
"I have been working as a diplomat in Iran and Algeria and then in the foreign affairs department of the Ministry of Telecommunication. I participated in negotiations in 53 countries."

✉ Str.Calea Victoriei 142, Sc.D, Ap.22, Bucuresti, 71101 ✆ (90) 505302 ✍ French ♥ football ⌂ starting 1992

VOICULESCU, Elefterie - Emil and Florica (wife)
     Film director / Teacher (retired)
"I practiced different jobs between 1946 and 1968, when I became a student at the Institute for Theatre and Cinema. I graduated in 1973 and now direct films, documentaries and commercials."

✉ Sos.Fundeni 2, Bl.11 B, Sc.A, Ap.28, Bucuresti, 73531 ✆ (90) 276319 ✍ French, Italian ♥ writing (I published a lot of books) ⌂ yes

VOINEA, Cristian   b.12/24/60   Mechano - Chemical engineer
"I was born in Bucharest, in an intellectual family. I grew up like all other children in the 'golden era'. In 1988 I married Rodica and I can say I made a good choice. We have no children yet."

✉ Str.Trestiana 5, Bl.9, Sc.2, Ap.66, sector 4, Bucuresti ✆ (90) 758774 ✍ English, German ♥ tennis, skiing ⌂ yes

BUCURESTI

VULPESCU, George Dragos   b.12/17/70   Student at the Faculty of Chemic Technology

"My parents are geologists and so I came to love the mountains. In a serene day when there is no cloud in the sky, you can see the Black Sea from the highest mountain Moldoveanu (2500 m)."

✉ Str.Aleea Tincani 1,Bl.F12,Sc.A,Ap.10,sector 6, Bucuresti, 77349 ✆ (90) 266755 ✎ French ♥ music (Chopin, Beethoven, Bach, Brahms), pop music, trips in the mountains, skiing ⌂ yes ☆ board

WINKLER, Adalbert   b.04/04/30   Musician (composer, pianist and conductor)

"Born in Aiud. Music studies from the age of 5. After finishing secondary school continues his musical studies in Leningrad (USSR) in "N.A. Rimsky-Korsakov" Conservatory. Written many compositions: opera, symphonies, instrumental and vocal music."

✉ Str.Tomis 6,Bl.H4,Ap.12, Bucuresti, 74544 ✆ (90) 476017 ✎ English, German,, French, Russian ♥ literature, theatre, tourism, sports ⌂ yes ☆ breakfast

ZAHARIA, Mariana   b.08/15/44   Nurse

"I am married and I have a 14-year-old son. My husband, Mircea, is 46 and he is a doctor. Our son Valeriu is a pupil. He speaks English. We are a hospitable family and we desire much to have friends in other countries."

✉ Str.Brasov 22,Bl.Z132,Sc.A,Ap.18,sector 6, Bucuresti ✆ (90) 457765 ✎ English ♥ music, film, stamp collecting (my son) ⌂ yes ☆ breakfast

ZAMAN, Constantin   b.01/16/59   Research worker

"I was born in Turnu Severin. I studied two years at the Maritime Institute in Constanta, but, in 1980 I was eliminated because I tried to run away from Romania. I continued my economic studies in Craiova and graduated in 1984. Now, I work as a researcher"

✉ Str.Riul Doamnei,Bl.M1,Ap.46, Bucuresti ✆ (90) 774134 ✎ English, French, Spanish ♥ yoga, opera, voyages ⌂ yes

ZANFIR, Mihaela and Radu (husband) b.01/12/63
   Economist / Engineer
   "Despite the isolation imposed by Ceausescu, we had a constant interest in France and its culture."
   ✉ Bd.Pionierilor 51,Bl.64,Ap.43,sector 4, Bucuresti
   ✆ (90) 753411 ✍ French, English ♥ pop and disco music, sports, trips to the countryside ⌂ yes

ZILISTEANU, Ion Radu b.10/28/58 Engineer, Mathematician, Journalist
   "Born in Bucharest. Secondary school at "Saint Sava". Between 1978 and 1983, student at the Polytechnical Institute of Bucharest. Head graduate, mechanical (motor vehicle) engineer. Between 1986 and 1990, studies of Math at University of Bucharest."
   ✉ C.P.82-38,Bucuresti 82, Bucuresti, 75650
   ✆ (90) 834937 ✍ English, French ♥ music, literature, travels ⌂ Yes

ZIMEL, Ana - Lucia b.07/06/48 Teacher
   "Born and brought up in Bucharest. Since 1971 I teach French to pupils aged 8 to 18. I am married to an electro-mechanic engineer, great cinema fan. No children, but I like children. I love my job."
   ✉ Str.D.Bolintineanu 5,Ap.41,sector 3, Bucuresti, 70448 ✆ (90) 159208 ✍ French, English
   ♥ reading, listening to classic music, travelling
   ⌂ yes

BUSTENI

> *" ... a famous resort in the Carpathians, on the Prahova Valley ... and see Peles Castle in Sinaia - a royal residence ... "*

BALTA, Mihai and Marilena (wife) b.10/18/40 Builder (he)/Economist (she)
   "We are married; we have a four year old son."
   ✉ Str.Clabucet 34, Busteni, 2185 ✆ (973) 20082
   ✍ French ♥ tourism, motorcars, photography, numismatics ⌂ yes ☆ board

DRAGUSIN, Mihai   b.10/05/58   Engineer
"1984 - end of studies; 3 years in investments, 3 years in automations"
✉ Str.Parintele Lucaci 1, Busteni ✆ (973) 21227
✍ French, English ♥ crossword, puzzle, dancing, trips

BUSTENI - POIANA TAPULUI

ALEXANDRESCU, Cornelia
and Traian (husband)   b.12/16/41   Teacher (drawing) / Economist
✉ Str.Amurgului 16, Busteni - Poiana Tapului, 2178 ✆ (973) 20355 ✍ French ♥ (she) art, cooking, classical music, fashion; (he) reading, sports, travelling by car ℍ yes ☆ breakfast

BUZAU

BOICU, George Cristian   b.04/22/59   Engineer in computers
"I married my present wife, Lucia, in 1983 (she is born in 1961 and an economist). I graduated from the Polytechnical Institute in Bucharest in 1984. We moved to Buzau in 1985, because my wife worked there. In 1986 our son was born - Lucian."
✉ Cartier Dorobanti,Bl.33H,Ap.11, Buzau, 5100 ✆ (974) 32866 ✍ English, French (a little) ♥ tourism, disco music, video movies, sports ℍ yes, in Bucharest too ☆ board

CIORCILA, Liana.   b.11/22/38   Architect
"My husband is also an architect. We have a twenty year old daughter. I am working at the Institute of Technical Projects in my town."
✉ Str.N.Balcescu,Bl.26,Ap.12, Buzau ✆ (974) 31834 ✍ French, Russian ♥ literature ℍ yes 1-2 persons

LUNGU, Marcel   b.05/20/59   Economist
"I graduated from the Faculty of Cybernetics in Bucharest in 1983. I am also a journalist at a local

newspaper. I also work as a guide since 1990 for French groups."

✉ Str.Unirii,Bl.P6A,Ap.10, Buzau, 5100 ✆ (974) 12698 ✍ French ♥ my job, the French, being a disk-jockey in the greatest discotheque of Buzau **H** yes

ROMULUS, Nutu   b.02/28/22   Economist (retreated) and guide

"I am married. I worked as a bank inspector 30 years."
✉ Str.Oltului 55, Buzau, 5100 ✆ (974) 27232
✍ French ♥ tourism **H** yes

BUZIAS

> *" Buzias is a very nice town, with mineral waters in the park. Rheumatism and heart diseases are treated here. We have beautiful mounains and caves. "*

BALOGH, Nicoleta   b.04/18/61   Engineer

"I was born in a small town in Transylvania. I studied in Oradea and Bucharest to become engineer in horticulture. I work in a vineyard farm. I am married for 8 years and have two children. My husband is a mechanical engineer."

✉ Str.Bacova 342, Buzias ✍ French, Hungarian
♥ gardening, the mountains, travelling, evenings with friends **H** yes

CALARASI

> *" A small town on the Danume shore. One can take walks by the river, fish, and visit the town's surroundins.   The Black Sea coast is near. "*

ACHIM, Irina   b. 10/18/76   Pupil

"I am a pupil in the 8th year. My parents are judge and teacher. I have no brother or sister. We all agreed to

accept visitors from abroad, preferably for a young girl with her parents."

✉ Str.Cornisei,Bl.D3,Ap.8, Calarasi, 8500 ✆ (911) 22459 ✍ French, English ♥ I like moving in clean air. I play handball ⌂ yes

MANEA, Cecilia-Nicoleta b.11/23/57 Building engineer
"I teach technical courses in a high school. My husband, Dorin, is a building engineer too and works in a design institute. He loves literature, tennis, painting. I have a daughter (11) and a son (2)."
✉ Bd.1 Mai,Bl.A36,Sc.D,Ap.18, Calarasi, 8500 ✆ (911) 12983 ✍ French ♥ nature, fashion, knitting ⌂ yes

CARACAL

DIACONESCU, Florina b.07/12/47 Teacher
✉ Str.Antonius Caracalla,Bl.E,Sc.3,Apt.6, Caracal, 0800 ✆ (945) 11123 ✍ French ♥ literature, history, voyages ⌂ yes

CIMPIA TURZII

" ... near the Apuseni mountains (20 - 40km) and to Cluj ..."

FLOREA, Gligor b.01/04/46 Teacher (French)
✉ Str.Garii 2, Cimpia Turzii, 3351 ✆ (953) 68467 ✍ French ♥ tennis, rugby, literature ⌂ yes, we have a big house ☆ board

REPCIUK, Vladimir b.11/21/30 Engineer
"I have been working for 20 years as a translator of technical documentation. My wife worked as a bookkeeper and retired a year ago. We have a 31 year old daughter and a 27 year old son, both engineers and not married."
✉ Str.Liliacului 1a, Cimpia Turzii, 3351 ✆ (953) 67597 ✍ Russian, German, French ♥ philately ✄ stamps ⌂ yes, in Radauti also ☆ we can get painted eggs

CIMPINA

> " ... see the Nocolae Grigorescu, perhaps the greatest Romanian painter ..."

APOSTOL, Viorel   b.05/20/58   Electrician

"*I am married and have two daughters : Laura (8) and Andra (4).*"

✉ Str.Ecaterina Teodoroiu,Bl.23,Ap.33,Jud.Prahova, Cimpina, 2150 ✍ French ♥ football, music (Smokie, Dire Straits), electrotechnics, literature ⌂ yes

BANU, Carmen   b.07/06/70   Locksmith

"*I was born in Cimpina. My grandmother raised me until the age of 7. I have been studying English and French in private. I am attending the courses of the Ecological University and am working in a plant in Cimpina. I live together with my parents.*"

✉ Str.Schelelor,Bl.6,Sc.B,Ap.33,Jud.Prahova, Cimpina, 2150 ✆ (973) 31588 ✍ English, French ♥ knitting, gardening ⌂ yes

RIZESCU, Adelaida   b.02/01/39   Engineer

"*I am a profound believer, I respect all religions. My father was a pilot, my mother a clerk. My husband (the best in Romania) is also an engineer. My daughter also. We just founded a private enterprise of electronics and auto.*"

✉ C.P. 83,Jud.Prahova, Cimpina, 2150 ✆ (973) 34761 ✍ French, English ♥ gossip, tourism, seeing monuments and museums, reading (literature, extraterestrial civilizations, UFO, etc) ⌂ yes, in a nice house with garden in Summer. ☆ breakfast, transport with car.

CIMPULUNG-MOLDOVENESC

PLATON, Leila - Rodica   b.07/02/58   Physician

"*I am married to Radu, who is a computer engineer. We have a daughter, Minola, born 11/02/84. I work as a* specialist in contagious diseases and epidemiology at the hospital in Cimpulung. We live in a large villa."

✉ Str.Martisorului 5 ,Jud.Suceava, Cimpulung-Moldovenesc, 5950 ✆ (988) 11666 ✍ French, English ♥ music, reading, knitting, sewing, dancing ⌂ yes ☆ breakfast

ROTARU, Magda   b.02/02/52   Economist

"*I have a sister and a brother. I have license for translating into English and French.*"

✉ Calea Bucovinei 79 ,Jud.Suceava, Cimpulung-Moldovenesc, 5950 ✆ (988) 13505 ✍ French, English, German ♥ music (I play the piano), foreign languages (I study Arabic and Japanese), oriental civilizations, literature, fashion ⌂ yes

CISNADIE

CARPADE, Tania   b.09/13/57   Bookkeeper

"*I worked after graduation of high school as a pedagogist in a school and enjoyed the work. I worked then in tourism as a guide. When I returned to my town, I could not continue this kind of work, although that is what I would like; I still have hope.*"

✉ Str.Fundatura Viilor 11, Cisnadie, 2437 ✆ (925) 62285 ✍ English, German, Esperanto (a little) ♥ reading, dancing, walking ⌂ yes

SANDOR, Hans Georg   b.02/07/57   Worker

"*I am married and have two children. I am 1.72m high, blond and have blue eyes. I graduated from an art school. I love painting and music.*"

✉ Str. 1 Mai Nr.55 ,Ap.8 ,Jud.Sibiu, Cisnadie, 2437 ✆ (925) 62836 ✍ German, English (a little) ♥ swimmimg, walking ⌂ yes ☆ board

CLUJ-NAPOCA

> " ... 500,000 people, beautiful medieval buildings and churches, dating since roman times ... the National Theatre, Opera, Orchestra, Art and History Museums, the Botanical Gardens ... History of Pharmacy, House of Emil Isac ... the second largest town in Romania ..."

ALB, Sorin b. 08/03/64 Chemist engineer
"*I was born in a family of workers. My father was a driver and my mother a dressmaker. As a child I studied piano for six years. I finished faculty last year and work as a chemist engineer in Cluj. I live with my mother. I am not married.*"
✉ Str.Mehedinti 62-64,Bl.D3,Sc.I,Ap.27, Cluj-Napoca, 3400 ✆ (951) 65807 ✍ English, French
♥ photography, skiing, mountain hiking, basket-ball, theatre, opera, reading ⛺ yes for 1-2 people ☆ board

ALEXANDRU, Tiberiu b.01/13/55 Engineer
"*I was born in Turda, a town in the Cluj county. I studied computers in Timisoara. I graduated in 1978 and since I have been working for an electronic company.*"
✉ Str.Tatra 12,Ap.22, Cluj-Napoca ✆ (951) 24704
✍ French, Russian, Hungarian ♥ reading, politics
⛺ yes

ARION, Dorin b. 12/20/57 Engineer - software programmer
"*I am married; my wife, Mirela, is 31; she is also an engineer in computer programming. We have a 7 year old daughter, Oana, who also speaks English. We are a very happy family.*"
✉ Str.Gheorgheni 2,Ap.24, Cluj-Napoca, 3400
✍ English, French ♥ computer programming, painting
⛺ yes

BAN, Daniela b. 06/06/63 Doctor
"*I graduated the Faculty of Dentistry in Cluj in 1986. I'm married to an architect since 1987 and we have a*

boy aged 2. I'm working now in a polyclinic here in Cluj."

✉ Str.Muscel 9/1, Cluj-Napoca, 3400 ✆ (951) 45433 ✍ English, German (a little) ♥ my profession, classic music, painting, good movies. my husband likes interior design and graphic arts ⌂ yes ☆ board

BOZAC, Cita b. 01/01/40 Translator
✉ Str.Donat II, Ap.38, Cluj-Napoca, 3400 ✆ (951) 82558 ✍ English, French ⌂ yes

CRISAN, Rares b. 10/07/65 Student

"*My father is a lawyer and my mother is a teacher of French. I have no brothers or sisters. I study medicine. We live in a four room flat.*"

✉ Str.Bucium 11,Ap.7, Cluj-Napoca ✆ (951) 62701 ✍ French, English ♥ reading, music, travelling, sports ⌂ yes

GRAUR, Mircea b.03/27/56 Engineer - mechanic designer

"*I was born in this city where I did all my studies. I learned from my father to paint and draw. I like to paint landscapes in oil, from my trips, and to draw portraits with pencil. I am married and have two boys aged 9 and 6.*"

✉ Str.Agricultorilor 20,Bl.D-IV,Sc.IV,Ap.54, Cluj-Napoca ✆ (951) 60758 ✍ English, French (a little) ♥ trips, artistic photography, painting, drawing, literature; table tennis, volleyball, chess, I practised judo for three years; I began to practise Hatha Yoga ⌂ no

GRECEA, Daniel   b.01/15/61   Surgeon
"I work at the "First Surgical Clinic" in Cluj-Napoca. I have two daughters, Monica and Alina, 4 and 2 years old and my wife is a doctor too."
✉ Str.Caliman 2, Cluj-Napoca, 3400 ✆ (951) 88891
✍ English, French ♥ classic music - I play violin - , rock music (Genesis, Pink Floyd, Rush, Jethro Tull), literature (Dostoievsky, Tolstoy, Orwell, Graham Greene). I play tennis, football; mountain climbing. my dream is to see the Himalayan mountains, to conquer everest ⌂ yes

HANGANU, Horatiu   b.10/11/72   Pupil
"I am still a pupil at the high school for natural sciences."
✉ 109, Donath; Bl.P2,Ap.35, Cluj-Napoca, 3400 ✆ (951) 88809 ✍ French, English ♥ sports (tennis, volleyball, skating), nature, voyages, light music, theatre, cinema

IANCU, Zeno-Sabin   b.11/26/33   Engineer
"My wife is an engineer too. We have two sons : one of them is an architect, the other one is going to become an engineer. We live in a house with yard and a little garden."
✉ Str.Seceratorilor 5, Cluj-Napoca, 3400 ✆ (951) 43286 ✍ French ♥ gardening, beekeeping ⌂ yes

IVAN, Veronica   b.01/23/55   Schoolmaster
"I live alone. I am divorced for 7 years."
✉ Str.Dimbovitei 85,Bl.D17,Sc.2,Ap.89,Jud.Cluj, Cluj-Napoca, 3400 ✍ French ♥ music, tourism, children, sensitive people ⌂ yes

KALLO-PETI-FERKO, Akos   b.06/04/57   Manager
"I was born in Cluj. After graduating from high school and after serving in the army, I started working here, in Cluj. In 1990, I organized a travelling agency called "K-Tours"."
✉ Bd.1 Decembrie 1918 128,Bl.D,Ap.14, Cluj-Napoca, 3400 ✆ (951) 85750 ✍ English, German, Hungarian, Romanian ♥ football, tennis ⌂ yes, through the agency ☆ colour TV; board

CLUJ-NAPOCA

MARINESCU, Dumitru Titi   b.01/30/42   Teacher (Romanian language)

"I was born in a family of physicians in Cluj. I studied here, I teach here, I live here in a three room flat where I feel perfect. I am not married, I am alone, but I have my hobbies and my holidays."

✉ Str.Girbou 17,Ap.47, Cluj-Napoca ✆ (951) 62428
✍ French, Italien, Hungarien ♥ swimming, painting icons on wood and glass, opera ⌂ yes ☆ board

MUDURE, Mihaela   b.11/07/54   Teacher

"My mother was a biology teacher and my father was a surgeon. I also had a brother, engineer, who was killed in the Revolution (December 21 1989). I studied in Cluj, highschool and University. I am married. We have a girl aged 7 and a boy aged 13."

✉ Str.Almasului 3R,Ap.5, Cluj-Napoca, 3400
✆ (951) 70111 ✍ French, English ♥ literature, opera, music, cooking ⌂ yes

MUNTEA, Cornel   b.04/09/52   Engineer, University Teacher

"I was born in a small village where I finished elementary school. I graduated highschool in Cluj-Napoca and then the Polytechnical Institute in Bucharest. I am married and have two young girls."

✉ Str.Venus 25,Bl.31,Sc.1,Ap.19, Cluj-Napoca, 3400 ✍ French ♥ reading, journalism, theater, voyages ⌂ yes

MUSTE, Marian   b.03/14/55   Lecturer with the Polytechnical Institute of Cluj, Hydraulics Dept.

"I graduated in 1980 from the Civil Engineering Faculty of Cluj; since 1982 I joined the staff of the Polytechnical Institute of Cluj as an assistant professor, from this year as a lecturer at the same institute, teaching Hydraulics and Fluid Mechanics."

✉ Str.Pata 33,Bl.B1,Sc.I,Ap.8, Cluj-Napoca, 3400
✆ (951) 40641 ✍ English, German, Hungarian
♥ tourism, sports (tennis, swimming, football), politics, music, entertainment ⌂ yes ☆ breakfast

NODITI, Gilda   Geologist engineer

"*I am 28. I always wanted to meet people from different countries and make friends. Unfortunately this is was not possible until the revolution in December 1989.*"

✉ Str.Pata 11-15, Ap.34, Cluj-Napoca, 3400
✆ (951) 44123 ✍ English, French (a little) ♥ travelling

OLTEAN, Dora   b.11/17/67   Secretary

"*I learnt English and German as a child. I graduated from the German high school four years ago. I am very close to my family and live together with my parents. I have many friends and love making new ones.*"

✉ Str.Padin 23, Ap.31, Cluj-Napoca, 3400 ✆ (951) 62317 ✍ German, English ♥ swimming, reading, walking ⌂ yes

PARAIAN, Calin Florian   b.11/04/68   Student

"*I was the first at the admission exam at the Medicine Faculty in Cluj. I want to become a surgeon. Between 1987 and 1990 I also worked as a guide for the Travel Agency in Cluj.*"

✉ Str.Ec. Teodoroiu 10, Cluj-Napoca, 3400
✆ (951) 31007 ✍ English, French, Italian ♥ travelling, trips in the mountains, dancing, books ✂ stamps ⌂ yes ☆ board

PODOABA, Cristina   b.09/02/66   Student

"*I study medicine. I love studying and I have to work hard. I have no boyfriend at the moment. I am talkative and I would like to meet people.*"

✉ Str.Bolintineanu 16A, Cluj-Napoca ✆ (951) 46735
✍ French ♥ reading, talking about life, sports (swimming, jogging, tennis) ⌂ yes (I live in a big house)

POPESCU, Mircea   b.01/31/25   Opera Singer

"*I am alone in the world. I had a 5 person family, but now I have got nobody.*"

✉ Aleea Borsec 2, Sc.1, Ap.4, Cluj-Napoca, 3400
✆ (951) 41582 ✍ French, English, Italian ♥ opera, jazz, fishing, corresponding with friends ⌂ yes

SZEKELY, Stefan   b.06/11/46
- ✉ Str.Padin 10,Bl.C12,Ap.38, Cluj-Napoca, 3400
- ✆ (951) 64200 ✍ Hungarian ■ yes

TRENEA, Tiberiu Romy   b.05/03/56   Architect
"I was born in Satu Mare, a town in Maramures, in the north of the country. I finished highschool in Satu Mare and then I graduated the Faculty of Constructions in Timisoara, then I continued my studies at the Architecture Institute in Bucharest."
- ✉ Str.Anatole France 29, Cluj-Napoca, 3400
- ✆ (951) 47184 ✍ Hungarian, French, English
- ♥ fishing, photography ■ yes, in Cluj, Satu Mare and Maramures ☆ round trips of these places in Summer

VASIAN, Mircea   b.12/25/28   Scientific rresearcher
"My father was a Catholic priest. I studied agriculture and economy at Cluj and Bucharest. I am a Pg.D. in management. I specialized abroad in the field of preservation by cold."
- ✉ Str.Alex.Vlahuta 17, Cluj-Napoca, 3400 ✆ (951) 83701 ✍ French, Italian, English (a little) ♥ travelling, doing things around the house, tennis ■ 2-4 persons in Buc.,4 rooms in the mountains-1400m ☆ board

COMANESTI

> *"Mother Nature is very pretty here. The Ciobanis forests are always green. Also, Slanic Moldova is a wonderful resort. Come to us with pleasure!"*

SPANU, Natalia   b.02/24/44   Teacher
"We are teachers in the small town of Comanesti."
- ✉ Str.Aleea Parcului,Bl.C7, Ap.7,Jud.Bacau, Comanesti, 5475 ✆ (933) 71004 ✍ French, English
- ♥ painting ■ Yes ☆ breakfast

Constanta

> " ... the oldest town in Romania ... I should exaggerate the beauty of my city: natural, but not necessary ... the aquarium, dolphins, Tomis harbour, the resorts ... a museum of archeology ... a new university ... many museums ... a harbor on the Black Sea coast ..."

BDULA, Turgay   b.09/17/68   Student

"I was born in Braila in a family of Turkish people. I am Turkish by nationality and Romanian by citizenship. I am a student at the Polytechnical Institute in Bucharest."

✉ Bd.1 Decembrie 1918 Nr.3, Bl.F17, Ap.43, Constanta, 8700 ✆ (916) 73278 ✍ English, French ♥ football, swimming, chess, car driving ■ yes

ICIOLLA, Helmuth   b.08/15/43   Engineer

"I was born in Constanta, studied in Timisoara and work now as the chief of the department of building dwellings in Constanta. My wife teaches French in a school. We have no children. We have a cat and I would like to have a dog too."

✉ Str.Dacia 48, Constanta, 8700 ✆ (916) 15748 ✍ German, French, English ♥ sports (swimming, riding the bicycle), literature, history, music ■ yes (I own a house with 5 rooms and a garden) ☆ breakfast

UMBAC, Robert   b.05/04/74   Pupil

"I want to correspond with boys from other countries."

✉ Str.Pictor Grigorescu 86, Constanta, 8700 ✆ (916) 46469 ✍ English ♥ football ■ yes

URCEA, Mihaela   b.06/07/75   Pupil

"I am a 15 year old girl whose life until now hasn't been too much different from the boring, uneventful life of any other Romanian teenager. In spite of this I still have

a strong wish to find out more about our world and about it's people."

✉ Str.Dobrogei 35, Constanta, 8700 ℂ (916) 12622 ✍ English ♥ tennis, dance, gardening, opera, philately 🏠 housing

BUSCA, Valeriu   b.05/28/58   Operator helio

"I graduated from the marine military high school, and started studying at the Marine Institute, but suffered an accident. The dream of knowing the whole world will now become possible."

✉ Bd. Aurel Vlaicu 94,Bl.A.V.10,Sc.A,Ap.44, Constanta, 8700 ✍ French ♥ trips, swimming, playing chess, riding the bicycle, photography, writing poems 🏠 yes, but starting 1992

CHIRIAC, Irimia   b.11/18/41   English teacher

"Conditions of life obliged me to learn many professions like: sailor, teacher, guide, plumber. At the moment I work as a teacher in a high school. My wife, Lida, works as a doctor assistant in a hospital. My son Adrian is 22 years old and is a student."

✉ Str.Dobrila Eugeniu 5,Bl.N,Sc.5,Ap.31,Tomis Nord, Constanta, 8700 ℂ (916) 42878 ✍ English, German 🏠 yes

CODREANU, Mariana   b.03/27/71   Student

"Last Sunday I could see my name on the list of the University in our town. So, I'm a student, the fourth admitted. My parents are very proud of me. My father is an ecomomist, he works with an enterprise that sells books and is interested in business."

✉ Al.Gradinilor 1,Bl.O,Ap.30, Constanta, 8700 ℂ (916) 40582 ✍ English, German, French ♥ playing tennis, skiing, reading, watching movies, dancing, getting brown, knitting, travelling, climbing, playing chess, driving, teaching maths or foreign languages, laughing, discussing and having fun 🏠 yes ☆ trips by car

DATCU, Eduard Chemist
"*I am 22. I am a qualified guide. I want to meet young people especially from France, where I would like to travel, but also from Italy, England, West Germany.*"
✉ Bd.1 Mai Nr.1, Bl.H9,Sc.B,Ap.48, Constanta, 8700 ✍ French, English, Italian ♥ sports, aerobic music, trips ♖ yes

DOBRA, Valentin Driver
"*I am 19 years old. My dream is to become a sailor. I want VERY MUCH to correspond with somebody in English. Thank you!*"
✉ Str.Arcului 11,Bl.F6,Sc.B,Ap.22, Constanta, 8700 ✍ English ♥ music, sports, reading, writing poems

DULIU, Tinca b. 01/08/38 Teacher
✉ Alea Stejarului 7,Bl.20,Sc.B,Ap.3, Constanta, 8700 ✆ (916) 61979 ✍ Greek, Russian ♥ travelling, Greek music and dance ♖ yes

ENACHIOAIE, Adrian b.07/08/52 Biologist
✉ Sos.Filimon Sirbu 54,Bl.A4,Ap.10, Constanta, 8700 ✆ (916) 24978 ✍ English ♥ tennis, gardening, sports, theatre, films, languages, sailing

ENESCU, Elena b.07/10/30 Pensioner
"*My husband died in 1989. I have a daughter living in Ploiesti and two grandchildren aged 13 and 7. Because my pension is very small, I make knitwear.*"
✉ Bd.Tomis 299,Bl.3B,Sc.A,Ap.6, Constanta, 8700 ✍ French ♥ children, dogs ♖ yes

FILIMON, Luiza-Maria b.05/07/54 Shorthand writer
"*I graduated from high school and from a school for secretaries, shorthand typing and foreign trade. My husband is a radio operator on board of a vessel. We have a one year old daughter. I have a dog called Black, a car and a small flat.*"
✉ Bd.1 Decembrie 1918 Nr.2,Bl.L69,Sc.D,Ap.74, Constanta, 8700 ✆ (916) 23742 ✍ English, French ♥ opera, visiting exhibitions, reading poetry, cactus ♖ yes ☆ breakfast

CONSTANTA

GHEGELIU, Alexandru   b.10/26/36   Engineer
"Married; a daughter of 2; invalid retired from a left hemiparesis; operating experience in naval communication and navigation radio appliances."
✉ Str.Faget 92, Constanta, 8700 ✆ (916) 62852
✍ English, French, Russian ♥ chess, economics, politics ⌂ yes

GHITA, Anka   Teacher
"For the moment, my husband and I are teachers in a small town, Calarasi, half way between Constanta and Bucuresti. We consider we are a young family (34 and 38). We have a house with a flower garden in Tuzla, on the Black Sea coast."
✉ Str. Stefan cel Mare 67,Sc.A,Ap.5, Constanta
✆ (916) 64032 ✍ English ♥ playing games (cards, Monopoly, Scrabble), travelling, sports, reading
⌂ yes ☆ while student, I worked as a guide

IONESCU, Leila   b.09/15/59   Medical assistant
"I can dance, sing, make facial massage and cosmetic masks. I have a three room flat."
✉ Tomis Nord,Bl.D3,Sc.A,Ap.35, Constanta, 8700
✆ (916) 43436 ✍ English, French, Italian ♥ music, dancing ⌂ yes

IONESCU, Rodica   b.02/06/28   Retired
"I am an assistant of obstetrics and gynecology, now retired. My husband was a lawyer. He died 7 years ago. I have a daughter, doctor, who lives with me. My flat is near the Sea."
✉ Str.Remus Opreanu 12,Ap.17, Constanta, 8700
✆ (916) 15659 ✍ French, English, German (a little)
♥ music, shows, walks on the coast ⌂ yes ☆ breakfast

NENCIU, Gheorghe   b.07/01/50   Mechanician
"I graduated from high school and from a three years mechanical school. I am married and have two children. I live 50m away from the Black Sea."
✉ Str.Pescarilor 1,Bl.PA8,Sc.B,Ap.50, Constanta
✍ German (a little), French (a little), English (a little)
♥ chess, football, music, dancing, entertainment
⌂ yes ☆ board

NICOLESCU, Daniel b.03/29/74 Pupil
"I have no brother or sister. I study in highschool. I play football at FC Constanta. Maybe I'll become a football player!"
✉ Aleea Daliei 2, Ap.3, Constanta, 8700 ✆ (916) 24868 ✍ English, French ♥ travelling, mountain climbing, music, walking in the park, films, games ♨ yes ☆ board

PETCULESCU, Andi 'b.10/20/68 Student at Physics University Bucharest
"A couple of years ago one of my neighbours lent me Johnny Cash's "21 Foot-Tappin' Greats" and that started it all; ever since I've been a most resolute admirer of country & western music and brought in a very strong desire to know the American culture."
✉ Bd.Alex.Lapusneanu 116,Bl.X2,Ap.10, Constanta, 8700 ✆ (916) 41898 ✍ English, French ♥ physics, American English, American culture & way of life, country music, tennis, volleyball ♨ yes

PETRE, Ovidiu - Octavian b.07/11/47 Engineer in Oenology
"I studied in Constanta and Galati. I worked 16 years in the Wine Research Company Murfatlar and for the last 4 years I've been working in a large wine production enterprise in Constanta. Married since 1986, no kids; I like to travel."
✉ Str.Mihai Viteazu 57, Constanta, 8700 ✆ (916) 63398 ✍ French, English, Italian ♥ sports, dance, opera, walks in picturesque places ♨ yes ☆ board

PETROVICI, Ioan b.01/23/40 Chemical engineer
"I graduated from faculty in 1976 in Iasi, the town where I was born. In 1970 I married a nurse. Since 1980 we have been living in Constanta, close to the famous resort Mamaia. We have an 11-year-old son."
✉ Str.Hortensiei 1B,Bl.ME1B,Sc.A,Ap.6, Constanta, 8700 ✆ (916) 49622 ✍ Italian, Russian ♥ tennis, trips, jazz music ♨ yes ☆ breakfast

POSTARU, Vasile b.01/01/44 Engineer
"Born in Ostrov, county Constanta. Elementary school in Casimcea, county Constanta. High school 1957-

1966 in Cimpulung. Naval Academy in Baku, U.S.S.R."

✉ Str.Eugen Dobrila 20,Bl.Y,Sc.C,Ap.52
Post address: P.O.Box 1018 - 8700 Constanta, Constanta, 8700 ✆ (916) 43936 ✍ English, German, French ♥ deep diving, trips, learning foreign languages, dance, tennis, reading ■ yes

PREDUSEL, Iulius   b.04/29/30   Painter

"My wife is 54. We are both retired. I worked in tourism and I am also a painter. We have a 3 room flat in a nice aerated district. We have a son aged 35, married. He lives separately."

✉ Bd.Alex.Lapusneanu 116,Bl.X2,Ap.13, Constanta, 8700 ✆ (916) 48051 ✍ French ♥ philately ✂ stamps ■ yes

TAMPU, Violeta and Gelu (husband)
   Cosmetician/Engineer

"I was born in Constanta and am 23 years old. My husband was born in Bacau and is 31. Our flat is empty in summer. You can have a wonderful time on the Black Sea coast"

✉ Str.Filimon Sirbu 92,Bl.SR7,Sc.B,Ap.69, Constanta, 8700 ✍ German, English, French ♥ trips, cinema, music, literature ■ yes ☆ board

TANASESCU, Mihaela   b.12/30/67   Student (Medicine)

"I was born in Ploiesti, near Bucuresti. My father was an officer, he retired in 1988. My mother is a housewife. I have a brother seven years older than me. He is a musician. I studied in Constanta, Tirgu-Mures and Bucharest. I have two more years study"

✉ Str.Costache Burca 16,Bl.M12,Ap.20, Constanta, 8700 ✆ (916) 65993 ✍ English, French ♥ arts, swimming, dancing, everything connected to beauty and love ■ Yes ☆ board. Mother cooks Greek, Armenian, etc. food.

TOFAN, Lucia   b. 01/04/59   Teacher

"I was born in Constanta; mother - teacher, father - decorator, a brother - student in Bucharest. I graduated from the Faculty of Biology at the University in

Bucharest. I am married to Eduard - a surgeon. We have a three years old son - Lucian."

✉ Bd.1 Mai Nr.68,Bl.UM1,Sc.C,Ap.35, Constanta, 8700 ✆ (916) 40101 ✍ English, French ♥ tourism ⌂ yes ☆ breakfast

VOINESCU, Stefan   b.03/21/42   Engineer

"I graduated from the Polytechnical Institute in 1964. I have been working as a manager ever since. I have tho daughters, aged 22 and 14."

✉ Str.M.Kogalniceanu 27,Ap.15, Constanta, 8700 ✆ (916) 15216 ✍ French, English ♥ tennis, art, tourism ⌂ yes

ZEGA, Daniela   b. 10/17/60   Air traffic controller

"I am married and have a child. My husband is 32 and also an air traffic controller. I worked as a tourist guide too. We own a three room flat in Constanta."

✉ Str.B.P.Hasdeu 106,Bl.H6,Sc.B,Ap.34, Constanta, 8700 ✆ (916) 57264 ✍ English, French ♥ movies, windsurf, contemporary literature (English, American, French) ⌂ yes ☆ breakfast

CORABIA

> " ... in the center of Oltenia ... many museums, and neighborhoods ... played an important part in Romania's history ... "

GOIA, Marcela - Mariana   b.01/03/54   Teacher

"I am married and have 3 children aged between 1 and 12. My husband is a physician gynecologist at the hospital in Corabia. I am a teacher for the highschool in the same town."

✉ Str.General Tell 59,Jud.Olt, Corabia, 0875 ✆ (945) 60757 or 61180 ✍ French ♥ my job, children, voyages, gardening (we have a vegetable garden), the flowers, the animals, music, stamp collecting ✂ stamps ⌂ yes, in Corabia, Brasov or Ploiesti. ☆ board

COVASNA

JACAB, Istvan   b. 08/31/61   Electromechanic
✉ Str.Brazilor 5/15, Covasna ✆ (923) 40787
✍ Hungarian, German ♓ yes

CRAIOVA

ASSOCIATION "ALLIANCE FRANCOPHONE",
"Association aiming at: enlarging friendship with Francophone persons or associations, studies and cooperation in various fields, the stimulation of Francophone spirit, consolidation of friendship between peoples, realization of an United Europe."
✉ Str.Nicolae Titulescu,Bl.5,Sc.1,Ap.3,Jud.Dolj, Craiova, 1100 ✆ (941) 74806 (work: 7800 Ext.2036) ✍ French, English,, Italian, Bulgarian,, German, Russian, ♓ Call Stelian Giubelan, president, at given nr.

ALECU, Cosmin   b.11/29/67   Student in medicine
"I was born in Carbunesti,Gorj and spent my childhood in Ticleni. Gorj is a marvelous place, the "Mioritic Space" which marked my way of thinking. School and faculty in Craiova."
✉ Str.Paltinis,Bl.K6,Ap.7, Craiova, 1100 ✍ Spanish, French, English (a little) ♥ all good music (classic - Bach, Beethoven, Wagner, Chopin, Rachmaninov, Brahms, Mendelsohn, Mozart, Verdi);, modern (Depeche Mode, Falco, Pet Shop Boys, Jean Michel Jarre); traditional Romanian, Iberic, Latin-American music;, dancing, theatre, American and Russian literature, Romanian poetry (Eminescu) ♓ yes

ANGHEL, Constantin Gabriel   b.05/17/68   Student
"I am a student at the University of Craiova, very busy and fond of reading. I study economics and I love meeting people."
✉ Bd. 1 Mai,Bl.22,Sc.2,Ap.2, Craiova, 1100
✆ (941) 20554 ✍ French ♥ trips, music, sports
♓ yes ☆ breakfast

CAMENITA, Alexandru   b.04/01/42   Physician (neurologic surgeon)

"I am married and have two sons. My wife is a physician too. We have never been members of the communist party. I don't smoke. I don't drink. I would like to establish connections with French friends (maybe neurosurgeons)."

✉ Str.Alexandru Macedonski 30, Craiova, 1100 ✆ (941) 32871 ✍ French, Russian, English ♥ sports (tennis) ⌂ yes wherever in Romania ☆ board

CAMENITA, Radu   b.01/04/44   Mechanic engineer

"I work as chief of technical staff in an enterprise for irrigation. My wife Diana, 39, is an engineer in electronics and works in a research institute. We have two children: a girl aged 10 and a boy aged 6. We share a 10 rooms house with my brother."

✉ Calea Bucuresti,Bl.8,Ap.11,Jud.Dolj/ or: Str.Alexandru Macedonski 30,Jud.Dolj, Craiova, 1100 ✆ (941) 46680 or 44632 ✍ French, English ♥ tennis, history, trips, reading ⌂ yes ☆ board

CEOROIANU, Mariana   b.07/24/57   Teacher

✉ Calea Bucuresti,Bl.A6,Sc.2,Ap.6, Craiova, 1100 ✆ (941) 44083 ✍ French, English ♥ knitting, symphonic music ⌂ yes

CIUCULESCU, Stefan   b.08/10/36   Dentist

"I graduated from faculty in 1962. Since 1966 I have been working in Craiova. I am member of the International Association of Stomatology and I took part in several congresses."

✉ Calea Bucuresti,Bl.B6,Sc.2,Ap.4,Jud.Dolj, Craiova, 1100 ✆ (941) 46498 ✍ French, Russian, Italian ♥ philately, chess, football, theatre, history ⌂ yes

CLONDA, Traian Petru   b.06/04/37   Engineer

"I was born in Oradea. I graduated in 1962 from the Agronomic Institute in Craiova and later specialized in Italy. I wrote books and articles."

✉ Str.N.Titulescu,Bl.E4,Ap.7,Jud.Dolj, Craiova, 1100 ✆ (941) 15608 ✍ French, Italian, Hungarian ♥ basketball, tourism ⌂ yes

CRAIOVA

DUTA, Doraliu Eugen   b.05/23/72   Student

"Height : 1.86m. Weight : 82kg. I have brown hair and chestnut eyes. My mother is professor at the Horticulture Faculty in Craiova. My father died in a car crash when I was 3 months old. He was a physician. My actual father is a lawyer."

✉ Piata Unirii,Bl.N,Ap.64, Craiova, 1100 ✆ (941) 14257 ✍ English ♥ music, computers, mathematics, swimming, basketball, foreign languages ✂ coins, stamps ⌂ yes, in Olanesti too

GAVRILA, Ion   b. 05/06/30   Engineer (retired)

"I was born in a village near Craiova. I did my secondary studies and Faculty in Craiova. I am married, my wife is an engineer and teacher, I have a daughter, also an engineer. She is married and has a little daughter. She lives in a neighbouring block."

✉ Cartier Rovine,Bl.J28,scara 1,Ap.8,Jud.Dolj, Craiova, 1100 ✆ (941) 89146 ✍ French ♥ gardening (vegetables and flowers) ⌂ yes ☆ breakfast

ILIESCU, Dumitru   b.05/29/27   Teacher of mathematiques

"I have been teaching mathematics for more than 30 years in a big high school in Craiova. I am retired now."

✉ Cal.Bucuresti,Bl.E1,Sc.1,Ap.19, Craiova ✆ (941) 34552 ✍ French ♥ trips (especially in the mountains), desire to know the historical past and the landscapes of other countries ⌂ yes

IONESCU, Emilian Angel   b.06/02/69   Car mechanic

"My childhood was sad: lack of joy, toys, sun, even of food. It was a real dog life. Now I work at a big auto-service in Craiova and I become better and better every day."

✉ Str.Brazda lui Novac,Bl.16,Sc.4,Ap.1, Craiova ✆ (941) 58380 ✍ English, French ♥ dancing ⌂ yes

LUGOVOIU, Romeo-Mircea   b.03/26/51   Computer engineer

"Height : 1.72m. I have brown hair and blue eyes. I am married to Eugenia, who is a teacher of history. We have *a little daughter , five years old, called Andrada-Fabiola."*

✉ Cartier Valea Rosie,Bl.C6,Sc.2,Ap.4, Craiova, 1100 ✆ (941) 24402 ✍ English, French ♥ travelling, mountain tourism, photography, human relations ⌂ yes ☆ bed and breakfast

MIRESCU, Simona-Mirela   b.01/21/58   English teacher

"I became English teacher in 1981, I teach in my town, Craiova. I'm married (my husband is an economist) and I have one child (one year old). I have a large house (4 rooms) and a studio flat nearby."

✉ Str.Petre Ispirescu,Bl.9,Sc.2,Ap.1, Craiova, 1100 ✆ (941) 45192 ✍ English, French, Italian ♥ post cards (old and new), travelling, reading (literature and politics), flowers, music (clasical and modern), swimming ✂ postcards ⌂ yes ☆ board; trips through the country.

NICULESCU, Titiana   b.01/09/67   Lawyer

"I live with my parents and sister. I studied law in Bucharest. My childhood and youth were happy enough, youth always finds its light. And this light is love, friendship, art, game, nature..."

✉ Piata Garii,Bl.K3,Ap.17, Craiova ✆ (941) 12692 ✍ French, English, German (a little) ♥ cinema ⌂ yes ☆ board

PARIS, Irina   b. 05/07/62   Engineer

"I am not married."

✉ Str.Cl.Bucuresti,Bl.A8,Sc.1,Ap.7, Craiova, 1100 ✆ (941) 42515 ✍ French, English ♥ tourism ⌂ yes

POPESCU, Jean-Lucian   b.04/06/54   Engineer

"I finished my studies in Craiova. Between 1982-1983 I took part with a group at shows organized all over the country (over 600 performances). Since 1990, I started to write for a newspaper in Craiova."

✉ Str.George Enescu,Bl.B22,Ap.10, Craiova, 1100 ✍ French, English ♥ philately (I can offer Romanian stamps since 1965);, literature, theatre ✂ stamps ⌂ yes

RACEANU, Theodor　　b.03/03/48　Automation engineer
"I was born in the country side. Later I studied in Bucharest. Since 1970 I work in a chemical factory. I am married and I have two sons (11 and 10 years old). My wife Mariana is also an automation engineer and works in designing."
✉ Bd.23 August,Bl.A2,Ap.59, Craiova, 1100
☏ (941) 34257　✍ English, French　♥ travels, philately, numismatics　H yes　☆ lunch

STANCU-MURTAZA, Andorina　　b.05/25/53　Chemist
✉ Str.Dezrobirii,Bl.A28,Ap.4,Jud.Dolj, Craiova, 1100　☏ (941) 44083　✍ French　♥ opera, philately
H yes

URSACHE, Elena　　b.12/21/32　Retreated
✉ Str.Brazda lui Novac,Bl.I6,Sc.5,Ap.14,Jud.Dolj, Craiova, 1100　✍ French　♥ tourism, music
H yes

CRISTURU-SECUIESC

> *"... monuments, parks, a resort with salted water 2km away, where you can listen to birds singing ..."*

CONSTANTINESCU, Marie　　b.12/12/64　Tourism agent
"I am married. My husband, Cornel, is an engineer."
✉ Str.Gheorghe Doja 9,Jud.Harghita, Cristuru-Secuiesc, 4180　☏ 51543　✍ French　♥ sports, tourism, music　H yes

CURTEA DE ARGES

> *" ... a small mountain town, with good people and good mountain air. It has a rich historic past and a 15th century monastery. ... Dracula's castle is in the neighborhood! "*

CURTEA DE ARGES

BALOC, Adrian b.03/27/60 Electronic engineer
"Thirty years old, married, two children and I have no car."
✉ Str. 23 August,Bl.F11,Sc.A,Ap.3, Curtea de Arges, 0450 ℂ (977) 14761 ✍ French, English ♥ tennis, fishing, nice girls ⌂ yes ☆ board

PRUNA, Viorel b.03/16/50 Internist physician
"I am married and have a 16 year old son. My wife is an engineer and also 40 (we were schoolmates from the 4th form). I work at the Curtea de Arges Hospital as chief of department. Until now, I could travel only in Bulgaria, Hungary and G.D.R.."
✉ Bd. R.S.R. Bl.F12A,Sc.A,Ap.8,Jud.Arges, Curtea de Arges, 0450 ℂ (977) 14622 ✍ French ♥ travelling, nature, monuments with their history, people with their customs ⌂ yes ☆ board, entertainment, travelling all over Romania

RADU, Petre b. 11/26/54 Chief of store; Football referee.
"My father died when I was 5 and my mother died when I was 16. When I was a schoolboy I had to help mother at work to make a living. I tried to play football and study in Bucharest but could not do both. Now I have a very good job ; married, two children."
✉ Str.Victoriei,Bl.P3,Sc.C,Ap.33,Jud.Arges, Curtea de Arges ✍ English (a little) ♥ football, music, rummy ⌂ yes ☆ board

SOCOLOVSCHI, Anca Cornelia b.08/26/58
Engineer
"I graduated from the Electrotechnical Faculty in Craiova in 1982. Since then, I work at I.P.E.E. Electroarges in town. I am married and have no children. My husband is an engineer too."
✉ Str.23 August,Bl.F11,Sc.A,Ap.4, Curtea de Arges ℂ (977) 14589 ✍ English, French ♥ climbing, travelling, good music and movies, gardening ✂ stamps ⌂ yes ☆ board

STATESCU, Vlad b.03/09/73 Pupil
"My mother is an English teacher and my father is a lawyer. I'd like to be an engineer in energetics,

mechanics or electronics, I have not decided yet. I am looking forward to my college life in a new, democratic society."

✉ Str.Negru Voda 137, Curtea de Arges ✆ (977) 13924 ✍ English ♥ sports (football), music, dancing, shows, physics, english, travelling, politics
⌂ yes

DARMANESTI

BADEA, Virgilius b.09/07/22 Engineer (retreated)
"Since my wife died, I am alone. I want a sincere, religious friendship. I started building together with my wife and using our own money and work a hermitage for nuns. I would appreciate help in finishing it."
✉ Comuna Darmanesti,Jud.Arges, Darmanesti, 0403
✍ French (a little) ♥ forestry, religion

DEVA

" ... in the west ... many riches like the gold mines at Brad, iron mines at Teliuc, coal mines, forests, and wonderful people ... "

BENTA, Viorel-Dan b.07/26/64 Computer Engineer
"I am married. My wife, Monica, is a computer engineer too. We have a two year old son. For the moment we live together with my parents in Deva, but we will move to Timisoara where we own a flat on Str. 1 Decembrie, Bl.90A,Ap.12, tel 961/62686 pc 1900."
✉ Str.Minerului,Bl.P2/5, Deva, 2700 ✆ (956) 21656 ✍ French, English, German ♥ skiing, trips (I prefer the mountains), ecology (I am a member of the ecologist movement) ⌂ yes ☆ breakfast

COCA, Ovidiu b. 02/14/56 Doctor
"I am married. My wife is a doctor too."
✉ Str.Simion Barnutiu 2,Jud.Hunedoara, Deva, 2700 ✆ (956) 11361 ✍ French ♥ culture
⌂ yes ☆ board

CRISOVAN, Peter - Valerio   b.03/16/58
   Commercial worker

"I am married and have a boy aged 1. Nothing interesting about me."

✉ Bd.Dacia,Bl.33,Sc.A,Ap.40, Deva, 2700 ✆ (957) 70306 ✍ English, French, Hungarian (a little) ♥ movies, gardening, opera, stamp collecting, records, magazines ✄ stamps ⌂ yes ☆ breakfast

LAZAR, Dorica   b.03/08/53   Economist

"I was born in Brad, a town 40 km away from Deva. I studied in Brad and Timisoara. I am not married."

✉ Str.M.Eminescu,Bl.K,Sc.B,Ap.20, Deva, 2700 ✆ (956) 22876 ✍ French ♥ literature ⌂ yes ☆ breakfast

DOBRESTI

STANCU, Iulia   b. 07/12/68   Teacher

"I was born in the village of Dobresti. I graduated the "Normal School" (preparing schoolteachers) in 1987 in Cimpulung. I teach in my village. I am married and I have a little boy. I live with my parents. They were also teachers, now they retired."

✉ Sat Dobresti,Jud.Arges, Dobresti, 0352 ✆ 35 A ✍ English, French ♥ music, dancing, embroidery ⌂ yes

DOROHOI

STOICA, Corneliu-Silviu   b.05/21/54
   Electrotechnical Engineer

"My wife (35) is a dentist. We have a daughter aged 9 and a son aged 5."

✉ Str.A.I.Cuza 8,Ap.9,Jud.Botosani, Dorohoi, 6850 ✆ (986) 15949 ✍ French, German, English (not well) ♥ tennis, philately ✄ stamps ⌂ yes, 4-5 persons ☆ board

DR.PETRU GROZA

> *" Our town is small, placed in a valley surrounded by mountains. The mountains are easy to climb, and there are many caves. Winter sports can be practiced until April. "*

FLORUTA, Adrian b.03/19/54 Engineer

"I was born in Oradea. I studied in Timisoara at the Polytechnical Institute. I graduated in 1979. I am married. My wife is a teacher and we have two children : a girl 6 years old and a boy 3 years old."

✉ Str.Garii 1 c/1, Dr.Petru Groza, 3638 ℭ (992) 31315 ✍ English, Hungarian, French ♥ bridge, walking in the mountains in summer and autumn, skiing ; car driving ♓ yes ☆ board

DROBETA TURNU SEVERIN

MIHUT, Margareta Maria b.09/08/46 Teacher of chemistry

"I am alone, I have never been married, I have a big house, I have been living in this town for 38 years. I teach chemistry and in my free time I work as a guide."

✉ Piata Unirii 8, Jud.Mehedinti, Drobeta Turnu Severin ℭ (978) 12218 ✍ German, French ♥ dance, literature, travelling ♓ yes ☆ breakfast

VISAN, Dragos Gabriel b.06/08/74 Pupil

"My parents are economists. We live in Dudas Cerneti, a village close to Drobeta Turnu Severin. I want to study medicine. I don't hear well and I would be very grateful to the person who could help me get a hearing device."

✉ Dudas Cerneti 53, Jud.Mehedinti, Drobeta Turnu Severin, 1500 ℭ (978) 21947 ✍ French ♥ music, walking ♓ no

FAGARAS

> " ... a medieval fortress in the center of town ..."

DINCA, Arnold b.03/14/55 Master chemist
"I am married to Cornelia and we have four children aged between 4 and 12. We both work in the chemical industry."
- ✉ Str.Cimpului,Bl.1/C/14, Fagaras, 2300 ✍ French
- ♥ paintings reproduced on stamps ♂ yes ☆ breakfast

METEA, Toma Agronomist engineer
"I am 31 years old. My wife, Carmen, is an economist. We have a seven years old daughter - Ruxandra. We are ordinary people. We fight for friendship and understanding among people."
- ✉ Str. 6 Martie,Bl.8,Ap.19, Fagaras, 2300 ✍ French
- ♥ trips, sports, music ♂ yes

POPESCU, Claudiu b.12/27/60 Mechanic engineer
"I am married; my wife is a mechanic engineer too. We have a three year old son."
- ✉ Str.13 Decembrie nr.58,Jud.Brasov, Fagaras, 2300 ✆ (920) 13433 ✍ English ♥ skiing, painting, travelling ♂ yes

RATA, Daniela b. 02/14/53 Chemist
"I am married to Olimpiu (41), an economist and a good husband. We work in the same chemical plant in Fagaras. We have no children."
- ✉ Str.Titu Pertia 29,Jud.Brasov, Fagaras, 2300 ✆ (920) 11752 ✍ French, German ♥ reading, trips, music, gardening ♂ yes ☆ board

FOCSANI

> " ... many museums, and taste the wines for which this region is famous ..."

ACASANDREI, Stefan-Eugen b.12/24/57 Clrrk
- ✉ Str.Diviziei 3,Ap.1,Jud.Vrancea, Focsani, 5300
- ✍ French ♥ book lover (bibliophile) ♂ yes

FOCSANI

CASU, Eugen - Andrei   b.11/17/51   Chemical engineer
"I am not married. I have no brothers. My parents were teachers. Now, my mother is retired and my father is dead."
✉ Bd.Unirii 53,Bl.B,Sc.1,Ap.9,Jud.Vrancea, Focsani, 5300 ✆ (939) 22076 ✍ French, Russian ♥ ralleys, painting, tourism in the mountains, vine-growing, fruit-tree growing ⌂ yes, in Bucharest too ☆ board, trips by car,any other service asked before

GEORGESCU, Petre   b.01/26/21   Physician
"I was imprisoned for 5 years for political reasons during the dictatorship. I love people and society. I am married. I have a son who is a physician too and who is married to a physician."
✉ Strada mare a unirii 2,Jud.Vrancea, Focsani
✆ (939) 22226 ✍ French ♥ classical music ⌂ yes

GRAVENFELS, Robert   b.04/15/72   Student at the Faculty of Electronics and Telecommunications
"I was born in Focsani. I graduated highschool here in July 1990 then I was admitted to Faculty."
✉ Str.M.Kogalniceanu 2,Ap.25,Jud.Vrancea, Focsani
✆ (939) 16210 ✍ French, English, Italian (a little)
♥ photography, electronics, voyages ⌂ yes ☆ two rooms and garrage in the centre of town.

PUSCA, Ion   b.   12/18/41   Director of the Wine Enterprise of Focsani; Ph.D.in oenology; Official expert for O.I.V.
"Ion Pusca comes from an old family of vine cultivators. He studied in Panciu, Onesti and Iasi, where he graduated from the Faculty of horticulture. Between 1970-1975 he studied at the Faculty of Trading in Bucharest."
✉ Str.Unirea Principatelor 7,Ap.4, Focsani, 5300
✆ (939) 23654 (work: 21510 or 21700) ✍ French, Italian, Spanish ♥ vineyards, history, tourism
⌂ yes ☆ board

ULEA, Camelia   b. 10/13/57   Chemical engineer
"In 1981 I graduated from college and married Radu, whom I divorced a year later. In 1989, I met Radu again, and we are together since. I work with the Health

Department and he is an engineer specialized in computers."

✉ Str.Cotesti 12,Ap.6,Jud.Vrancea, Focsani ✆ (939) 28389 ✍ French ♥ games, voyages ⌂ yes ☆ board

GALATI

> " ... on the Danube ... a beautiful harbor ... from here one can reach the Danube delta, a remarkable natural attraction ... yead your footsteps to the heart of the mountains, and you will discover the fantastic ... "

ARITON, Viorel   b.07/01/53   Electronic engineer

"From childhood I lived in a cosmopolitan society: Greeks, Jews, Poles; I had friends among them and I was acquainted with different kinds of living. In 1977 I settled in Galati, where I work with computers. My wife, Doinita, is an economist & programmer."

✉ Str.G.Cosbuc - Tiglina 2 - Bl.CS5,Ap.32, Galati, 6200 ✆ (934) 38716 ✍ English, German, Russian ♥ reading books, knowing about man (medicine, psychology, human society, history), oriental philosophy and civilization, tennis ⌂ yes

BANEA, Rodica   b.06/24/44   Teacher

"I am married; my husband is an engineer. I have two children, a daughter aged 22, studying science and literature, and a son aged 15. I teach Romanian literature to pupils between 12 and 16 years old. I am sociable. I like to chat and housekeeping."

✉ Micro 17,Bl.C1,Ap.4, Galati, 6200 ✆ (934) 42771 ✍ French, Russian ♥ gardening, flowers, Gobelins, reading, classic music ⌂ yes

BARBU, Roza-Manuela   b.09/18/72   Pupil

"I have the beautiful age of 18. I am a dreamer and melancholic nature. I am 1.68 m tall, brown long hair *and very black eyes. I shouldn't say I am agreeable, but pleasant."*

✉ Tiglina III,Bl.L,Sc.1,Ap.10,Str.Lebedei 3, Galati, 6200 ✆ (934) 53098 ✍ French ♥ dance, fashion, music, poetry, theater ∎ yes ☆ bed and breakfast

CIUCHI, Roxana   b.02/13/74   Student

"My mother taught me to love all the beautiful things in the world. I want to study foreign languages at the university. I resemble Shirley Temple, the American star. I have green eyes and I like nice clothes. I trust the future."

✉ Str.Melodiei 18,Bl.B4,Ap.36, Galati, 6200 ✆ (934) 32795 ✍ English, French, German (a little) ♥ foreign languages, piano playing, psychology, dancing, sports, reading and writing poetry ∎ yes

COSTACHE, Doru   b.07/19/53   Teacher of physics

"I graduated from faculty in 1977 and since I teach physics in a secondary school in Galati. In 1979 I married Ecaterina, who is a dentist. She speaks French. We have two children : Roxana (9) and Alexandru (1)."

✉ Tiglina I Bl.PS 13 B,Ap.81, Galati, 6200 ✆ (934) 35894 ✍ English ♥ travelling by foot in the mountains, reading books, listening to music (classical) ∎ yes

COSTIN, Gabriela - Ana   b.04/30/70   Student

"My father is an economist, my mother is a clerk and my sister is a student. There haven't been very important events in my life until now, except for the revolution in December 89. But I am young and I hope to have an interesting life."

✉ Str.Constructorilor 9,Bl.B1,Ap.16,Tiglina II, Galati, 6200 ✆ (934) 50954 ✍ French, English ♥ history of the Second World War, foreign languages, music, fashion, travelling, sports ∎ yes

DAMIAN, Valeriu   b.02/16/51   Engineer

"I studied in Galati and worked for 5 years at the shipyard here. For the last 10 years I have been

teaching at the University in Galati. I am married and I have two children."
✉ Str.Reforma Agrara,Bl.C6C,Ap.6, Galati, 6200
✆ (934) 50019 ✍ French ♥ tourism, sports, humour
🏠 yes ☆ anything necessary for a pleasant stay

DIMA, Mircea   b. 12/15/69   Student
"I study siviculture. I live with my parents in a house with 5 rooms near the centre of the town. My mother is a technician and my father is a commercial agent."
✉ Str.Democratiei 49, Galati, 6200 ✆ (934) 16588
✍ French, English ♥ fishing, sports, music, voyages, religion, gardening, history 🏠 yes ☆ breakfast

DOBRE, Maria   b. 04/28/43   Technician (dentist)
"I have a 22-year-old daughter and two brothers, both priests. We are of orthodox religion."
✉ Str.Brailei 19,Bl.R3,Ap.31, Galati, 6200 ✆ (934) 31776 ✍ English ♥ classical music, theatre, arts, travelling 🏠 yes ☆ board

DUMBRAVA, Viorica   b.08/08/28   Bookkeeper (retired)
"I am a widow for 20 years. I have two children: a daughter, student in Timisoara and a son who works in railway transport. I studied secondary school in French. I like to travel."
✉ Micro 38,Bl.Y7,Ap.45, Galati, 6200 ✆ (934) 25251 ✍ French ♥ trips, opera 🏠 yes ☆ breakfast

GASPAR, Rodica - Ana   b.09/03/31   Teacher of physics
"I studied; I am a mother; I have two sons; I am divorced; I am retired."
✉ Str.Republicii 130,Ap.27, Galati, 6200 ✆ (934) 15674 ✍ French ♥ opera, mountains, travelling, tennis

GROSU, Sorin   b. 06/23/55   Ship mechanic
"I graduated the high school with humanistic profile which gives me the desire to look for friendly relations with all the people in the world."
✉ Str.Siderurgistilor 15,Bl.SD10A,Sc.2,Ap.26,Jud.Galati, Galati, 6200
✆ (934) 51435 ✍ French, English ♥ beekeeping
🏠 yes

GALATI

IORGA, Oltea b. 03/19/34 Engineer
"I was born in Galati, my parents were intellectuals. I live alone. My husband died last year. I have two sons, one is a physician, the other an engineer. I travelled a lot in my country."
Str.Republicii 116,Ap.25, Galati, 6200 © (934) 13194 ✍ French, English, Russian ♥ music of good quality, literature, trips to the mountains. I was leader of a mountain trips club ∏ yes ✰ board

MANOLE, Dan-Mihai b.01/29/62 Engineer
"I have been working since 1986, first on a ship and since a year at the University in Galati. I am married and have an eight month old son."
Str.Textilistilor 4,Bl.Q3,Ap.29,Micro 19, Galati, 6200 © (934) 42058 ✍ German, French, English (satisf.) ♥ the mountains, photography, reading ∏ yes, for friends ✰ board, guide

MOLDOVAN, Mariana Engineer
"I graduated from the Faculty of Naval Constructions. I was married. Now my husband is gone and I am alone. I have a 14-year-old son."
Str.Cezar 20A, Galati © (934) 29510 ✍ French ♥ voyages; Romania is a beautiful country. one can travel here to see many interesting and wonderful places ∏ yes

NEGRU, Ion b. 01/30/57 Designer
"I am married and we have a 5 years old son. We work in building. We have a flat that we could offer to our friends."
Micro 21,Bl.M4,Ap.14, Galati © (934) 47383 ✍ French ♥ nautic sports, fishing ∏ yes

OLTEANU, Octavian Georgel b.02/24/56 Engineer
"I work in the industry of river sailing on the Danube. I often travel in the country either for my job or personal interests. I own a small agency of international tourism."
Str.Brailei 38, Galati, 6200 © (934) 11682 ✍ English, French, German ♥ touristic guiding, touristic maps collecting, vessel models making, fishing ✂ tourist maps ∏ yes ✰ board

GALATI

PRODROM, Ion and Tereza (wife)   b.01/19/19
   Doctor (retired) ; wife: Engineer (retired).
"We have two children: Ioan Matei, born 11.24.66, student at the Polytechnic University in Galati; speaks German, French, English, and Andrei, born 01.23.69, student at the same University."
· Str.Republicii 130,Ap.7, Galati, 6200 ℂ (934) 15399 ✍ French, German, Greek ♥ we like to travel a lot; we travelled to Bulgaria, Poland, Hungary, Germany, Austria, Italy, Greece, ancient history and mythology ∎ yes. We prefer people from small towns/villages.

RIPA, Minodora   b.06/11/56   Engineer, professor assistent at the University of Galati.
"I did all my studies in Galati. I worked for 4 years in mechanic design and then became assistant at the Faculty of Mechanics. I am not married."
· Mazepa 1,Bl.Salcia 2,Ap.106, Galati, 6200 ℂ (934) 11919 ✍ French ♥ reading, knitting, voyages ∎ yes

SCUTARU, Rodica   b.10/14/53   Stomatology technician
"I am married to Traian Scutaru, born 1952. He is a taxi driver. We have a daughter, Adina, born in 1976, feb. 4th. She plays the guitar. We also have a son, Florin, born in 1977, oct. 10th. He practices Judo."
· Micro 40,Str.Piersicului 13,Bl.J7,Sc.III,Ap.56, Galati, 6200 ℂ (934) 24996 ✍ French, English ♥ travelling, literature, history of arts, music, paintings, embroidery ∎ yes ⚂ board

SMARANDA, Paul   b.09/12/53   Teacher
"I teach Mathematics in a highschool in Galati. I am married and I have two children, a girl aged 11 and a boy aged 13. My wife teaches Mathematics in the same highschool."
· Micro 18,Bl.C5A,Ap.1, Galati, 6200 ℂ (934) 49689 ✍ French ♥ mathematics, painting, animals, reading ∎ yes

GALATI

TASCA, Mihai   b. 04/29/46   French teacher

"I studied foreign languages. I teach French in a high school in Galati. I live in a three rooms flat with a wonderful view upon the Danube."

✏ Str.13 Iunie,Bl.Malina II,Ap.39, Galati, 6200
✆ (934) 13369 ✍ French, Italian ▮ yes ✯ board

URSACHE, Zoica - Sonia   b.01/02/29   Teacher of Romanian and Psychology.

"I am retired now, but feel very young and keeping an agreeable aspect (1.76 m tall and 71 Kg). I am married, my husband is an economist. I like to watch TV, visit friends and having them in my house. My husband is practical, I am romantic. Never jealous."

✏ Micro 17,Bl.H,Ap.37, Galati, 6200 ✆ (934) 42646 ✍ French, German, Russian (a little)
♥ voyages, making tourist albums, knitting, opera, modern music (Nana Moskouri) ▮ yes ✯ breakfast; trips in the country.

VERGA, Petrica   b.07/13/51   Telephone-operator

"I am not married. I have no children. I have been working at the Post Office since I graduated from high school. I would like to correspond with people in the West, men and women, married or not."

✏ Tiglina 2,Bl.I2,Ap.66, Galati, 6200 ✆ (934) 50483 ✍ French, English, Italian ♥ shows, poetry, conversation, trips, shopping ▮ yes (modest)

ZAMFIR, Ion - Constantin   b.05/23/51
   Electromechanic engineer

"I was born in Timisoara. My father came to Galati with his job in 1957. I studied in Galati and I work in a metallurgy plant for 18 years. My wife is also an engineer. We have two children, a girl aged 13 and a boy aged 11."

✏ Str.Siderurgistilor, Bl.SD4A,Ap.12, Galati, 6200
✆ (934) 23381 ✍ French, Italian ♥ visual arts (I am a self-made painter), ecology, tourism ▮ yes

GIURGITA

> " ... *local habits as they really are, not the way they show on TV* ... "

PLUGARESCU, Liviu b.07/24/65 Engineer
"*I graduated the Polytechnic Institute of Cluj-Napoca. I have a brother. We are very hospitable. My house is in the countryside 40 Km from the town Craiova. I am not married. I consider friendship above all. I'd like to make a lot of young friends.*"
· Str.Crinilor 247, Jud.Dolj, Giurgita, 1232
✍ English ♥ tennis, music ‖ yes

GIURGIU

> " ... *70,000 people ... historic resonances like the ruins of the fortress of Mircea the Old, a Turkish tower, a Greek church, the forest of Balanoaia* ... "

BALTARETU, Ioana b.06/29/29 Bookkeeper (retreated)
"*I worked as bookkeeper between 1948 and 1984. I have a son (35, engineer) and two grandsons, aged 5 and 9.*"
· Str.Ecaterina Varga 14, Giurgiu, 8375 © (912) 16029 ✍ Italian ♥ music, foreign languages, cinema, gardening, corresponding, postcards, children ‖ not now, but after corresponding - yes

SIMIONESCU, Virginia b.03/06/54 Economist
"*I am still living on my own "island" of silence and solitude. I was and still am (in spite of my age) a "dreaming eyes child". Me and my generation, we would change the world, but "THEY" gave us only false promises, lies and hatred, keeping us in dark.*"
· Str.Dunarii 45, Giurgiu © (912) 16932 ✍ French, Italian, Spanish ♥ music (Vivaldi, Bach, Beethoven, Rachmaninoff, Tchaikovsky, but also the Beatles, Bee-Gees, Leonard Cohen), poetry (Minulescu, Eminescu, Hafez, Fr.Villon, Ronsard, Baudelaire, Poe, Yeats), flowers, animals, nature ‖ yes

TONCA, Mirella b.08/20/56 Econoimist - computer programmer

"I was born in Giurgiu. I have a sister, born in 1943. I live with my little daughter and my parents. I graduated the Faculty of Cybernetics and Economy in Bucharest, in 1979. I got married in 1979, but my husband left me in 1986."

- Str.Partizani 37, Giurgiu, 8375 © (912) 11432
✍ French, English ♥ computers, painting, music, ballet, aerobic, swimming, bycicle riding, travelling
❚❚ yes ✭ board

HATEG

> *" ... near the Retezat Mountain, in a beautiful and interesting zone... equidistant from the Roman castrum of Sarmizegetusa, the Dac fortress of Costesti, and medieval castles "*

BAJURA, Aurelian b.10/07/39 Motor mechanic

"I work with a local company. My wife is a clerk. Our son is an engineer and lives together with his wife who is a physician in Arad."

- Str.Tudor Vladimirescu,Bl.17A/30,Jud.Hunedoara, Hateg, 2650 © (957) 70177 ✍ English ♥ trips, electronics ❚❚ yes, for 3-4 persons ✭ lunch

CIORA, Aurel b. 01/13/50 Engineer
- Str.T.Vladimirescu,Bl.30B,Ap.67, Hateg, 2650
✍ French ♥ painting ❚❚ yes

DOBREAN, Ioan b.07/28/64 Engineer

"I graduated from the Polytechnical Institute in Bucharest. I am married to Simona, who is a teacher. We have a two years old son, Marian, whom we love very much."

- Str.Mihai Eminescu 54,Jud.Hunedoara, Hateg, 2650 © (957) 77013 ✍ English ♥ cars, mountains, music ❚❚ yes

IOSIF, Liziana - Radita b.08/29/63 Teacher

"I studied in Timisoara and now I teach foreign languages in a village near Hateg. I live together with my parents, but I hope I'll have my own flat by next year. I am not yet married."

- Str.Aurel Vlaicu,Bl.P31,Ap.23,Jud.Hunedoara, Hateg, 2650 © (957) 70466 ⇆ English, French ♥ foreign languages, sewing, embroidery, driving, music, reading ∎ yes ✗ board

MOCANU, Adrian b.05/24/63 Electrician

"I work in a hydro-power plant. I graduated highschool in 1981. In the next year I obtained my driving license. In that year I married Elena in May."

- Str.Piata Unirii,Bl.48,Ap.27,Jud.Hunedoara, Hateg, 2650 © (957) 70912 ⇆ English ♥ music, adventure movies, philately (beginner), tourism ∎ yes

NEICONI, Mircea Sorin b.10/11/65 Student

"I am a student. I study in Timisoara. I am 24 years old. I live with my wife - Adelina, aged 24, and my parents. We have a one year old daughter - Magdalena. I am an evangelical christian."

- Str.Florilor 32,Jud.Hunedoara, Hateg, 2650 © (957) 70089 ⇆ English ♥ mountain climbing, table-tennis, I love the Bible ∎ yes

HIRSOVA

" ... the ancient ruins of Carsium, the Turkish church Djamia, beautiful and savage places ...,,

MANOLESCU, Daniel Constantin b.05/11/64
  Aquaculture Biotechnologist Engineer

"I graduated University of Galati in 1987. I have worked in research activity at Galati University, Con-

stanta Fishing Corp., Aquatical Research Centre from Galati. I am 1.80 m tall, 74 Kg weight."
- Str.23 August 36,Jud.Constanta, Hirsova, 8773
- (918) 71084 English, French, Italian (a little)
- dancing, music, travells, literature, sports, biological investigations, ancient history, scientific expeditions
- yes board; car

HUNEDOARA

> " ... the Castle of the Corvins, the Cincis lake, the fortress of Deva, the defile of Lainici, the defile of Surduc ... the Romanian dishes virsli, mici, and sarmale ... "

AMITITELOAIE, Gheorghe b.01/01/44 Metallurgic engineer

"I was born in Cernauti. I have 10 years of experience in the field of special treatments for steel. I have been married for more than 16 years. My wife is a teacher of biology in a secondary school. We have a son (15) and a daughter (14)."
- Str.Avram Iancu 10,Ap.48, Hunedoara, 2750
- (957) 13559 English ♥ travelling ∎ yes

BECHERETE, Ion b.03/30/27 professor-foreman (retired)

"I worked in a factory and for the last 27 years I worked in education as teacher. I am pensioned since last year. I practiced sports as gliding and plane flying. I am now building an ultra-light airplane. I am a beekeeper. My wife is also retired."
- Str.C.Negruzzi 4A, Jud.Hunedoara, Hunedoara, 2750 (957) 13752 Hungarian, Romanian
- ♥ sportive aviation, gliding, any kind of flying, apiculture, literature (short stories, poetry, epigram)
- yes board

BROASCA, Cosmin Nicolae b.02/06/73 Pupil

"There are no important events in my life. I appreciate the western cultural values because the most important

part of my cultural education was formed with the help of "Radio Free Europe"."
- Str.Roma 3, Hunedoara, 2750 © (957) 18004
- ✍ English ♥ cycling, tennis, informatics, music, films ❚❚ yes ✗ board, guide

NICOLAE, Corneliana
"I am married and have six children."
- Aleea Obor 9,Jud.Hunedoara, Hunedoara, 2750
- ✍ French ♥ sports ❚❚ yes ✗ board

HUSI

OVAC, Oana   b. 05/17/76   Pupil
"My father is an engineer, my mother is a chemist. I have two sisters : Raluca and Alina and a brother - Octavian."
- Str.Episcopiei 1,Jud.Vaslui, Husi, 6575 © (984) 72718 ✍ French, English, German ♥ arts, poetry, literature, music, travelling, making friends ❚❚ yes

PLESEA, Gheorghe   b.08/01/50   Physician (cardiologist)
"I was born in the west of Romania. I studied medicine at Timisoara (1969-1975); General practitioner in the country side 5 years; 3 years of secondary studies in Bucharest (internal medicine), then cardiologist in 1989. Married, two children."
- Str.Dobrogeanu Gherea 3,Bl.6,Sc.B,Jud.Vaslui, Husi, 6575 © (984) 71290 (work: 71467)
- ✍ French, English, Italian ♥ sports (water-polo, rugby, skiing), arts (literature, photography, cinema), electronics, tourism (mountains by foot) ❚❚ yes

IASI

> " ... founded in 1354, with a national theatre, opera, university, and mediaeval architectural monuments ... the historical capital of Moldavia ... sculptures of Brancusi, the painted church of Voronet ... a most attractive region ... The city of great loves ... situated on seven hills, like Rome ... center of Moldavian culture ..."

ALBISTEANU, Silvia - Maria   b.09/26/74   Pupil

"I am a pupil studying in the 10th year at the highschool "M.Eminescu", philology - history. I have 3 brothers: Micky, aged 18, Alex, aged 11 and Andrei, aged 8 months. My mother is a physicist and my father is a farming engineer."

• Str.Barboi 1,Bl.F1,Ap.1, Iasi, 6600 ✆ (981) 49843 ✍ French, German ♥ sports (tennis), theatre, philately, swimming, dancing, music, nature, postcards collecting ✂ postcards ∎ yes

ANGHELACHE-LUPASCU, Ivona   b.10/04/49
   Physician gynecologist

"I was born in Iasi. My parents are doctors. My husband is 45. He is a Mechanic engineer. We are the happy parents of a baby boy of 4 months. I am a real subject for paranormal perceptions. I had experiences of premonitions about myself, also relatives."

• Str.Penes Curcanul 9,Ap.3, Iasi, 6600 ✆ (981) 42628 ✍ French, English, Russian ♥ predicted Cernobyl catastrophy, (inherited gift from my grandmother), interested in telepathy, horoscope, life in clean air, voyages, my husband and I travelled to France, Japan, Eastern European countries ∎ yes

ARSENE, Robert - Andi   b.07/29/65   Automobiles engineer

"I am born in Iasi, the ancient capital of Moldova. My hair is dark, I am 1.74 m high and weigh 70 Kg. I work in the automobiles industry."

· Str.Ursulea 13, Iasi, 6600 ℂ (981) 47490
✍ French, English ♥ auto - sports, music, literature, voyages. I like to live, to dance, to know the world and meet new people ❚ yes

BACIU, Antoneta   b.01/17/62   Mechanical Engineer

"I am working in a factory. I am married. My husband is a mechanical engineer too. We have a 4 year old daughter."

· Soseaua Arcu 81,Bl.T7,Sc.A,Ap.13, Iasi, 6600
✍ French, English ♥ travelling, making friends, rock music, classical music, theatre, cinema, reading
❚ yes ✗ breakfast

BARSANESCU, Paul   b.06/12/51   Mechanical Engineer

"I am a mechanical engineer and lecturer at the Polytechnic Institute of Iasi. My wife is a chemist and she is lecturer at the same Institute. We have one child, a boy. He is 10. He also likes stamps. We have a 5 rooms flat."

· Al.Gradinari 4,Bl.H33,Ap.6, Iasi, 6600 ℂ (981) 74311 ✍ English, French, Italian ♥ opera, symphonic music. I have many records, philately
✂ stamps ❚ yes

BIRZOI, Ion   b.   07/23/44   Teacher

"I teach English for 22 years. I have 4 children : Ingrid (22), Niki (20), Sorin (15), Andreea (4). Ingrid is married and has a two years old son. My wife, Rodica, is a chemical laboratory assistant."

· Sos.Arcu 63,Bl.T11,Sc.C,Ap.1, Iasi, 6600
ℂ (981) 40026 ✍ English ♥ children education, politics, table and field tennis, boxing, philately, light music, flowers, correspondence, travelling, friendship
❚ yes

IASI

BOAZU, Sorin   b. 02/27/55   Engineer
"I studied civil building in Iasi. I work now in a research institute. My wife, Rodica, teaches at the faculty for Civilian Buildings in Iasi. We have a six years old child."
  Aleea Rozelor 2A,Bl.X2,Ap.12, Iasi, 6600
  (981) 36867 ✍ French ♥ tourism, sports, music
  yes ☆ board

BOBOC, Irina   b. 06/24/74   pupil
"height: 1.60 m; eyes:brown; hair:brown"
  Str.Carpati 2,Bl.908,Ap.32, Iasi ✍ Italian
  ♥ music

BUTUCEA, Iulia   b.07/08/57   Economist
"I am not married. I want to correspond with people and travel."
  Str.Cucu 20,Bl.309,Sc.B,Ap.12, Iasi, 6600
  (981) 79833 ✍ English ♥ reading, theatre, cinema
  yes ☆ breakfast

CILA, Emil Corneliu   b.10/25/41   Physicist
"I was born in Ploiesti, Prahova. I studied in Iasi. In 1971 I followed courses of cybernetics in Paris for C.I.I. I've been working since in hardware for computers. I founded in Iasi the "A.E.C. Alphatronics", for electronics, computers and consulting."
  Str.Roman Voda 15,Bl.N1,Sc.B,Ap.14, Iasi, 6600
  (981) 52081 ✍ French ♥ numismatics, voyages
  yes

CONDREA, Octavian   b.01/20/58   Engineer
"IO was born in a settlement near Iasi, Podu Iloaiei. I came to live in Iasi with my parents when I was a little boy. I did all my studies here, including university. I am married for 10 years but we have no children yet. I research thermic motors."
  Str.Ciurchi 117,Bl.B1,Sc.B,Ap.13, Iasi, 6600
  (981) 73527 ✍ French ♥ cars, theatre, films
  yes

DASCALU, Aurelia   b.11/02/38   Secretary in a highschool
"I am retired now. I have two children, a son, Ovidiu and a daughter, Vasilisa. They are both married and have their children."
 • Str.Sf.Andrei 4, Iasi, 6600 ℂ (981) 10421
 ✍ French, English, Italian ♥ theatre, music, gardening, tourism (I am a guide), I like to write poems
 ❙❙ yes ☆ I am an excelent cook!

DRISCU, Mihai Corneliu   b.07/02/54   Architect
"I studied architecture in Iasi and Bucharest and now work in a design institute. My wife is also architect and we have two children aged 5 and 3."
 • Str.Anastasie Panu 17,Bl.Ghica Voda 2,Sc.B,Ap.23, Iasi, 6600 ℂ (981) 43477
 ✍ English, French ♥ design, pictures, rock music
 ❙❙ yes

DUMITRESCU, Ana   b.06/19/35   Teacher of Romanian
"I am a widow since 1978 when my husband died of a heart attack. I have two sons: Florin, mechanic engineer, he lives separately; and Catalin, student in electrotechnic. They both like trips by car, fishing, philately, music, basketball."
 • Str.23 August 44,Bl.B-1,Ap.37, Iasi ℂ (981) 41881 ✍ French, English ♥ writing ❙❙ yes

FECIORU, Viorel   b.04/01/57   Engineer
"I have been a building engineer for 5 years. I love my town."
 • Str.Decebal 34,Bl.D4,Sc.A,Ap.6, Iasi, 6600 ℂ (981) 31623 ✍ French, Spanish ♥ nature (gardening, flowers), music, dancing, operetta, travelling, meeting people ❙❙ yes

FILIPPOVSKAIA, Alexandra   b.02/20/24   Teacher of French
"I taught at the University in Iasi. Now, I am retired. I am divorced since 1964. I have no children. Sometimes I translate poems."
 • Bd.Stefan cel Mare 7,Bl.A2,Sc.A,Ap.33, Iasi, 6600 ℂ (981) 45184 ✍ French, Russian, English (a little) ♥ painting, literature, travelling ❙❙ yes

GROSU, Radu - Grigore b.01/30/56 Engineer

"*I am an electrotechnical engineer and work in a research institute. I am married. My wife works as a technician in the same institute. we have two children : a 14-year-old daughter and a 13-year-old son.*"

• Al.Sucidava 4,Bl.264,Ap.15, Iasi, 6600 ✍ French, English ♥ tennis, voyages, literature, music, computers, physics, foreign languages ‖ yes ✗ board

HARAMITA, Paul - Lucian b.10/17/68 Computer operator in an institute of computing and industrial buildings

"*My father is a technician. My mother is retired now. I studied electronics in the high technical school and in 1988 I graduated a course in computers. I visited France in 1984, Germany and U.S.S.R. in 1989 and Italy in 1990.*"

• Bd.Independentei 25,Bl.C1-5,Sc.C1,Ap.22, Iasi, 6600 ✆ (981) 13011 ✍ English, German ♥ tennis, painting, philately ‖ yes ✗ bed and breakfast

IVASIUC, Paula b.02/05/49 Teacher of German language

"*I was born in Brasov. My parents still live there. I attended the German school. I graduated from University in Iasi, where I got married. My husband is an engineer. I work in an office for translations.*"

• Aleea Decebal 11,Sc.B,Ap.4, Iasi, 6600 ✆ (981) 39133 ✍ German ♥ everything new: movies, music, travelling; knitting ‖ yes

LERESCU, Dana b.11/01/67 Student - Medical school

"*I am a student since 1986, now in the 5th year. My husband too. I have good marks, I like to learn. I live with my husband, my parents and my grandmother in a 6 room house with a garden.*"

• Str.Buna Vestire 3, Iasi, 6600 ✆ (981) 13587 ✍ English, French, German ♥ music, sports (basketball, handball, badminton, swimming), cooking; I like to organize parties;, learning foreign languages ‖ yes, for a person or two.

LUCHIAN, Stefan and Mariana (wife)   b.10/08/27
Agriculture engineer; Professor (of Chemistry) (wife)
"We are three, me, my wife aged 56 and my daughter, Patricia-Elena, aged 19, student in medicine."
· Str.Nicolina 9,Bl.A4,Sc.A,Ap.5, Iasi, 6600
✆ (981) 32327 ✍ French, English ♥ gardening, opera, theatre, film, opera, theatre, chemistry, physics (wife), medicine, reading, opera, theatre, philately, dancing, music (daughter) ∎ yes ✰ breakfast

MANOLACHE, Dan   b.07/03/57   Mechanic engineer
"My wife Juliet is also 33. We have a daughter Oana aged 8. I work in a big food factory. My wife, a teacher of Romanian language, works now at the University Library "Al.I.Cuza" (established 1870) of Iasi. We live in a little house with a garden."
· Str.M.Kogalniceanu 7, Iasi, 6600 ✆ (981) 15589
✍ English, French ♥ music (country folk music, dance music), feature film, horse opera, documentary, video shows, books, taking walks in the woods, picnics, animals (we have two dogs) ∎ yes ✰ board, autotransport, touristic guide, parties.

MANOLE, Dumitru
and Iulian-Robert (son)   b.12/11/50   Painter / Pupil
"I attended in the last 21 years several courses in chemistry, medicine, arts. I am a painter and had many exhibitions. I love democracy and my hobbies. My son is a pupil and a sportsman. He took part in a lot of contests."
· Str.Piata Voievozilor 16,Bl.C3,Sc.B,Ap.33, Iasi, 6600 ✆ (981) 50202 ✍ German ♥ father: painting, sculpture, travelling, tailoring. Son: tennis, basket-ball, athletics, chess, electronics, travelling, physics, mathematics ∎ yes ✰ breakfast

MOROSANU, Iocasta - Iosefina   b.03/20/71
"I graduated highschool but failed the exam for the University (French -Romanian literature) because of the Romanian! I'll try again, and if I don't make it I want

to make a marionette theatre. I have a sister, Lavinia-Suzana, aged 17."

⁜ Sos.Nationala 194,Bl.D,Sc.C,Ap.28, Iasi, 6600
✆ (981) 36234 ✍ French, English ♥ I adore tennis, swimming, philately, French language, marionette theatre ✂ stamps ∎ yes ✯ breakfast

NEGREA, Magda   b.02/18/48   Teacher of French at a highschool

"I am from Iasi. I worked many years in Piatra Neamt, a town 150 Km far from here. I have a 6-year-old son, who gives me a lot of unrest and satisfaction."

⁜ Str.Dochia 2B, Iasi, 6600 ✆ (981) 16016
✍ French, Italian ♥ reading, illustrated magazines, philately, corresponding with nice people all over the world ∎ yes

NICOLA, Alexandrina   b.04/13/24   Physician/ Bachelor of Medical Science

"Since 1950 I have been working at the Clinical Hospital of Lung Diseases in Iasi. I divorced my husband in 1962. I have no children. I own a 3 rooms flat in the centre of the city and a car."

⁜ Bd.Stefan cel Mare 7,Bl.A2,Sc.A,Ap.19, Iasi, 6600 ✆ (981) 42855 ✍ French, German ♥ literature (fiction, medical), theatre, opera, symphonic music, travelling ∎ yes; a family of two, non-smokers. ✯ breakfast

OLTEANU, Radu - Tudor   b.12/12/55   Engineer

"I am the son of Basil, lawyer, and Anne, teacher. I have a sister lawyer. My wife is a teacher of Romanian. We have two sons (6 and 2) and a daughter aged 4. I work in an enterprise that produces electronic equipment. I also deal in real estate."

⁜ Str.Ciric 6,Bl.Z1,Sc.A,Ap.4, Iasi, 6600 ✆ (981) 77563 ✍ French ♥ music: As a student I was succesful with my compositions ∎ yes ✯ board

PALADE, Diana   b.01/20/70   Computer operator

"*Height:1.73m. I have brown eyes and brown hair. I love travelling and would gladly offer housing to a family who would like to know my country.*"

· Str.Uranus 50,Bl.C3,Ap.6, Iasi, 6600 © (981) 31853   French, English ♥ dancing, music, trips, opera ■ yes

PIUCA, Dan   b.   08/27/51   Economist - Analist

"*I am married and I have a daughter aged 14 who loves the French and the English languages.*"

· Sos.Arcu 67,Bl.T3B,Sc.A,Ap.13, Iasi, 6600
© (981) 14215   English, French, Italian ♥ sports (football), politics, international affairs, philately (stamps concerning sports events and arts) ✄ stamps ■ yes ✗ breakfast

POINESCU, Monica   b.05/04/61   Mathematics teacher in a highschool

"*I was born in Iasi where I did my studies; graduated from University in 1981, Faculty of Mathematics. I am now divorced and I live with my little boy Edi, who is 3 years old.*"

· Piata Unirii 5,Sc.B,Ap.31, Iasi, 6600   English, French, German (a little) ♥ reading, classic music (Bach), travelling, climbing mountains, skiing and swimming ■ yes ✗ guide for the monasteries in North

POPOVICI, Gabriela   b.05/05/68   Student in Fine Arts (sculpture)

"*I have now new conditions of freedom. There are many beauties in the world that we were not permitted to know, not even through images in magazines and books.*"

· Sos.Stefan cel Mare 32, Iasi, 6600 © (981) 48398   French ♥ painting (Christian icons) ■ yes

POSTICA, Romeo - Radames b.06/09/70
   Electromechanic
"I started school in 1977. I work since 1989 and in parallel with work I attend courses of secondary school (last year)."
• Bd.D.Cantemir 2,Bl.P3,Sc.C,Ap.9, Iasi, 6600
℗ (981) 37597 ✍ English, French ♥ tourism, dance, electronics, literature (fiction and SF)

RUSCANU, Dumitru b.06/24/49 Physicist
"I have been married for 15 years. My wife is a teacher; we are of the same age. We have a large family : 4 children. I work in a laboratory at the University in Iasi."
• Bd.Independentei 27,Bl.C1-5,Sc.C2,Ap.30, Iasi, 6600 ℗ (981) 19165 ✍ French, English ♥ shows, gardening ∎ yes ✕ breakfast

STAN, Sylvie b. 03/19/53 Teacher
"I was born in Tecuci in a modest family. I have two sisters. After graduating from high school in Tecuci, I studied philology in Iasi. In 1975 I married an economist - Liviu. We have two daughters : Sabina (14) and Cristina (4). We live in a 3 room flat."
• Bd.Republicii 18,Bl.904A,Ap.5, Iasi ℗ (981) 23826 ✍ French ♥ the French language, reading, travelling ∎ yes ✕ breakfast

TARABUTZA, Vasile - Corneliu b.05/07/38
   Electromechanic engineer
"Between 1942 and 1964 I lived in Radauti (Bucovina), so that I know all the old and famous monasteries there. I work now in the field of designing. I have a daughter (22, married, medical assistant) and a son (20, car mechanic). My wife is an economist."
• Str.Dobrogeanu Gherea 8A,Ap.2, Iasi, 6600
℗ (981) 46407 ✍ German, Russian ♥ music, chess, literature ∎ yes ✕ I can accompany the tourists and provide housing

TASCA, Ioan b. 08/02/43 Teacher of Foreign Languages
"I was born in Iasi. I studied here and now I teach French. While a student, I worked as a tourist guide for

foreign groups (French, Swiss, German, Belgian). I am impassioned about agriculture and own a small farm (Galata) for 20 years."

· Str.Podisului 3 (Galata), Iasi, 6600 © (981) 76259 ✍ French, German ♥ agriculture (cows, horses, fowl, dogs), vineyards. I inherited a small farm where I like to work ✗ I offer my services for tourists visiting Romania.

TODOSI, Gabriela   b.06/14/56   Physician

"*I was born in Iasi from a family of intellectuals. I practice medicine in a village 5 Km far from Iasi. My husband, of the same age, is a doctor too and we have two children, girls, aged 11 and 7. We live in the centre of the city.*"

· Str.Th.Pallady 9, Iasi, 6600 © (981) 16379 ✍ English, Italian, French ♥ medicine, travelling, music and my children; we like to make friends with good people ‖ yes

ULIANOV, Ciprian   b.06/10/68   Student (medicine)

"*I have a car and I'm driving very well. Also I have a house with 4 rooms and I can spend money (I work in my free time and my father is a doctor, my mother a lawyer). I am a pleasant person and I like to make conversation (politics, history, arts...)*"

· Bd.Independentei 30,Bl.Y5,Ap.17,Jud.Iasi, Iasi, 6600 © (981) 14164 ✍ French, English, German ♥ travelling (I traveled to Soviet Union, Bulgaria, Yugoslavia, Hungary, Austria, Italy), music (opera, Chopin, Rachmaninov, Brahms, Ravel), modern music (pop, rock, slow); sports (tennis, swimming, football), I am a good dancer and I like to dance ‖ yes; I prefer a doctor or a student of my age.

UNGUREANU, Dumitru   b.11/09/28   Economist

"*I worked as an economics manager in a plant in Iasi. I am retired now. My wife, Ernestina, is a researcher at the Institute for Socio-Humanitarian Sciences in Iasi.*

We have no children. We live in a 3 room flat right in the centre of the city."

∴ Bd.Independentei 15,Sc.1,Ap.2, Iasi, 6600
© (981) 13930 ✍ French ♥ reading, listening to music, walking, trips into the mountains ∥ yes(for a family of French intellectuals;no child) ☆ trips by car

VARLAM, Ioan   b. 09/06/26   Economist

"I come from a farmers' family. I studied in Birlad and in Bucharest (the Academy of High Commercial and Industrial Studies). I worked mainly as highschool teacher. I am married to Marioara Varlam, zootechnic engineer."

∴ Str.Decebal 14A,Bl.X10,Ap.5, Iasi, 6600
© (981) 38206 ✍ French, Italian ♥ culture, music, etc ∥ yes

ZANOSCHI, Christache   b.07/18/49   Physician

"I graduated from the medicine faculty in 1974. I am married and have a son. I've got a house with 5 rooms and a car."

∴ Str.Pinului 9, Iasi, 6600 © (981) 17605
✍ French, English ♥ getting on in English ∥ yes
☆ board, car

JIMBOLIA

GRINDEAN, Marcela   b.07/19/52   Technical drawer

"married, a nine-year-old son"

∴ Str.Republicii 1B, Jimbolia © (962) 50797
✍ German, Serbian ♥ literature ∥ yes

LUGOJ

" ... a little town, but quite nice and old, with the river Timis ..."

BALOMIRI, George and Rodica (wife) b.02/08/25
   Physician and musician/Pediatrist
   "*I am also a painter and sculptor. I translated poems from French and German into Romanian.*"
   ∙ Str.Bojinca 8, Lugoj, 1800 ℂ (963) 11710
   ✍ French, Italian, English ♥ opera, philately
   ♊ yes

ILIN, Ligia b. 11/12/58 Riding trainer (phisical education teacher)
   "*I graduated from Physical Education Institute in 1981. In 1987 I won the Balcanic Riding Championships in Sofia. My husband is also a riding trainer. I have a daughter named Laura. I like to have many friends and I prefer them to be older than I.*"
   ∙ Str.Cotu Mic,Bl.3C,Ap.2,Jud.Timis, Lugoj, 1800
   ✍ English, French ♥ riding, swimming, dancing, reading, opera and classical music ♊ yes (in a 4 room appartment by the river) ☆ board

MANGALIA

> "*Mangalia is a small ton on the sea side, 50km from the Bulgarian border. One should visit the Black Sea coast, the museums, the Turkish church, and at 150km the Danube Delta. At 5km from town are the villas of Ceausescu.*"

MIHAI, Gabriela Cashier
   "*I was born in 1952. I am married and have two children, a little boy aged 7 and a little girl of 6. My husband is pensioned because he had an operation on the backbone.*"
   ∙ Str.Libertatii 8.,Jud.Constanta, Mangalia, 8727
   ✍ Italian ♥ flowers, children ♊ yes

MEDGIDIA

MICULESCU, Sergiu b.07/27/51 French teacher
   "*I live in a town with 60,000 inhabitants, 35 Km far from the Black Sea. I am married, my wife is a dentist.*

I studied at the University of Bucharest. We have no children yet."

✉ Str.Tineretului 12,Jud.Constanta, Medgidia, 8650
✆ (918) 14757 ✍ French, English (a little) ♥ books and reading, music, arts, history, tennis, tourism
H yes ☆ board; tours by car

MEDIAS

> " ... the tower where Vlad Tepes (Dracula) was emprisoned ... baroque buildings ... the ecological disaster in Copsa Mica ... "

BRUSANOWSKI, Paul   b.04/04/72   Student
"I am the only child of my parents. I study theology in Cluj, because I think it is very interesting to find out about faith, God, history of religion. I would be glad to discuss any problem concerning our lives with people abroad."
✉ Str.Sibiului 20, Medias, 3125 ✆ (928) 13327
✍ German, English (a little) ♥ history, geography, theology, music H yes

GHEMES, Dan   b. 08/03/55   Engineer
"I was in conflict with Ceausescu's political regime. Since 1990 I am the leader of the youth organization of the Peasant Party in Medias."
✉ Str.Cluj 4,Ap.15,Jud.Sibiu, Medias, 3125
✆ (928) 13949 ✍ French ♥ literature, history, numismatics, voyages H yes ☆ breakfast

MIERCUREA-CIUC

MOLDOVAN, Emil   b.01/05/48   Engineer
"I graduated from college in 1971. I studied electromechanics. I work in the field of machine building. I am married and have a daughter born in 1978. I own vacation houses in the most beautiful places."
✉ Bd.Timisoarei 26,Ap.8, Miercurea-Ciuc, 4100
✆ (958) 20075 ✍ Hungarian, German, French (a little) ♥ photography, music H yes, in exchange

MIHAI VITEAZUL

> *" My village is situated by the river Aries, near Cheile Turzii and the well-known Scarisoara cave."*

POPA, Lizeta   b. 12/08/58   Mechanic technician
"*I studied at the Polytechnical Institute in Cluj. I work in a factory in Turda. I am married and have two sons aged 8 and 4. My husband is an electrician. We live in a house with garden.*"
  Str.Garii 956, Mihai Viteazul, 3352 ✍ French
♥ history, tailoring ⌂ yes ☆ board

MINECIU UNGURENI

BARBU, Dianne   b.03/23/62   Teacher of history and philosophy, writer
"*I was born in Mineciu Ungureni. I studied in Bucharest. I am a poet too. I have already published a book. In 1989 I won the European contest "Health.Peace.Humanity"*"
  Str.Pietii 519,Jud.Prahova, Mineciu Ungureni, 2104 ✆ 10 ✍ French ♥ history of mentalities, history of south-east European countries, history of the French revolution, music, poetry, painting, dancing
⌂ yes ☆ guide

MIZIL

OANCEA, Elena   b.01/10/54   Teacher of french
"*I graduated from the University in Bucharest in 1977. I am teaching French in a village next to Mizil. My husband works as an engineer at the mechanical plant in the town. We have a 8 year old daughter. We love honest people.*"
  Str.N.Balcescu 217,Bl.7,Sc.B,Ap.15,Jud.Prahova, Mizil, 5025 ✆ (972) 50659 ✍ French, Russian
♥ reading, exchanging opinions ⌂ yes, for serious persons ☆ board

MORENI

> " ... one must get to know the quiet nature which surrounds my small town ...."

DUTA, Marian   b. 04/07/53   Architect

"*I studied architecture and urbanism. I designed houses and urban areas. I am married and we have a daughter aged 13. She speaks German. I spend my holidays in the Danube Delta, a unique wonderful place in Europe.*"

∙ Str.Neptun 7,Bl.I,Ap.4, Moreni, 0271 ℂ (926) 65407 ✍ French ♥ voyages, music of good quality, arts, fishing, ecology ∎ yes ✰ a tour to the Danube Delta.

STANESCU, George   b.03/10/53   Designing technician

"*I am married to an economist; have a daughter 2 years old. I work in a company which produces containers and equipment for oil industry, large span bridges, high pressure gas cyliders, etc. I worked as a guide for the Inernational Travel Agency Mamaia.*"

∙ Str.22 Decembrie 1989,nr.30,Bl.160/A,Ap.115, Moreni, 0271 ℂ (926) 65118 ✍ English, Italian, French ♥ travelling, reading in foreign languages, classic music ✂ pens of all kinds (fountain pens, pencils, ball pens, etc.) ∎ yes ✰ board and cover other expenses

MOTRU

POPESCU, Clement   b.03/02/38   Mining Engineer

"*I came to this county in 1966 and have been working as an engineer in Motru since. I am married. My wife is a geological engineer. We have two children, both students in Bucharest. I will retire in 1992 and I will have plenty of time for tourism.*"

∙ Bd.Trandafirilor 14,Jud.Gorj, Motru, 1416 ℂ (949) 61766 ✍ French, Russian ♥ music, arts, chess ∎ yes, for 4 persons ✰ board

NUCET

JURCUT, Dan b. 10/15/62 Engineer
"*I work as an engineer in Petru Groza. I am married.*"
· Baita 212, Nucet, 3641 ℂ 61 - Nucet ✍ French
♥ tennis ‖ yes

OLTENITA

CONSTANTIN, Gelu b.03/22/47 Technician in electric equipment; foreman
"*I am married. My wife is a physician. We have a daughter, aged 21, who works in a textile factory, and a son aged 12. We are a united family, we love the truth and respect our fellowman whoever he might be.*"
· Str.Alex.Iliescu 46-48,Bl.G2,Sc.A,Ap.12, Oltenita, 8350 ✍ French, Russian, German (a little)
♥ tourism, fishing, photography, electronics, energetics, car racing, fashion ‖ yes ✰ board

GEORGESCU, Marcel Operator projectionist
"*I was born in Oltenita. I am 30. I worked as an electrician at the shipyard here after I graduated from high school. I was not satisfied with this job and attended a school for foreign languages. Then, I studied to become a cinema projectionist operator.*"
· Bd.Republicii 62,Bl.E.Sc.A,Ap.11,Jud.Calarasi, Oltenita, 8350 ℂ (919) 11843 ✍ English, French, Italian ♥ tennis, heavy-metal and disco music, electronics, electricity, literature, foreign languages, travelling, watching TV, in two words: to live ‖ yes

ION, Georgeta b. 12/01/61 Seller
"*I graduated from high school and worked at the shipyard in Oltenita in an electrotechnic laboratory. I didn't like this job, so I studied again attending a commercial course. I was employed in a shop for ladies since 1983 and I like this job.*"
· Str.8 Mai Nr.178,Jud.Calarasi, Oltenita, 8350 ℂ (919) 12067 ✍ English, Chech ♥ travelling, reading, tailoring, knitting ‖ yes

ONESTI

> " ... surrounded by mountain resorts ... "

FORNICA-LIVADA, Gabriel   b.05/26/58   Teacher
"*I studied in Bucharest at the French highschool, then at the University. I worked as a teacher in a small village for four years, then I took a job in a chemical plant. I want to teach again now. I am married and have three children.*"
 Calea Marasesti 28/17, Onesti, 5450 French, German, Turkish ♥ arts in general, music (symphonic, opera, folklore, but also modern), painting, literature, theatre, photography, tourism (I am a guide interpreter for French speaking people)
yes ☆ board; tours by car in Summer.

SBARCEA, Corneliu   b.02/14/59   Worker
"*I am married and have a seven year old daughter. I live in Onesti in an elegant district, in a three room flat.*"
 Str.A.I.Cuza,Bl.15,Sc.A,Ap.18, Onesti, 5450
 French ♥ travelling, music, tennis   yes

SFARAIALA, Doru - Virgil   b.02/03/38   Doctor
"*I am married for 31 years. My wife is as old as me. She works as chief anaesthesist in Onesti hospital. I worked as doctor in a small village between 1961-1965, then in a hematology centre in Bucharest between 1965-1970 where I was also the director.*"
 Str.Perchiului 2/3, Onesti, 5450 © (933) 12335
 French, Italian ♥ bridge, tourism by car (I travelled also to USSR, China, India, Pakistan, Turkey), literature (political economy, geography)
yes

ORADEA

> " ... the first Romanian town tourists travelling on E60 can visit ... 200,000 people, and lays over the river Crisul Repede ... thermal waters ... "

BIRSAN, Simona Daciana b.01/23/72 Pupil
"I want to study medicine starting next year"
- Str.Portile de fier 1,Ap.23, Oradea, 3700
℃ (991) 34305 ✍ English, Hungarian, French (a little) ♥ swimming, gymnastics, films, music ✂ stamps ▮▮ yes (?)

BRANZAS, Fl.Ioan b.01/08/37 Teacher of French
"I was born in the village of Sumugiu, Bihor county. My parents were peasants. They came to Oradea in 1935. I have two children, twins, boys, they are 16. They speak French and Hungarian. I live with them. Their mother abandoned them at 6 months."
- Str.L.Salajan 105/A,Bl.A2,Ap.29,Jud.Bihor, Oradea, 3700 ℃ (991) 37231 ✍ French, Russian, Hungarian ♥ flowers and flower arrangements, heraldics, folklore (dances, tales, legends) ▮▮ yes, only for two persons. ✰ breakfast

COCEAN, Gheorghe b.09/20/30 Retired
"I was an army officer between 1951 - 1981. Retired with the rank of colonel."
- Str.Sovata 56,Bl.C/4,Ap.7,Jud.Bihor, Oradea, 3700 ℃ (991) 44868 ✍ Hungarian, English (a little) ♥ gardening, swimming, music ▮▮ yes ✰ bed and breakfast

GAL, Alexandru b.06/30/57 Analist computer programmer.
"I am married. I graduated the Economic Cybernetics faculty of the Academy of Economic Studies in Bucharest."
- Str.Vladeasa 741B PB10,Ap.18,Jud.Bihor, Oradea, 3700 ✍ English, German ♥ music, politics, computers ▮▮ yes

TONT, Dan - George b.12/23/57 Engineer
"My father, Teodor, is a physician, my mother, Maria, is a chemist. I am married. I have a one year old daughter - Diane. My wife, Gabi, is an engineer too. We work in the health department in Felix. I like to meet people, talk, communicate."
- Str.Magheru M-7,Ap.1,Jud.Bihor, Oradea, 3700 ℃ (991) 37380 ✍ English, French ♥ tennis ▮▮ yes

ORASTIE

> *" ... the heart of the Cacic civilization near Orastie ... Brancusis sculptures in Tirgu Jiu ..."*

GRADINARIU, Augustin   b.07/20/53   Technician

"I was born in Orastie, a small town, I studied in two secondary schools. I am married, I have a child 10 years old. He writes letters to children in France and Belgium. We own a house in Orastie."

- Str.Viilor 38.,Jud.Hunedoara, Orastie, 2600
- ✆ (956) 47241 ✍ German, Russian, English
- ♥ chess, philately, corresponding with people from other countries ■ yes ✗ breakfast

PETRIC, Gabriel   b.08/15/56   Teacher

"I studied Romanian and French. I founded the pop/rock group EQUINOX. I published philosophic essays and articles dealing with the history of the guitar. I intend to found an independent society for international tourism."

- Str.A.Iancu 4.Ap.5.,Jud.Hunedoara, Orastie, 2600
- ✆ (956) 41814 ✍ French, English ♥ music (rock, jazz), guitar, literature, philosophy ■ yes

ORSOVA

> *" ... come here, and discover the unknown! ..."*

STUPARU, Anca   b.03/31/74   Pupil

"I study French and English in Timisoara. My parents are teachers. I have an eleven years old brother - Mihai."

- Str.23 August Nr.28.,Jud.Mehedinti, Orsova, 1543
- ✆ (979) 61475 ✍ French, German ♥ music, literature, foreign languages ■ yes, in exchange

ELICAN, Venuela   b.10/22/66   Typist

"*I took part in the Revolution in December in Timisoara, and since I value life more. I want to live to love the Beautiful. I want to feel the joy of living.*"

• Str.Decebal ,Bl.A3 ,Sc.A,Ap.19 ,Jud.Mehedinti, Orsova, 1543 ℂ (979) 61450 ⌕ French, English
♥ flowers, tennis, theatre, dancing, everything
⌂ yes

OTELU ROSU

" *My town is small, with 15,000 people, and situated near the Caransebes, on the picturesque Bistrita Valley.* „

OSCAIU, Tiberiu   b.05/15/28   Teacher of Romanian language and literature

"*I was born in Timisoara. I studied in Cluj. I traveled a lot to France, Spain, Italy, Germany, Greece, Turkey. I made a museum of literature in the highschool I work in.*"

• Str.Republicii 25 ,Jud.Caras-Severin, Otelu Rosu
ℂ (965) 30807 ⌕ French ♥ I am founder of the "Cine Club" in my town and lead the society "Science and Philology" ⌂ yes ✗ breakfast

PIATRA NEAMT

" *... a crossroads in Romanian history, still full of old monuments and monasteries ...* „

RNAUTU, Amilcar   b.11/04/57   Railways engineer

"*I was born in Cimpina, on the Prahova valley. After graduating from the Polytechnical Institute in Bucharest, I worked 4 years in Miercurea-Ciuc and* ➘

Tirgu Mures, in Transylvania. Then I got married and moved to Piatra Neamt. My wife is a doctor."

• Str.Calugareni 3,Bl.F34,Sc.B,Ap.19,Jud.Neamt, Piatra Neamt, 430 ✍ French, English ♥ I like to work with my hands and I like to think that one who has two hands and a head can do everything;, mountains, skiing, photography ∎ yes ✰ breakfast

BANU, Sorin   b.   03/21/58   Electromechanic

"*I am a young man who works and I have two children, a daughter aged 10 and a son aged 2. My wife is a librarian.*"

• Str.Darmanesti 80,Bl.K10,Sc.B,Ap.88,Jud.Neamt, Piatra Neamt, 5600 ✆ (936) 27763 ✍ French, English ♥ philately ✂ Stamps. ∎ I live in a two room flat.

CEZARIUS, Mitrea   b.10/24/66   Mechanical Engineer

"*In 1988 I became an engineer. I am married to a student. She is going to become a physician. So far we have no children,*"

• Str.Progresului 121,Bl.48,Ap.8,Jud.Neamt, Piatra Neamt, 5600 ✆ (936) 29737 ✍ English, French, German (a little) ♥ literature, music, sports, everything that fits our age ∎ yes, for a young family ✰ board, guide

EDITH, Paulon   b.07/20/62   English teacher

"*I am of Hungarian origin and presently I live in Romania. I graduated from University in 1985. I am not married and have no children.*"

• Str.Borzesti,Bl.E8,Ap.1, Piatra Neamt ✍ English ♥ English, pop music ∎ yes

LOGHIN, Lidia and Corneliu   b.12/27/32   Doctor (retired), Economist (retired)(husband)

• Str.George Cosbuc 1,Ap.3, Piatra Neamt, 5600 ✆ (936) 16086 ✍ English ∎ yes

MERTICARU, Mihai   b.06/20/48   Teacher

• Str.Paharnicului,Bl.4,Ap.46, Piatra Neamt, 5600 ✆ (936) 13567 ✍ French, Italian, Russian ♥ philately, travelling ∎ yes, in the countryside too ✰ board

TAZLAOANU, Florenta   b.04/09/46   Biology teacher
"I teach biology at school in a settlement near Piatra Neamt. I am divorced."
- Aleea Ulmilor 16,Bl.E5,Ap.2, Piatra Neamt, 5600
✆ (936) 25391   ✍ French, Russian   ♥ reading, dance, tourism, music   ❚❚ yes   ✗ board

TERBESCU, Dumitru   b.10/26/42   Teacher (sports)
"I studied in Bucharest. In Piatra Neamt, I worked first as a trainer, then as a teacher. I am married. My wife teaches mathematics."
- Str.Ecoului Bl.K15,Ap.8,Cartier Precista, Piatra Neamt ✆ (936) 12328   ✍ French, Russian
♥ skiing, football, tennis, music, dancing   ❚❚ yes
✗ board

PIETROASELE

"Wine!"

APOSTOL, Mario   b.08/13/61   Private
"Diabetes"
- Com. Pietroasele, Jud.Buzau, Pietroasele, 5172
✆ 137   ✍ English   ♥ reviews   ❚❚ yes

PITESTI

BACIOIU, Ion   b. 02/22/66   Electrician
"I work in a plant of drinkable water. I am not married and live with my parents. I am a nice fellow and I desire to make acquaintances."
- Str.Craiovei,Bl.19,Sc.B,Ap.15,Jud.Arges, Pitesti, 0300 ✆ (976) 40254   ✍ English, French (a little), Bulgarian (a little)   ♥ football, other sports, music
❚❚ yes

GHEORGHE, Florin   b.06/15/59   Engineer
"I was born in Constanta. Now, I am living in Pitesti and working in a centre of research in horticulture. I an not married."
- Str.Negru-Voda,Bl.E2,Sc.C, Pitesti, 0300 ✆ (976) 39526   ✍ English, French   ♥ flowers, travelling, cars and driving   ❚❚ yes   ✗ guide, car

PITESTI

GIONEA, Petruta   b.07/29/55   Schoolmaster
"My husband is a chemist technician. We have two sons : Marius (11) and Ovidiu (8). We invite you to visit us."
· Str.Prundu,Bl.B5A,Sc.C,Ap.5,Jud.Arges, Pitesti
✆ (976) 48620 ✍ French ♥ tourism, sports, philately, music ‖ yes

IVAN, Gabriel   b. 08/26/76   Pupil
"Height:1.68m. I am brown eyed. I learn good. I have many friends. I have a 15 years old sister called Adina."
· Str.Exercitiu,Bl.A8,Sc.C,Ap.11,Jud.Arges, Pitesti, 0300 ✆ (976) 23769 ✍ French ♥ music, reading, sports ‖ yes

NEACSU, Cristian (CRIC)   b.08/25/61   Painter and cartoonist
"Since 1987 I took part in more than 40 exhibitions. In Pitesti I had 5 personal exhibitions. In 1989 I was present in France with my paintings in February and with my caricatures in September."
· Str.Craiovei,Bl.53,Sc.A,Ap.31, Pitesti, 0300
✆ (976) 33059 ✍ French, English ♥ painting and art in general, cartooning, travelling ‖ yes

NITULESCU, Monica   b.08/22/66   Student
"I study medicine."
· Bd.Republicii,Bl.D6,Sc.A,Ap.8, Pitesti, 0300
✆ (976) 33021 ✍ French ♥ the French language, music, reading, sports, travelling ‖ yes

POPOV, Mircea Dorin   b.01/27/46   Engineer
"I studied physics at the University in Bucharest. I am chief of a research team studying the radiated nuclear fuel. I have been married since 1977 and have two daughters aged 10 and 12. My wife works as medical assistant."
· Cartier Gavana III,Bl.B7,Sc.B1,Ap.7, Pitesti, 0300 ✆ (976) 84051 ✍ French, English, Russian ♥ books, computer games, tourism, philately ‖ yes ✗ board

STEFANESCU, Gheorghe   b.04/23/40   Veterinarian doctor
"I work as a veterinarian doctor in the agricultural sector. Between 1981-1983 I was in Somalia, working

for a Romanian-Somalese project. I am married and I have two daughters, aged 21 and 16."

· Cartier Trivale,Bl.63,Sc.A,Ap.7,Jud.Arges, Pitesti, 0300 ✆ (976) 27276 ✍ Italian, French ♥ tennis, swimming, foreign languages, painting, classical music ∎ yes

TATU, Luana b. 05/14/75 Pupil

"I am 15 years old and attend the tenth form at a high school in my town. I want to become an economist and work in the field of foreign trade."

· Str.Victoriei,Bl.A5,Ap.17,Jud.Arges, Pitesti, 0300 ✆ (976) 34024 ✍ English, French ♥ corresponding with persons all over the world ✂ postcards ∎ yes (maybe)

TEODOREANU, Alina b.08/18/64 Chemist

"I graduated from the Faculty of Pharmacy in 1988 with almost 10. I would like very much to correspond with young people all over the world."

· Bd.Republicii,Bl.D6,Sc.A1,Ap.12, Pitesti, 0300 ✆ (976) 30078 ✍ French, English ♥ travelling, reading, music, art ∎ yes

VALCEANU, Maria b.08/29/51 Teacher

"I teach in Pitesti, but I am also a journalist and a writer. My husband is a vet. We have a flat in Pitesti, a farm in the countryside, a house in the mountains. We would very much like to have friends abroad."

· Str.Cimpineanu,Bl.3,Sc.C,Ap.3, Pitesti ✆ (976) 33019 ✍ French, English ♥ literature, painting ∎ yes, during vacation ✈ trips by car

PLOIESTI

" ... highly industrialized, and therefore ugly, but is a good starting point for a trip through the Prahova valley, which is one of the most beautiful touristic areas of Romania ... "

PLOIESTI

ALEXANDRU, Cristina-Alina b.06/24/69 Electonist
"I graduated from school in 1988 and am working in a refinery."
- Str.Brumarelelor 4,Bl.130,Ap.13,Jud.Prahova, Ploiesti ✆ (971) 39748 ✍ English, French
- ♥ trips, books, fashion, cars ⚑ yes

ANTONESCU, Petre b.01/02/17 Lawyer
"I was a political prisoner between 1948 and 1955, when a military court declared me innocent. I retired in 1977."
- Sos.Stefan cel Mare 29, Ploiesti, 2000 ✆ (971) 48725 ✍ French, Italian, German (a little) ♥ tourism in the mountains ⚑ yes

CARLAN, Eugenia b.12/13/33 Economist
"My husband and I, we are both pensioners. Our only son died in a car crash in 1986, when he was 30. Our grandson, Andrei (8) lives together with his mother."
- Str.Gloriei 3,Bl.205,Sc.B,Ap.29, Ploiesti, 2000 ✆ (971) 34663 ✍ French, German (a little), Russian (husband) ♥ travelling ⚑ yes ✭ board

CHIRICA, Carmen - Tamara b.01/28/50 Teacher
"I teach Romanian and my husband teaches history (a family of teachers!). I have two children: Karina, aged 17 and Narcis, aged 16, pupils at a big highschool in Ploiesti. I wish to visit Europe with my husband. We have a hose with 5 rooms and a garden."
- Str.Romana 136, Ploiesti, 2000 ✆ (971) 23996 ✍ French, Italian ♥ history of literature, tourism, dance ⚑ yes ✭ trips over the country.

CIOBANU, Iulian b.12/23/38 Engineer - computer programmer
"Civil Building Institute in Bucharest. Activity : building sites, building design companies and since 1970, working with computers. Married to Carmen; a daughter, Dana (21) - student. I have a house in the mountains and a car."
- Str.Stefan Gheorghiu 14, Ploiesti, 2000 ✆ (971) 42276 ✍ French, English, Italian ♥ travels, music, philately, reading books and magazines, country escapades ⚑ yes

DIMA, Iulian Dimitrie b.08/03/48 Teacher
"My wife works as a clerk. I am a founder of the "Association of Human Rights" in Ploiesti. As a first aim, we want to help the orphanages, the hospitals and the asylums for old people. Any humanitarian aids wold help."
  Str.Rodica 3, Jud.Prahova, Ploiesti, 2000 © (971) 74056 ✍ French ♥ history, tourism, sports
  ‖ yes

DIMITRIU, Roman b.08/23/55 Chemist engineer
"Dimitriu Roman is also a teacher at the University in Ploiesti. His wife, Mariana is a chemistry engineer too. They have a daughter, Ioana, 10 years old, and a boy, Alexandru, 3 years old."
  Bd.Republicii 100A, Bl.11A, Ap.15, Ploiesti, 2000 © (971) 38075 ✍ English, French

DONE, Ioan and Yolanda (wife) b.06/06/50 Metallurgic engineer / Translator of French
  Intrarea Caminelor 3, Bl.27A, Ap.6, Ploiesti
  © 62015 ✍ French ♥ he : stamps, jazz, films, video, travels, she : languages, video, travels

DRAGOMOIR, Ion b.11/15/52 Foreman
"I am married and I have three children. We want to be the messengers of friendship with those who want to know Romania."
  Str.Democratiei 36, Ploiesti, 2000 ✍ French
  ♥ gardening, fishing, trips ‖ yes ☆ board

DUMITRESCU, Virgil b.01/11/53 Engineer
"I liked maths very much, because sometime people must be exact. I am not very rich, neither too poor. My richness is in my soul and in my heart. I am married. My wife Dana is 34, technician. I have not children, though I'd like to."
  Bd.Republicii 173, Bl.26A, Ap.6, Jud.Prahova, Ploiesti, 2000 © (971) 61386 ✍ English, French, Italian (a little) ♥ music of the 60's and 70's (Beatles, Pink Floyd, Rolling Stones, Led Zeppelin, Eric Clapton, B.B. King, J. Joplin), films, history, especially of WW2 ‖ yes

GOLBAN, Eugen   b.05/31/44   Economist

"Golban Eugen is an economist at a mining enterprise in Ploiesti. His wife Nina is 42. They have two sons, Dan, aged 22 who is a student and Bogdan, aged 18."

Str.Marasesti 410,Bl.13,Sc.A,Ap.14, Ploiesti, 2000 © (971) 51582 ✍ English

GRIGORAS, Ioan Dan   b.06/04/56   Engineer Assistant professor

"I received the BS and MS degrees in petroleum engineering from the Petroleum and Gas Institute of Ploiesti in 1981. Since 1987 I teach Reservoir Engineering, Reservoir Simulation, Computer Programming, Management."

Str.Milcov 6, Ploiesti, 2000 © (971) 71681 / 72423 ✍ English, French ♥ computers, modern music, audio & video equipment, travels, cars
⌂ yes ☆ breakfast

IACOB, Nicolas   b.12/05/67   Student

"I study machine building in Iasi."

Str.Negru Voda 53, Ploiesti, 2000 © (971) 43237 ✍ French, German ♥ interior design, tourism, tennis, swimming, music, cars, painting, graphic, sculpture
⌂ yes

JIANU, Alexandru
and Raluca (daughter)   b.02/13/24   Surgeon

"I am 26, unmarried, I work in a computer centre, I live with my parents. My father Jianu Alexandru, 66 years old, is a pensioner surgeon. My mother Jianu Steliana is also 66."

Bd.Republicii 100A,Bl.11A,Ap.3, Ploiesti, 2000 © (971) 36211 ✍ English, French, German

LAZAR, Iosefina   b.02/04/55   Translator

"Intellectual family (mother-teacher, father-doctor, sister-physicist). Graduated in English-French (1978). Two years of highschool teaching, then translator at a

*big plant in Ploiesti. Married; two-years-old daughter.
I also work as private interpreter."*
- Str.13 Decembrie Nr.18,Bl.G3,Ap.13, Ploiesti,
  2000 ✆ (971) 72441 ✍ English, French ♥ literature - a passionate reader of all kind of literature, curious mind ⌂ accomodation for max. two persons ☆ a modest breakfast

MAZILU, Stelian b.05/01/48 Mechanical engineer
"I am married to Christine, who is a mathematician, works in the computer industry and speaks very good French. We have a 12 years old son who loves tourism and sports. I work in an institute designing refineries."
- Str.23 August Nr.42 B,Ap.3, Ploiesti, 2000
  ✆ (971) 42848 ✍ French, English ♥ classical music, trips, basketball ⌂ yes ☆ car

MIHAIL, Mircea b.01/14/51 Chemist
"My parents are chemists; they are retired now. My brother works as a chemist engineer. I am not married."
- Str.Levantica 1,Bl.13,Ap.22,Jud.Prahova, Ploiesti,
  2000 ✆ (971) 70670 ✍ French, English (a little)
  ♥ philately, numismatics, tennis, opera, gardening, fishing, photography, tourism ⌂ yes ☆ breakfast

MINCU, Valeriu b.09/10/37 Engineer
"I was born in Radauti (Bucovina). I studied in Bucharest. Since 1962 I have been working in an institute for oil mining and refinement in Ploiesti. I travelled a lot for business and studying."
- Str.Buna Vestire 22, Ploiesti, 2000 ✆ (971)
  22816 ✍ English, German, Russian ♥ tennis, gardening, symphonic music, playing piano, bridge

MINDRU, Cicerone U.V.Test Operator
"I graduated highschool in Bucharest. I took part in the revolution in December. I am a friendly person, kind, romantic, with good manners, not married."
- Str.Baraolt 19,Bl.44,Sc.D,Ap.62,sector 7, Ploiesti,
  2000 ✍ French ♥ classic music, photo art, aquariology ⌂ yes ☆ breakfast

PLOIESTI

MOCANU, Vivianne b.01/14/58 Teacher
"*Since 1981 I am a B.A. in English and French. I work as a teacher of Foreign languages. I have a 6 years daughter who speaks English.*"
Str.Rodica 2,Sc.C,Ap.33, Ploiesti, 2000 © (971) 26655 ✍ English, French, German ♥ foreign languages, travelling ♖ yes

NEGULESCU, Raluca b.07/03/67 Student
"*I am studying medicine. I have an older brother named John. I also have a dog, a caniche, named Trixi. We love him very much. When I was 5 I went with my parents to India, in a small town called Durgakiole, near Calcutta. I stayed there two years.*"
Str.23 August Nr.71, Ploiesti, 2000 © (971) 42172 ✍ English, French ♥ chess (I play chess for 7 years and became a master). I also like travelling ♖ yes

NICOLESCU, Marian Roman b.09/13/41
  Mechanical engineer
"*I am senior design engineer in the field of petrochemical engineering. I hold a MS degree and a PhD degree in mechanical engineering. I worked abroad, mainly in Jordan. I am married and I have a child. My wife is a chemical engineer.*"
Aleea Pajurei 1,Bl.A3,Ap.7, Ploiesti, 2000 © (971) 47009 ✍ English, French ♥ trips in the mountains, swimming ♖ yes ☆ board

NITOIU, Gabriela b.07/14/68 Secretary and Data Processing Operator
"*I had the chance of getting a good, serious and profound education despite of the conditions offered by our society; my father was an economist skilled in foreign trade and my mother is a Bachelor of Arts. I live with my mother.*"
Str.Lapusna 8, Bl.31-H,Ap.15, Ploiesti, 2000 © (971) 44192 ✍ English, French, Italian ♥ music, literature, movies, travels ♖ yes

PARASCHIVOIU, Marius b.07/10/67 Student
"*Between 1977 and 1981 I was a football player at "Petrolul" Ploiesti. In 1985 I was admitted at the*

Faculty of Trade. Then I followed the military stage. While a student I was a member in our paper's editorial stuff. I will graduate this autumn."
- Str.Brumarelelor 5, Bl.122, Sc.G, Ap.122, Jud. Prahova, Ploiesti, 2000 © (971) 31366 ✍ English, Spanish ♥ philately, sports (table tennis, football, swimming), literature, music, mountain trips ‖ no

POPESCU, Cristian   b.06/17/60   Designer
"I am married and I have a beautiful girl 3 years old. I graduated an arts school and I do a lot of caricatures, paintings, design, sculptures."
- Sos.Nordului 11, Bl.101, Ap.69, Ploiesti, 2000 © (971) 30244 ✍ French, English ♥ arts ‖ yes ☆ bed and breakfast

POPESCU, Daniela   b.11/30/45   French teacher
"My husband teaches sports. We have no kids. We'd like to exchange accommodation with a middle aged couple, a serious family, intellectuals who speak French."
- Str.Gh.Dimitrov 12, Bl.85, Sc.B, Ap.16, Ploiesti, 2000 © (971) 56692 ✍ French, English (a little) ♥ we like to travel (me and my husband). I like the finesse of people, their good sense and education, music (opera, ballet), theater, sport ‖ yes, in exchange ☆ board

POPESCU, Dumitru   b.03/21/39   Mechanical engineer
"I graduated from the Polytechnical Institute in Bucharest. I work in a Design Institute. I was a lot abroad, on business and travelling. I have two sons, both studying to become engineers."
- Str.Traian Vuia 16, Ploiesti, 2000 © (971) 20934 ✍ English, French ♥ classic music ✄ stamps ‖ yes ☆ breakfast

POPESCU, Valeriu   b.08/17/32   Economist
"I am married; we have two children."
- Str.Maramures 9, Jud.Prahova, Ploiesti, 2000 © (971) 22542 ✍ French ♥ tennis, rugby, voyages, museums, tourism, music, flowers, opera ‖ yes

PLOIESTI

PUSCASU, Daniel - Robert   b.08/04/67   Student

"I was born in Ploiesti. My father is from Iasi and my mother from Tirgoviste. I will finish Electronic engineering studies next year (1991)."

Ansamblul Eroilor,Bl.15G,Sc.A,Ap.5,Jud.Prahova, Ploiesti, 2000 ✍ English ♥ I am captivated by flying, almost impossible to do in Romania. However, I made 13.5 hours of piloting, computers, music, girls ♊ yes

RADU, Daniela   b.02/13/90   Chemist

"I am a modest woman. I am not married. I'd like to meet many men from all over the world."

Piata 16 Februarie, Bl.A EST,Sc.B,Ap.23, Ploiesti, 2000 ✆ (971) 42603 ✍ French, English ♥ voyages ♊ yes ☆ breakfast

RIZEA, Coralia   b.01/12/38   Teacher

"I teach Romanian language and literature. I learn English by myself. I am married. I have a daughter, Roxana, married, and a son, Liviu, a student in Timisoara."

Str.Tirnave 1,Bl.A,Sc.A,Ap.15,Jud.Prahova, Ploiesti ✆ (971) 37970 ✍ French, Russian ♥ folk music and dance ♊ yes

ROSU, Mihai   b.   04/23/55   Worker

"I was born in the town I live. I graduated from a vocational school. I have been working since I was 18. I married when I was 27 and in 1988 my only daughter was born."

Str.Tirgsor 1,Bl.79,Sc.A,Ap.14, Ploiesti, 2000 ✍ French, English (a little), Italian (a little) ♥ sports, electronics, painting, I love culture, science and religion (literature, music, philosophy, thanatology, history, of religion) ♊ yes ☆ board, taking care of a small child

SACAGIU, Sorin   b.03/17/74   Student
 Str.Gloriei 3A,Bl.25,Ap.12,Jud.Prahova, Ploiesti, 2000 ✆ (971) 32468 ✍ English ♥ listening to music, especially the Beatles; also New Wave, Disco, Reggae: New Kids on the Block, Prince, Janet Jackson, Paula Abdul, Bobby Brown, Phil Collins, Bad English, Bros, Kylie Minogue, The Sundays, Roxett, Sinead O'Conner, Fine Young Cannibals, Gloria Estefan; sound equipment, sports (football, tennis, basketball), science, literature ♖ yes

SARIU, Costin   b. 05/06/62   Mechanical engineer
"I was born in Ploiesti and I live here. I studied in Timisoara and Bucharest. I work in the design department of a plant producing equipment for the chemical industry."
 Str.23 August Nr.183, Ploiesti, 2000 ✆ (971) 57424 ✍ English, Russian, French ♥ skating, skiing, tennis, table tennis, dancing, mountain trips, miniature sculpture ♖ yes ✯ board

SAVULESCU, Daniel   b.11/17/61   Engineer
"I am married and I have a little daughter. Both me and my wife are engineers in oil industry and we want to live in peace and to visit a lot of countries."
 Str.Carpati 1,Bl.33F,Ap.27, Ploiesti, 2000 ✆ (971) 41267 ✍ English, French ♥ sports (football, swimming, tennis), climbing mountains, seeing the world ♖ yes, on the Prahova Valley too (Azuga)

SIRBU, Carmen - Adella   b.10/23/64   Physician
"I am married. My husband, Octavian, is a doctor too. We are waiting a baby this year."
 Str.Cercelus 13, Ploiesti, 2000 ✆ (971) 25037 ✍ French, English ♥ music, swimming, voyages ♖ yes ✯ board

TERECOASA, Cornelia   b.11/03/65   Engineer
"Sometimes I enjoy housekeeping."
 Str.Bobilna 95,Bl.A4,Ap.25,Jud.Prahova, Ploiesti ✆ (971) 23056 ✍ English, French ♥ dancing, badminton, swimming

TRENTEA, Alexandru b.11/23/58 Technician
"Meet my family: Florentina, my wife, 32, secretary; Sebastian, my son, 5 1/2; Corina, my daughter, 4. I work in "The large size bearings factory" in my town. I was born in Ploiesti. This town has 250,000 inhabitants and is 60 Km far from Bucharest."
Str.23 August 191.Bl.150D.Ap.3,Jud.Prahova, Ploiesti, 2000 © (971) 88559 ✍ English, French (a little) ♥ fishing, SF literature (Asimov, Arkadi & Boris Strugatski, Arthur C. Clarke, George R.R. Martin, Robert Sheckley, Herbert Franke, Philip K. Dick, Gerard Klein, Jean-Pierre Andrevon) ☗ yes

TROCARU, Adina b.09/17/69 Student in medicine
"Born at 9 months, grew up in happiness (1.70/62), looking for love of life. I have a collection of odd paintings (1900) in oil and a collection of Romanian stamps. I have a brother aged 22, student, interested in almost everything."
Str.Rudului 47, Ploiesti, 2000 © (971) 41568 ✍ English, French ♥ music (I studied piano), tennis, yoga, art, nature, astrology, psychoanalysis, parapsychology, Ikebana ✂ Romanian stamps, old paintings. ☗ yes

TUDOR, Monika b.08/22/67 Computer Scientist
"I married in March 1989; I gave birth to a girl, named Diana, in November 1989. This summer I divorced her father. Diana is staying with my grandmother. I live with my parents in a 5 rooms flat."
Str.C.D.Gherea 2C,Bl.A,Sc.A,Ap.24, Ploiesti, 2000 © (971) 41058 ✍ English, French, Italian (a little) ♥ dancing, listening to music ☗ yes

POIENI

" A nice village surrounded by hills and a forest, 26km from Iasi. One can meet here the Romanian peasant, known for his hospitality. Come and be enchanted by the beauty of the place. "

OLARU, Rictar   b.06/01/55   bookkeeper

"*I am married. My wife's name is Emilia. She is 32. We have two children: Claudiu-Adrian who is 3 and Claudia-Alexandra who is 1.*"

⁃ satul Poieni, comuna Schitu-Duca, Jud.Iasi, Poieni ✆ (981) 15 ✍ French ♥ gardening, football, music, dance ■ yes

PREDEAL

TRIPA, Ana Maria   b.10/20/65   Student

"*I was born in Oradea. I study medicine in Bucharest. I visited Bulgaria, Lybia, Malta, Italy, Austria, Hungary, Germany and France. In December 1989, I took part in the Revolution.*"

⁃ Str.Dimitrie Cantemir 2, Predeal ✆ (922) 56836 ✍ English, Hungarian ♥ tennis, swimming, skiing, art, cinema, theatre, literature, music ■ yes ✗ breakfast

PRISACA

" *... for those who love living in the countryside ...*"

TITARU, Maricela   b.01/16/55   Teacher (Romanian)

"*I studied Romanian language at the University in Iasi. My parents live in Bacau. I left the town and moved to Prisaca, where my husband had built a house. He is a bus driver. We have three children : Andy (8), Victor (6), Xenia (4).*"

⁃ satul Prisaca,comuna Beresti-Tazlau,Jud.Bacau, Prisaca ✆ 159 ✍ French ■ yes, for 1-2 families ✗ board, suggestions for trips

PUCIOASA

CIRSTOIU, Mihaela   b.02/27/76   Pupil

"*I am a pupil in the 9th form at the highschool in my town. My parents are engineers. I have a sister aged 10.*

I live with my family. I want to correspond in English with someone the same age (14) as me."
- Str.Republicii,Bl.B2,Ap.11, Pucioasa, 0275
- ✆ (927) 60682 ✍ English, French ♥ films, theater, books, music (pop, disco, classical), sports, tennis, skiing, swimming, watching football

RIMNICU-VILCEA

" ... a health-resort, with a partk, theatre, and cinema ..."

BERCEANU, Lucian - Victor   b.05/14/23   Teacher (retired)

"I was born in Bucharest, son of an important statesman. I studied piloting planes and worked as an instructor in 1951-53; took part in WW2; Auto Technic School 2 years; Pedagogic Institute 3 years; coach for aeromdelism, counselor at Sports Department."
- Str.Cozia,Bl.C6,Sc.B,Ap.7, Rimnicu-Vilcea, 1000
- ✆ (947) 19895 ✍ French, German ♥ aviation (I am an ex-glider and plane pilot), aeromodels (ex-champion), driving my Simca 1100 ♖ yes ☆ board

FLORESCU, Teodor   b.08/04/28   School master and engineer

"I studied in Corabia, Sibiu, Deva and Iasi. I was not member of the Communist Party. My father is a priest, 84 years old now. My wife is a chemical engineer. We own a nice house near the resort Caciulata-Calimanesti. We have no children."
- Str.7 Noiembrie,Bl.16,Sc.A,Ap.12,Cartierul Nord, Rimnicu-Vilcea, 1000 ✆ (947) 18199 ✍ French, Italian, Esperanto ♥ cycling, photography, chess, trips in the mountains ♖ yes

FUMURU, Ana Maria   b.09/10/77   Pupil

"I am 12. I am a pupil on the 7th form. I live in a beautiful house."
- Str.30 Decembrie 14, Rimnicu-Vilcea, 1000
- ✆ (947) 16672 ✍ English ♥ music, tennis and football ✂ stamps ♖ yes

GANESCU, Horia-Manuel b.01/31/64 Teacher of English and French

"I am a bachelor and I have neither brothers nor sisters. I studied piano since the age of 4 and wanted to become a concert pianist, but my parents didn't let me. At the age of 23 I graduated from the University of Bucharest (Bachelor degree in English)."

 Str.Rapsodiei 1,Sc.B,Ap.5, Rimnicu-Vilcea, 1000 ✆ (947) 13148 ✍ English, French ♥ classical music, reading, travelling, sports ✂ postcards ⌂ yes (I have 4 rooms) ✰ board

IRIMESCU, Dalila b.08/10/51 Teacher

"I was born in Rimnicu-Vilcea. I graduated from University in 1974 in Timisoara. I teach French in a secondary school. My husband is a teacher too. We have a seven years old daughter. We live in a workers' district."

 Bd.Tineretului 2,Bl.B1,Sc.A,Ap.26,Ostroveni 5, Rimnicu-Vilcea ✆ (947) 28486 ✍ French, English ♥ symphonic music, reading, travelling by foot ✂ postcards ⌂ yes (modest)

ONEATA, Costel b.05/12/62 Engineer

"I did not exist between 05.12.62 and 12.21.89. I hope to live from now on."

 Str.13 Decembrie,Bl.S7/3,Sc.A,Ap.10,Jud.Vilcea, Rimnicu-Vilcea, 1000 ✍ English ♥ symphonic music (Tchikowsky), progressive rock (Tangerine Dream, E.L.& P., Yes, Vangelis) ⌂ yes, also in Stoienesti, village nearby

RISNOV

> *" ... a roman citadel and a mediaeval citadel ... a monastery from the 12th century ..."*

DENDIU, Dan b. 09/05/60 graphician

"I graduated the high school of Arts and a technical school, and obtained a diploma of technician cartog-

rapher. I live in a house with my grand-parents in Risnov. I am a bachelor."
· Sos.Branului 25 ,Jud.Brasov, Risnov, 2221
✍ French ♥ philosophy, literature, history, astrology, religion, esoteric medicine, travelling ♨ yes ✗ bed and breakfast but only in Spring,Summer,Fall

PAPP, George   b. 11/19/54   Mechanic
"I am married and have two children in high school."
· Str.Nicolae Balcescu 10, Risnov, 2221 ✍ French, English ♥ I love poetry, I read and write much: I was even published ♨ yes ✗ breakfast

TERCIU, Olimpia   b.02/10/58   Postal agent
"I am married and have two kids."
· Str.Florilor 59, Risnov, 2221 ✍ French ♥ trips in the mountains, embroidery ♨ yes, in the mountains too (Pestera) ✗ breakfast

TUDOR, Mihaela - Georgiana   b.08/18/72   Chemist
"I would like to correspond with a young man aged between 18 and 25."
· Str.Eroilor 5 ,Jud.Brasov, Risnov, 2221 ✍ English, French, German ♥ fashion magazines, novels ♨ no

ROMAN

" ... in the middle of the Moldavia region, with the monasteries it is famous for ..."

BUBURUZAN, Gheorghe
and Maria (wife)   b.11/30/50   Physician / Dentist
"I studied medicine in Iasi and my wife in Cluj. We have two children : a son - Octavian and a daughter - Aurora, both pupils. Allow me to invite you to visit our beautiful country."
· Str.Smirodava,Bl.8 ,Ap.12 ,Jud.Neamt, Roman, 5550 ✆ (937) 21085 ✍ French, Russian, Hungarian ♥ fresh air, symphonic and religious music, tennis, trips in the mountains, photography ♨ yes ✗ breakfast

CORDUNEANU, Dana Engineer

"*I was born in 1956. My husband is the same age and is an engineer too. We have an eight-year-old son - Andrei.*"

Str.Smirodava 22/5, Roman, 5550 ⓒ (937) 21677 ✍ French ♥ literature, film, theatre, sports, travelling ∎ yes

GUSETU, Christian b.01/14/60 Engineer

"*I am not married (1,80m/83kg). My parents are intellectuals : my mother is a teacher and my father is an economist. Since 1985, when I graduated, I have been working at 'PETRO-TUB' Roman as an engineer.*"

Str.Nic.Titulescu 15/14, Jud.Neamt, Roman, 5550 ⓒ (937) 43865 ✍ English ♥ cycling, swimming, dancing, skiing ∎ yes ☆ bed and breakfast for max. 2 persons

SAG

> "*My village is 6km away from Timisoara. It is an old village of German origin.*"

BARAGAN, Costel b.06/21/61 Electrician

"*I was born here. I studied in Timisoara. I work at the "Bumbacul" factory (the cotton).*"

Str.II Nr.34, Jud.Timis, Sag, 1920 ⓒ 179 ✍ Italian, English, French ♥ tennis, table tennis, music ∎ yes

SATU MARE

> "*We have the highest building in the country, and a swimming pool with thermal waters.*"

REIT, Adriana   b. 03/14/61   Building engineer
"Height : 1.64m. Weight : 59kg. I work for a building company here in Satu Mare."
⁙ Micro 16, Brindusa G26/15, Satu Mare, 3900
✆ (997) 48273 ✍ English, Hungarian ♥ modern architecture (Japan), electronic music, abstract literature, Gershwin ☗ yes

Sebes

BARBONTA, Cristian and Diana (wife)   b.01/20/65
   Physician; Physician (wife)
"I was born in Oradea and graduated University in Cluj. Here I met Diana and got married after 2 years. We work in a hospital in Sebes. My parents are also doctors. We live in a nice house with a garden. We also have a weekend house. We have no kids yet."
⁙ Str.Calarasi 50,Jud.Alba, Sebes ✆ (967) 31754
✍ French, English, Hungarian, wife: English,
♥ tennis, skiing, basketball, music (opera, jazz, pop). wife: literature, theatre, painting, fashion, classical music, cinema (documentaries, comedies) ☗ yes

FARCASIU, Alexandru   b.07/28/50   Technician (car mechanic)
"I am married and I have two daughters, 15 and 13 years old. They both speak very good German."
⁙ Str.Spitalului 28,Jud.Alba, Sebes, 2475 ✍ English, German ♥ travelling, exchanging information, working in the garden and on the house ☗ yes. In Sebes and 25 Km away in my chalet ✰ complete accomodation.

Sfintu Gheorghe

" Whisky drinkers should taste 'palinca'."

KOCS, Janos   b.   03/21/56   Engineer
"I am married. My wife studied biology. We have two children ages 4 and 10. We are Szeklers, that is Hungarians from the east of Transylvania. We would like to

travel. We correspond with friends from Europe, Africa, Asia."

· Bd.Muncii 59,Bl.10,Sc.F,Ap.26,Jud.Covasna, Sfintu Gheorghe, 4000 ✆ (923) 21648 ✍ Hungarian, Romanian, English, Russian ♥ electronics, rock music, trips, photography, literature ✂ insects ⌂ yes ✯ board

NAGY, Lenke-Maria b.07/29/33 Notary
"My husband is a judge. We are both retired now. We have a son, physician, who also speaks a lot of foreign languages."

· Str.7 Noiembrie 2,Bl.3,Sc.G,Ap.20,Jud.Covasna, Sfintu Gheorghe, 4000 ✆ (923) 11510 ✍ French, Italian, English ♥ arts, fishing, trips, my husband loves hunting ⌂ yes, no food

SIBIU

> *" ... many tourist attractions: the Brukenthal Museum, the ancient salt mines of Ocna Sibului, the resort of Paltinis ... the museum of popular culture ... "*

BANCIU, Anca b. 11/30/57 Computer engineer
"My parents are pensioners. I have no brothers or sisters. I graduated from the Polytechnical Institute "Traian Vuia" in Timisoara. Now, I am working in hardware and software service. My firm is called "Magic Computer"."

· Str.Aleea Taberei 5,Bl.P22,Ap.4, Sibiu, 2400 ✆ (924) 46084 ✍ English ♥ excursions ⌂ yes ✯ board

BLAG, Petru b. 01/01/47 Engineer
"I was born in Zlatna, in a mountainous region. In 1970 I graduated from the Polytechnical Institute in Bucharest. My wife is 40 years old and works in a hospital. We have a 14-year-old son."

· Str.Gradinarilor 7, Sibiu, 2400 ✆ (924) 12025 ✍ German, French ♥ walking, tennis, gardening ⌂ yes

SIBIU

BUCUR, Simona b.05/24/63 Economist
- Str.Moldovei 32, Sibiu, 2400 ✆ (924) 48931
- ✍ German, English ♥ romantic music, sports, fashion, knitting, knowing different people ⦀ yes, for one person, after exchanging letters

CUPRIAN, Aurora Clerk
"I am 39 years old and my husband is 42 years old."
- Str.Mihai Viteazul 25, Sibiu ✆ (924) 26525
- ✍ French ♥ music, travelling, everything new and interesting ⦀ yes

GIURCULETE, Sorin b.01/30/66 Engineer
"I graduated the Faculty of Mechanics in Brasov. I work in a research institute. I am not married."
- Str.Lily Paneth 31, Sibiu, 2400 ✆ (924) 34035
- ✍ English ♥ photography. I am a good photographer. I made short short films about people's lives ⦀ yes
- ☆ bed and dinner

IORDACHE, Dan b.02/08/56 Teacher for English and History
"I worked as a teacher 1982-1990. Starting 21 December 1989 - "freelance" photojournalist; at present - photojournalist at "CONTINENT" magazine Sibiu. Short and plump. Beard. Generally good humored and tolerant. Married. 3 children and want more."
- Str.Negoi 76 C, Sibiu, 2400 ✆ (924) 32412
- ✍ English, French, Italian (a little) ♥ photography, painting and graphics, good science fiction, Anglo-Saxon and French literature, travels, handicrafts ⦀ yes, up to 5 pers, at my parents' house too
- ☆ board

ISTRATE, Corina b.08/26/56 Teacher
"I teach French and English."
- Str.Rahovei,Bl.8,Sc.B,Ap.38, Sibiu, 2400 ✆ (924) 22823 ✍ French, English ♥ music, reading, swimming, travelling ⦀ yes

LUPEAN, Olimpiu b.10/30/66 Student
"My father is a biology teacher and my mother teaches physics. I studied in Timisoara at the Polytechnical

Institute between 1986-1989. I quit to go to Cluj for studying economic sciences. Not married."
· Str.Pedagogilor 8, Sibiu, 2400 © (924) 11059 ✍ French, English, Italian ♥ literature, music, sports (ski, tennis, jogging), martial arts, oriental cultures (China, Japan), voyages, the sea, the sun, the mountains, dancing, animals, cinema ▌ yes ✭ breakfast

MARGINEAN, Ioan b.06/23/60 Physician
"I graduated the Medicine Institute in Cluj-Napopca. I am married and I have a child."
· Str.dr.I.Ratiu 5, Sibiu, 2400 © (924) 17861 ✍ English, French, German ♥ electronic music, skiing, computers, tourism ▌ yes, I have a house and a chalet. ✭ bed and breakfast

OLARIU, Constantin b.12/09/32 Engineer
"I am retired. I am married and have two children : a daughter (married) and a son. I find much pleasure in travelling and in meeting people."
· Str.Prof. Petru Spair 20, Sibiu, 2400 © (924) 23114 ✍ German, French, Russian ♥ football, basket, postcards ✂ postcards ▌ yes

PASCANU, Valer b.05/29/52 Engineer
"I have been working at the "Balanta" factory for 15 years. My wife works as a technician at the same factory. We have two children : Adina (13) and Calin (11). I know that not speaking well foreign languages is a handicap for me."
· Str.Poiana 2,Bl.43,Ap.13, Sibiu, 2400 © (924) 82186 ✍ Hungarian (a little), Russian (a little) ♥ I would like to work abroad ▌ yes, for a person

POP, Eugen b. 03/01/51 Physicien
"I finished the University of Cluj in 1975 and work in a factory that produces parts for automobiles, in Sibiu. I am married (my wife is an economist, born 1956) and have two boys, born 1984 and 1985."
· Str.G.Alexandrescu 6C, Sibiu, 2400 © (924) 28692 ✍ French, German, English ♥ gardening, jazz and symphonic music, trips in the mountains ▌ yes ✭ board

POPA, Liviu Rossano b.04/08/54 Clerk

"*I was born in Sibiu. I am married and have a child aged 6. I work as clerk in administration. My wife is 33. She also speaks French and English.*"

Str.Strandului 10,Ap.22, Sibiu, 2400 © (924) 11919 ✍ French ♥ literature, pop music, rock, reggae, dance ∎ yes

POTOLEA, Constantin b.05/30/34 Engineer

"*I was born in Galati. I studied at a military secondary school in Predeal, then the artillery school in Sibiu and the technic academy of engineers in U.S.S.R. I lived in Sibiu for 27 years.*"

Str.Lomonosov,Bl.2A,Ap.5, Sibiu, 2400 © (924) 27401 ✍ Russian, French, German ♥ beekeeping. I am a beekeeper for 15 years, sculpture ∎ yes ☆ board (in exchange or payed)

RADU, Daniela b.09/12/68 Student

"*I am student at the Faculty of Economic Cybernetics in Bucharest and in the same time I work as a clerk in a factory in Sibiu. I live with my mother in a very nice house, with a big yard and a nice garden.*"

Str.Traian Demetrescu 110, Sibiu, 2400 © (924) 34841 ✍ English, French ♥ astronomy, SF movies ∎ yes ☆ board

SANDRU, Bucur b.12/22/53 Trade and advertising

Str.Rahovei 18,Sc.II,Ap.30, Sibiu © (924) 24454 ✍ German, French ♥ cars, painting, music ∎ yes

SARLEA, Paul b. 04/15/63 Engineer

"*I am 1.93 m tall and weigh 85 Kg. I have two children.*"

Str.Baicoi 6, Sibiu, 2400 © (924) 33321 ✍ English, French (a little) ♥ sports, books, logic games, yoga

SAUCHEA, Constantin and Maria b.01/06/48 Clerks

Str.Mihai Viteazu,Bl.11,Ap.104, Sibiu © (924) 22190 ✍ German, English ♥ we like to have trips, parties and we are interested in new ∎ yes

SIMU, Cristina Maria b.03/29/53 Painting teacher

"*I am a drawing teacher and I organized some of my pupils in an art and literature circle called "Petals of Clearness"."*

- Str.Progresului 26, Sibiu, 2400 © (924) 31624 ✍ English ♥ flowers, nature, car, bicycle, painting, systems of education ∎ yes in Sibiu and in Sibiel ⭐ guide

TRITEAN, Sanda-Teodora b.06/11/71 Student

"*The names of my parents are Ioan and Mariana. I attended the courses of the German school and high school. Since 1990 I study Informatics at the University in Timisoara.*"

- Str.Manejului 4, Sibiu, 2400 © (924) 32653 ✍ German, English ♥ skiing, listening to music (Bruce Springsteen), dancing, travelling, knowing everything about foreign countries ∎ yes

VACARESCU, Lucian b.08/23/64 Engineer

"*I was born in a village where Germans lived and learned a little German from them. We moved then to town. I studied machine building in Sibiu and work in a plant as an engineer. I am married.*"

- Aleea Rosiorilor,Bl.1 ,Ap.25, Sibiu, 2400 © (924) 27857 ✍ French, German ♥ sports, music, travelling ∎ yes, for a short period of time

SIGHETU MARMATIEI

KOMAROMI-GHEORGHE, Rodica b.12/01/53 Teacher
- Str.Mihai Viteazul 27, Sighetu Marmatiei, 4925 © (995) 13084 ✍ French, English ∎ yes

SIGHISOARA

BARBU, Christian and Camelia   b.11/28/64   Electronic engineer / Economist

"*Camelia was born september 23 1966.*"

- Str.Mihai Eminescu 59, Jud.Mures, Sighisoara, 3050 © (950) 71576 ✉ English, French, German ♥ trips, parties, music, science ■ yes ☆ breakfast

MUNTEANU, Sorin and Mariana (wife)   Retired

"*We are retired. We want to rent our house for 30 days on these conditions: payment in US$ or DM; The house has furniture, two rooms, bathroom, kitchen; garden and garage.*"

- Str.Gheorghiu Dej 67, Sighisoara, 3050 © (950) 73866 ✉ Italian, German, Hungarian ♥ gardening ■ yes, only in conditions mentioned above.

SUCIU PETRU, Catalin   b.05/30/70   Worker

"*I learned German as a child. I work in a shirt factory in my town. I would be happy to offer accomodation.*"

- Str.Mihai Viteazu 21, Sighisoara, 3050 © (950) 73922 ✉ German ♥ reading, swimming, music, walking in the woods, meeting new friends ■ yes, in a five room house ☆ board

SINAIA

" ... *in the mountains of Bucegi, 130km from Bucharest ... the castles of Peles and Pelisor, where the king of Romania used to live ... called the 'Pearl of the Carpathians', one can go skiing in winter ... not far from Dracula's castle.*"

CLUCERESCU, Ioana   b.12/23/59   Engineer in wood working

"*I am 30. I live in a small town with my parents. I am not married and I like to have friends. I like the nature,*

the animals, the good music and I like very much to travel."
- Str.23 August Nr.8, Sinaia, 2180 © (973) 14491 ✍ French, English, Italian (a little) ♥ old music, tennis, skiing, other sports, travelling ❚❚ yes ✰ I can drive the car and be a good guide.

IORDANOVICI, Cezar and Rica (wife) b.01/30/18 Chemist
"I have been speaking French since childhood. I am retired now and live in a flat together with my wife."
- Str.Badea Cirtan 15, Sinaia, 2180 ✍ French ♥ tourism, climbing ❚❚ yes ✰ board

SERBULEA, Magda-Adriana b.08/15/38 Doctor
"Married, my husband is a magistrate."
- Str.Alexandru Vlahuta 1, Sinaia, 2180 © (973) 11532 ✍ French, Italian, English ♥ literature, poetry, tourism, Scrabble, cards, dice ❚❚ yes ✰ bed & breakfast

SINNICOLAU-MARE

VASS, Mariana Carmen b.09/11/62 Teacher (English)
"My husband is an engineer. I teach English. We have a two years old daughter - Alexandra Sorina. We live in a house with a garden, 62 km away from Timisoara."
- Str.Victor Babes 15 Jud.Timis, Sinnicolau-Mare, 1976 ✍ English, French, Italian ♥ film directing, journalism, theatre, music, astrology, flowers, children ✂ stamps, paper napkins ❚❚ yes

SLATINA

CIUCU, Sylvie b. 09/20/59 Economist
"I am married and have two children. My husband is 37 and works in a state enterprise as chief accountant."
- Bd.N.Titulescu,Bl.4,Ap.1,Jud.Olt, Slatina, 0500 © (944) 21663 ✍ French, English (a little) ♥ voyages, reading, knitting, cooking, music ❚❚ yes ✰ board

NICOLAINA, Ligia   b.06/22/73   Pupil
"height: 1.70 m; eyes: chestnut; hair: blond-chestnut. Favourite colours: blue, red, black. I wish to live my life with intensity and discover a great love."
· Bd.A.I.Cuza 20,Bl.GA16,Ap.8,Jud.Olt, Slatina, 0500 ✆ (944) 17921 ✍ French, English ♥ sports (tennis and skiing), dance, rock music (Bros, Bon Jovi, Madonna), SF literature ▮▮ yes ✗ board

TASCU-STAVRE, Iulian   b.11/09/33   Chemist
"I graduated from faculty in 1960 in Cluj. I work as a toxicologist. My wife teaches physics in a high school. I have a 24 year old daughter who graduated from the faculty of physics and a 21 year old son who is a student at the Polytechnical Institute."
· Str.Ionascu 16,Jud.Olt, Slatina, 0500 ✆ (944) 21953 ✍ French ♥ tourism, fishing, vine-growing ▮▮ yes, even for 2 families ✗ board

STRIMTURA

LIHET, Dumitru   Schoolmaster
· Strimtura 368,Jud.Maramures, Strimtura, 4934 ✍ French ♥ history, literature, folklore, sports, arts ▮▮ yes

SUCEAVA

" ... a starting point for visits to the monasteries Voronet, Sucevita, Moldovita, Humor, with famous interior and exterior paintings ... "

BELDEANU, Razvan   b.11/04/67   Veterinary technician
· Str.I.Gramada 5,Bl.B1,Sc.B,Ap.1, Suceava, 5800 ✆ (987) 13834 ✍ English ♥ picture, design, tennis, music, cars, wolf-dogs ▮▮ yes ✗ breakfast

GORCEA, Constantin b.06/04/59 Architect

"*I studied in Suceava and Bucharest, I am married and have a son.*"

∴ Str.Rulmentului 2,Bl.44,Sc.C,Ap.8, Suceava, 5800
✆ (987) 28837 ✍ French, English ♥ arts, philosophy
🛏 yes ✖ breakfast

ILIESCU, Mihaela b.11/08/60 English and French teacher

"*Beginning with 1984, the year when I graduated in Iasi, I taught English and French in highschools in Suceava. Since 1989 I've been working in the Library of our city. I have a guide license and accompanied groups of Romanian tourists abroad.*"

∴ Str.Vasile Bumbac 16,Ap.4, Suceava ✆ (987) 17113 ✍ English, French ♥ tourism 🛏 yes
✖ trips by car

MUSTEATA, Catalina b.03/06/68 Student at the Polytechnical Institute in Bucharest

"*I am born in Suceava. I am 1.58 m tall and weigh 58 Kg and I am very pretty. I have a married brother. My mother is dead. In the holidays I live at my father in Suceava. In term time I live in Bucharest in the student hostel.*"

∴ Str.Alexandru cel Bun 24,Bl.H3,Ap.9,Jud.Suceava, Suceava, 5800
✆ (987) 11115 ✍ English, French ♥ chamber music, books, dancing, skating, cooking 🛏 yes. In Suceava only on holidays.

TG-JIU

"*... the birthplace of Brancusi is in Hobita, 25km from Tg-Jiu ...*"

BLEJAN, Carmen Amelia b.05/10/62 Engineer

"*I am an aeronautic engineer. My father was an engineer (retired), my mother is a teacher. My brother, aged 24, is a student. I was born in Tg-Jiu, but after graduating from the Polytechnical Institute in Bucharest I moved to Craiova, 100 Km from Tg-Jiu."*

✎ Str.8 Mai Nr.6, Tg-Jiu, 1400 ✆ (941) 80435 (work: 929/11375) ✍ English, French ♥ gardening, swimming, travelling, meeting people ∎ yes

ISTRATIE, Claudia-Veronica b.11/01/74 Pupil

"My father -Emil- is a technician, my mother -Dorina- is a telegraph operator, my little sister Emilia is a pupil at the gymnasium and me, I am in the secondary school. I like very much to travel and to meet a lot of people. I also like English."

✎ Bd.Republicii ,Bl.4,Ap.9,Sc.1, Tg-Jiu, 1400 ✆ 16515 ✍ English ♥ music, dance ∎ yes

TALOI, Gabriela b.05/14/75 Pupil

"I was born in Tg-Jiu. My father is an engineer, my mother is a clerk and I have a 16 years old sister who is in high school. I am in high school myself. I love travelling and the French language, which I hope I'll improve."

✎ Str.Timis 63B, Tg-Jiu, 1400 ✆ (941) 18360 ✍ French ♥ dancing ∎ yes

TG.BUJOR

DUMITRACHE, Mirela b.02/10/68 Teacher

"I teach chemistry and physics in a secondary school. I am dark haired and eyed and 1.68m high."

✎ Str. Morii 35 ,Jud.Galati, Tg.Bujor, 6265 ✆ (930) 40340 ✍ French ♥ tennis, dancing, music, trips ∎ yes

TG.OCNA

" The monument of the heroes at Magura, the spa Slanic Moldova.,,

MOCANU, Viorica b.04/03/49 Music teacher

"*My husband is an engineer. We have a daughter aged 15, highschool student. We live in a small town in a picturesque region in the East of Romania.*"

- Str.Tudor Vladimirescu,Bl.D8,Sc.B,Ap.18,Jud.Bacau, Tg.Ocna, 5467
- ✆ (933) 40967 ✍ French ♥ music, flowers, dancing
- ∎ yes

TIMISOARA

> " ... *played a leading role in the anticommunist revolution in Dec. 1989; many spots where dramatic events took place ... 13th century origins ...* "

ARDELEAN, Vasile
and Elena - Maria (wife) b.09/08/38 Mathematics Teacher; Language teacher (wife)

"*My wife is born 09.08.38. We have two boys. I used to live in the North of the country then moved to Timisoara in 1975. I am a math teacher in a special school for blind children. My wife teaches language in a mentally handicapped children's school.*"

- Str.Doctor Stinca 63,Sc.B,Ap.4, Timisoara, 1900
- ✆ (961) 66316 ✍ Hungarian, German, English (a little) ♥ mathematics, gardening, arts, pictures;, Gobelins, knitting, foreign languages (wife) ∎ yes

CIRLAN, Horia and Emilia (wife) b.08/16/36
Designer Engineer /Chemistry Engineer (wife)

"*We offer comfortable housing and delicious cooking in a 3 room flat in the centre of the city.*"

- Str.Piatra Craiului 1,Sc.C,Ap.5, Timisoara, 1900
- ✆ (961) 36677 ✍ English, French, Hungarian
- ♥ bridge, gardening, opera, classical music ∎ yes
- ✗ board

TIMISOARA

CIRLAN, Radu and Mihaela (wife)   b.05/30/67
   Student/ Student (wife)
"We are married and living in a four room house with a garden."
· Spl.Tudor Vladimirescu 49, Timisoara, 1900
✆ (961) 14483 ✍ English, French, Serbian ♥ bridge, computers, basketball, tailoring ❚❚ yes ✰ board

HANDRA, Ioan   b.03/19/51   Engineer
"I work in an institute of metallic construction projects. I am married. I have a 17-year-old daughter."
· Aleea Rubinului 5,Sc.A,Ap.3, Timisoara, 1900
✆ (961) 22870 ✍ English, French ♥ football
❚❚ yes ✰ board

IONCELESCU, Mircea   b.05/22/63   Chemist engineer
"I have no brothers or sisters. I graduated from college in 1988. I am not married."
· Str.Buftea 2,Sc.C,Ap.2, Timisoara ✆ (961) 34089
✍ English ♥ tennis, travelling ❚❚ yes ✰ board

MAGDA, Andrei   b.12/28/54   Chemical engineer in
   polyurethans, microcelular elastomers
"wife: Magda Angela, age 33, chemical engineer; languages: English, German, French, Serbian. Child: Magda Adriana, age 5. I have a car. I have a 3 rooms apartment and a weekend house."
· Str.Cugir 2,Sc.B,Ap.8, Timisoara, 1900 ✆ (961) 39247 ✍ English, Hungarian ♥ travelling in foreign countries, trips in the mountains, pop music, TV, tennis, skiing ❚❚ yes ✰ guiding

SOLOMON, Edmund   b.05/15/30   Manager
"After the Revolution I organized a tourism organization-"PRIVATURISM". WE offered to invite tourists from all over the world, to assure them housing in private houses, free of charge, (possibly food too) on a reciprocity basis."
· Str.C.Brediceanu 8, Timisoara ✆ (961) 30859
✍ German, Hungarian, French (a little) ♥ tourism, opera, operetta, musical, light music, "Formula 1" races ❚❚ yes ✰ board

TOTOR, Nicusor   b.12/28/62   Engineer

"I was born here, in Timisoara. In 1987 I graduated from the Polytechnical Institute in Timisoara. I worked for three years in Resita, but now I am back home. I did not join any party. I can offer to anyone a great view of my beloved city."

- Piata Victoriei 7,Sc.D,Ap.13, Timisoara, 1900
© (961) 35753 ✍ English, Hungarian, Serbian
♥ tennis, music, theatre, science, human knowledge
♨ yes

TIRGOVISTE

LAZAR, Adrian   b.10/06/62   Technician

"I was born in Gura Ocnitei, Dimbovita county. I graduated from high school in Tirgoviste. Since 09/12/87 I am married to Daniela."

- Str.Matei Basarab 42, Tirgoviste, 0200 © (926) 17566 / 13571 ✍ German ♥ tennis, chess, swimming ♨ yes ✯ breakfast

PAVELESCU, Mihai   b.02/20/60   Musician

"I graduated in 1979 from the music high school. I taught music in a school in Tirgoviste. Now, I am a free professional musician. Married since 1985, I have a boy born in June 1989."

- Aleea Viitorului,Bl.9,Sc.F,Ap.109,Jud.Dimbovita, Tirgoviste, 0200 © (926) 33312 ✍ English, French (a little) ♥ great music, travelling, psychology, tennis ♨ yes, also Com.Gura-Ocnitei 389, cod 0217,Jud.Dimb.

TULCEA

" ... at the gates of the Delta, country of birds, fishes, weeping willows, and water lilies ...„

TULCEA

BANICA, Daniela   b.01/16/61   Teacher of Romanian language and literature.

"I was born in Tulcea, where I did my studies. For 7 years I've been a teacher of language and literature. I am married and have one child."

✂ Str.11 Iunie, Nr.4,Bl.3,Sc.A,Ap.16, Tulcea, 8800
✍ French, English (a little) ♥ literature, tourism, music, cultural issues ☗ yes

DAMIANOV, Radu   b.02/26/75   Pupil

"I am tall (1.82 m), I have black hair and black eyes. I like animals. I had a parrot but it died in an accident. I'd like to have a baby chimpanzee or a parrot."

✂ Str.Elizeului 27B,Jud.Tulcea, Tulcea, 8800
✆ (915) 17476 ✍ English, French ♥ cybernetics, computers, physics, swimming, music (Michael Jackson, Madonna, Janet Jackson, Elton John), animals ✂ postcards ☗ yes

IACOB, Roxana   b.11/14/63   Technical Drawer

"I live with my mother and my sister Alina who is student in Bucharest."

✂ Str.Pacii 121,Bl.128,Sc.A,Ap.9, Tulcea, 8800
✆ (915) 12978 ✍ English, French ♥ music (Pink Floyd, Genesis, jazz, Vivaldi, Chopin), philately, basketball, travelling ☗ no

SOLCA, Petru   b. 09/09/50   Teacher of English at "Scoala Normala" (a secondary school that prepares students to become schoolteachers)

"I attended the British Council Summer School for Teachers of English at the University of Nottingham; I worked as a translator for "Arcom" in Libya; My wife is a teacher of French. We have two children, a daughter aged 15 and a son aged 6."

✂ Str.M.Kogalniceanu,Bl.26,Sc.F,Ap.14, Tulcea, 8800 ✆ (915) 16431 ✍ English, French ♥ listening to music (jazz, rock, symphony), collecting records, photography ✂ records ☗ yes ✯ breakfast

STIUCA, Steluta   b.11/17/50   English teacher
"I teach English at a high school in Tulcea. My husband is a design engineer at 'The Danube Delta' design and research institute in Tulcea. My son is nine years old."
✉ Str.Portului 32,Bl.1B,Sc.B,Ap.25, Tulcea, 8800
✆ (915) 12967 ✍ English ♥ stamps ■ yes

TURDA

> *" Turda is a small town 30km away from Cluj, known as the 'Gate' to the Apuseni mountains."*

CRISAN, Sorin Tudor   b.05/29/74   Pupil
"I am a pupil on the tenth form."
✉ Str.Dr.Ioan Ratiu 36, Turda, 3350 ✆ (953) 11141 ✍ French, Russian ♥ tennis, chess, mathematics, skiing, literature ■ yes

JUCAN, Adrian   b.09/28/51   Master
"I am married. I have two lovely daughters : Andrea (12) and Adriana (10). My wife, Gerda (37) works at the Postal Office. I work at the quality department of a ceramic plant."
✉ Str.Macilor 17,Bl.M1,Ap.64,Jud.Cluj, Turda, 3350 ✆ (953) 12445 ✍ English, Hungarian ♥ travels, books, sports, people ■ yes ☆ yes

URLATI

TARINDA, Adina - Luminita   b.07/01/65   Engineer
"I am a young pretty girl who loves the country and nature. I live in a small town with 15,000 inhabitants but I work in Bucharest. My parents are teachers. I have an older brother also engineer who works in Ploiesti."
✉ Str.1 Mai Nr.30A,Jud.Prahova, Urlati, 2041
✆ (972) 71351 ✍ French, English ♥ music (classic, hard rock), literature, animals, trips to the mountains ■ yes ☆ board

VALENII DE MUNTE

> " ... 30km from Ploiesti and 80km away from Brasov ...,"

SANDU, Eugen - Mihail b.10/10/68 Chemic operator
"My whole life was marked by an affection of the hearing system. From a psychological point of view, this illness meant retreatment from life; I have almost no friends. I like thinking, analyzing, knowing human nature better."

⁕ Str.Andrei Muresanu 1 ,Jud.Prahova, Valenii de Munte ✆ (972) 82635 ✍ French ♥ tennis, exotic plants, reading, writing, geography ∎ no

VAMA

> " ... in Bucovina, in the North-East of Romania. Famous for monasteries ...,"

LUCAN, Gheorghe b.11/02/56 Constructions engineer
"I come from a family of workers who own a farm in Vama, a settlement 15 Km far from Cimpulung Moldovenesc. I finished Faculty in 1981. I am married since 1986 to Lucia Lucan. She is a doctor. She speaks French and German. We have a little boy."

⁕ Str.I.L.Caragiale 20 ,Jud.Suceava *or* Str.Ciprian Porumbescu 21A,Ap.2 ,5960 Cimpulung Moldovenesc, Jud.Suceava, Vama, 5969 ✆ (988) 12599 ✍ French ♥ photography ∎ yes.

VASCAU

BENE, Sorin b. 07/25/61 Prospector
"I am married to Magdalena. We have no children yet."

⁕ Str.Unirii 18 ,Jud.Bihor, Vascau, 3642 ✍ French ♥ nature, travelling, football ∎ yes

VASLUI

> "*The monument of Steven the Great is in the Central Square of Vaslui.*"

ANDREI, Gheorghe b.09/15/51 Agricultural Technician
"*I am married; I have two sons and a daughter.*"
- Str.Spatar Angheluta,Bl.211,Sc.D,Ap.18,Jud.Vaslui, Vaslui, 6500 © (983) 17993 ✍ French
♥ football, music, literature, nature ∎ yes

RUSU, Valeriu b. 04/20/58 Engineer
"*I was born in Vaslui. I work as an engineer in Bucharest. I live together with my wife, Nina, who is a chemist, in a two room flat in Bucharest. We have no children. We spend our vacations in Vaslui, together with my parents in a 4 room house (garden).*"
- Str.Eternitatii 38, Vaslui, 6500 © (983) 14457
✍ French, English ♥ cinema, classic and modern music, painting ∎ Y in Buc.:Str.I.Sulea 63,Bl.X1,Sc.C,Ap.113,sect.3

ZALAU

POP, Dumitru b. 10/19/62 Teacher of physics
"*In 1986 I graduated from the Faculty of Physics in Cluj. I worked as a teacher since. I have a four room flat, a garage, a car. I am married and have a boy.*"
- Str.Gheorghe Doja 19,Ap.2, Zalau, 4700 © (996) 32682 ✍ English ♥ trips in the mountains, badminton, computers ∎ yes

ZARNESTI

> "*... 'The Abisses of Zarnesti' - a picturesque defile, the Bran Castle ... one must taste the 'mititei' and 'sarmale'.*"

TUDOR, Viorel b.08/08/56 Engineer
"*I was born in Brasov. My parents were workers. I graduated from the University in Brasov. I am married. My wife works as an economist. We have two little*

daughters : Elena (6 years old) and Ioana (4 years old)."
- Str.Stefan cel Mare 7 ,Jud.Brasov, Zarnesti, 2223
- French, English ♥ literature, going on trips
- 1 room in Zarnesti, 3 rooms in Bran

Recommended Reading

Kiss the Hand You Cannot Bite
by Edward Behr
Hamish Hamilton, London 1991. This newly published excellent book about the rise and fall of the Ceausescus is a great source for Romanian political history. It reads like a thriller - highly recommended.

Marie, Queen of Romania
by Hannah Paluka
Weidenfelt & Nicholson, London, 1984. Well-written account of pre-World War II Romanian political intrigue.

Red Horizons
by Ion Pacepa
Coronet Paperback, Hodder & Stoughton, London, 1989. The book on the terrible stuff that went on in Romania by someone in a position to know. He defected from the Romanian Secret Service.

The Balkan Trilogy
by Olivia Manning
Now available in Penguin. A spy novel, a romance, and a top-notch historical novel, all in one. Set in pre-World War II Bucharest. Beautifully done.

Operation Autonomous
by Ivor Porter
Chatto & Windus Ltd, London, 1988. Porter was the spy described in fictional terms by Olivia Manning in 1939.

Eastern Europe, on a shoestring
by David Stanley
Lonely Planet Publications, Australia, 1989. This excellent guide contains 65 information-packed pages but much post-Ceausescu information is incorrect. For general information about traveling in Romania, it can be adequate.

Night Soldiers
Dark Star
by Alan Furst
Houghton Mifflin Company, Boston. Available in UK, France, Germany in paperback. Two novels that portray accurately the social and political climate in Europe just before the Second World War. Highly recommended.

Jim HAYNES

Born in Louisiana, schooled in Venezuela and Atlanta, Georgia, university at L.S.U., Tulane, University of Edinburgh, University of Paris. Created The Traverse Theatre in Edinburgh and the Arts Lab in London. Associate Professor of Media, University of Paris VIII since 1969.

An intrepid festival-goer, he has attended the Cannes Film Festival, the Edinburgh International Festival, the Lathi Writers' Reunion, the Frankfurt Book Fair, the Warsaw "Jazz Jamboree" and the Belgrade October Writers' Meeting for many many years, and has every intention of continuing to do so.

Other Books by Jim Haynes:
- *Traverse Plays* (editor)
- *Hello, I Love You!* (editor, with Jeanne Pasle Green)
- *Workers of the World Unite and Stop Working! A Reply to Marxism*
- *Everything Is! Soft Manifestos for Our Time*
- *More Romance, Less Romanticism*
- *A Tribute to Henry Miller* (editor)
- *Thanks for Coming! An Autobiography*
- *The Cassette Gazette*, an audio magazine (editor)

If you are interested in these books and other publications from Handshake Editions, please write, enclosing a self-addressed stamped envelope, for a complimentary catalogue.

Handshake Editions
83, rue de la Tombe Issoire
Atelier A2
75014 Paris, France

People to People and You

People to People guides are made up of information from people just like you. If you would like to be included in a future People to People publication, please take some time and as neatly as possible fill out the following form, and on a separate sheet of paper write a few lines about:

- Who you are - a short biography
- What you would recommend a traveler experience in your area
- What your passions, your hobbies, your interests are which others might share.

Personal Data:	
Family Name	
First Name	Birthdate
Address	
City	
Postal Code	
Country	
Telephone	
Profession	
Languages	
Accomodations:	(Yes/No Answers)
Can Exchange?	
Can Assist?	
Bed & Breakfast?	

I understand that Jim Haynès is editing a new kind of travel book and that I realize by participating in it I will receive letters and contacts with travellers and that I am committed only to the degree I wish to participate and that no other obligations are implied or demanded.

Signature	Date